Skillstreaming
in Early Childhood

A Guide for Teaching Prosocial Skills

THIRD EDITION

Ellen McGinnis

RESEARCH PRESS
PUBLISHERS

2612 North Mattis Avenue ■ Champaign, Illinois 61822 ■ [800] 519-2707 ■ www.researchpress.com

RESEARCH PRESS
PUBLISHERS

Copyright © 2012 by Ellen McGinnis

8   7   6   5   4   17   18   19   20   21

Copies of this book may be ordered from Research Press at the address given on the title page.

Composition by Jeff Helgesen
Cover design by Linda Brown, Positive I.D. Graphic Design, Inc.
Printed by McNaughton & Gunn, Inc.

ISBN: 978-0-87822-654-2
Library of Congress Control Number 2011932199

To Sara Winn, my daughter,
and an exemplary teacher of young children

Contents

PART 2
Skill Outlines and Homework Reports

Homework reports follow each skill.

Figures and Tables

Preface

Skillstreaming is now over 30 years old. Starting with its introduction in 1973 as one of the very first social skills training approaches, it has been widely used in the United States and beyond and is now in place in hundreds of schools, agencies, and institutions serving children and youth. This third edition of *Skillstreaming in Early Childhood* integrates what has been learned from research investigations over the past 10 years with training recommendations provided by many of the hundreds of teachers, administrators, youth care workers, and other practitioners who have used Skillstreaming.

The origins and development of the Skillstreaming approach afford an interesting context with which to understand the 21st-century incarnation of the program described in this book. The prevailing therapeutic approaches of the 1950s and 1960s (psychodynamic, nondirective, and behavior modification) held that an individual possessed effective, satisfying, or healthy behaviors but that these behaviors were simply unexpressed. In contrast, Skillstreaming represents a psychoeducational approach, viewing the individual in educational terms as a person in need of help in the form of skills training. Instead of providing therapy, the task of the skills trainer or teacher is the active and deliberate teaching of desirable behaviors to replace those less productive in nature.

Skillstreaming differs from the approaches of behavior theorists such as Albert Bandura (1973), who described the processes of modeling, behavioral rehearsal, and reinforcement implicit in the Skillstreaming approach but who also emphasized operant procedures such as prompting and shaping of behaviors. Although a strictly behavioral approach increases the frequency of a behavior, that behavior must already be within a person's repertoire. If the person does not have a grasp of the needed skill, operant procedures are insufficient to add that skill to the person's behavioral options.

The deinstitutionalization movement of the 1960s, which resulted in the discharge of approximately four million persons from mental health and other institutions into local communities, set the stage for acceptance of an alternative way of providing treatment. The realization was that the more traditional therapeutic interventions, which focused on looking inward to correct one's nonproductive actions (i.e., insight-oriented approaches), were ineffective for many individuals from lower socioeconomic environments, who constituted the majority of individuals discharged from institutions. The lack of effective methods to reach this population led Dr. Arnold P. Goldstein to develop Structured Learning Therapy (Goldstein, 1973), the precursor to Skillstreaming. Structured learning methods approached aggression, withdrawal, and other nonproductive patterns in a new way, as learned behaviors that can be changed by teaching new, alternative skills.

In addition to the growing importance of such structured learning methods in applied clinical work and as a preventive focus in community mental health, parallel developments in education clearly encouraged skills training. Specifically, a number of other approaches grew from the personal development context of certain educational movements—for example, progressive education (Dewey, 1938) and character education (Chapman, 1977). The goal of these approaches was to support the teaching of concepts and behaviors relevant to values, morality, and emotional functioning—in particular, values clarification (Simon, Howe, & Kirschenbaum, 1972), moral education (Kohlberg, 1973), and affective education (Miller, 1976). These three approaches, as well as other personal growth programs, combined to provide a supportive climate and context for skills training. These programs share a concern for personal development, competence, and social effectiveness. Clearly, education had been broadened well beyond basic academic content to include areas traditionally the concern of mental health practitioners.

Since its initial development as an intervention prescriptively targeted to low-income adults deficient in social skills, Skillstreaming has increasingly been used with many other populations. In the 1980s and beyond, Dr. Goldstein's skills training program, now known as Skillstreaming, was adapted to meet the needs of adolescents (Goldstein, Gershaw, Klein, & Sprafkin, 1980; Goldstein & McGinnis, 1997), elementary children (McGinnis & Goldstein, 1984, 1997), and preschool and kindergarten children (McGinnis & Goldstein, 1990, 2003) who exhibited aggression and other problematic behaviors. In addition to its use with children and adolescents, the Skillstreaming approach has been employed successfully with elderly adults, child-abusing parents, industrial managers, police officers, and others. Over more than 30 years of program use, a considerable amount of evaluation research has been conducted and reported. The results of these studies support the efficacy of Skillstreaming and have suggested means for altering and improving its procedures and materials. An annotated bibliography detailing Skillstreaming research is available on the Skillstreaming website (www.skillstreaming.com).

Acknowledgments

During the more than 40 years of his professional life, Arnold P. Goldstein (1934–2002) was a professor at Syracuse University, director of the Center for Research on Aggression, and wrote or coauthored over 90 peer-reviewed articles and 50 books. In the final year of his life, Dr. Goldstein founded the International Center for Aggression Replacement Training (ICART), which leads research and provides information and training to professionals throughout the world. At this point, Dr. Goldstein's work, including Skillstreaming, is used throughout the United States and in at least 16 other countries. Many people, myself included, cannot thank him enough for his efforts to help youth and adults with aggression problems and other challenging behaviors change to improve their lives and the lives of those who interact with them.

Three other persons share major responsibility for bringing Skillstreaming into existence and nurturing its development over these many years. Robert P. Sprafkin and N. Jane Gershaw helped originally codevelop the program and were prime contributors to enhancing both its early application and its initial evaluation. Barry Glick fully shared the effort to expand its boundaries to include especially difficult-to-reach adolescents. These colleagues well deserve special thanks and appreciation.

Thanks also to Shawnda Gorish and Julianne Woodhouse from Des Moines Public Schools, who provided many of the real-life scenarios included in the suggested content for modeling displays, and to Knut Gunderson, Sandnes, Norway, for his thoughtful review and suggestions from his training experience.

Gail Salyards and Russ Pence from Research Press provided the encouragement and understanding needed to complete this revision. Special appreciation and thanks to Karen Steiner, my editor, for her careful and sensitive reviews, changes, and recommendations, and for understanding the need to represent Arnie's spirit in this work.

Introduction

As preschool and kindergarten-age children enter school, they are faced with an uncommon set of routines, different expectations, and new relationships with both adults and peers. Young children are often challenged by the expectations to listen to adults and follow their directions; to share, cooperate, and interact in new ways with classmates; and to form new friendships. Growing up in today's world, young children require more support than ever before. School, family, and community violence continue to be pervasive concerns. Although the role of parents in the social development of children is one of the most critical pieces of school readiness, the stress on today's changing families often places more responsibility to seek support outside the family. As a result of financial necessity, public schools are often merging, resulting in larger, potentially less personal learning settings. Those who teach and work with young children continue to look for ways to provide support in responding to the effects of these social changes, as well as to address the very different environmental demands children experience.

SOCIAL SKILLS AND THE PRESCHOOL AND KINDERGARTEN CHILD

By age three, the age typically denoting the end of toddlerhood and the beginning of the preschool years, most young children are beginning to view themselves as part of a larger world—a world including demands that implicit and explicit skill competencies be mastered. Piaget (1962) has termed the ages between two and seven the preoperational stage, a time when children begin to contemplate their actions and become increasingly aware of how their behavior brings about either desired rewards from others—such as smiles, hugs, or words of praise—or undesired punishments—such as frowns, reprimands, or loss of privileges.

Allen and Marotz (2000) describe how language, cognitive skills, and social behavior of young children develop at various ages. During the preschool years, there is great change in all areas of the child's development. The child's verbal and cognitive skills develop rapidly, thus enabling the child to develop some control over his or her own behavior, solve problems, and express ideas verbally. During these years, the child is also making the transition from parallel play, in which the child engages in independent play while a peer does likewise, to more interactive and cooperative play. The child is also beginning to develop a sense of the needs of others (i.e., empathy) and is learning to cooperate and plan ahead. From kindergarten age (ages five and six) through age eight, more formal school routines are required, and the child acquires a strong interest in pleasing others and doing things right. Social interactions become more frequent and complex (Hartup, 1983), and friendships become increasingly more important.

Why need we be concerned with social skills deficits at such an early age? One central reason for teaching prosocial skills to young children concerns the new demands placed on them by preschool and kindergarten settings. With this important change, children must learn all at once to get along not only with one or two siblings or neighborhood friends but also with an entire classroom of other children and adults. Along with this increased social interaction comes the need for children to acquire a new set of skills.

Also at this time, quite abruptly, adult and group demands become far greater and more complex. The child is now required to direct attention to an other-selected activity, to sit among a group of other children in close proximity, to change activities according to an adult time frame, to follow a variety of instructions, and to interact cooperatively with other children across a changing variety of tasks and settings. Such demands are not typically included in the home environment in such a structured and consistent manner. Therefore, the young child's first encounter with preschool or kindergarten typically involves an array of foreign skills and behaviors.

In this regard, Chan and Rueda (1979) describe a "hidden curriculum" operating within schools. This curriculum involves the assumption that all children enter the school setting with similar experiences and values. In other words, it is expected that children will have developed certain language and cognitive skills by exploring their environments and that they will have acquired a set of student behaviors enabling them to respond appropriately to adult instructions. This assumption appears to be faulty. Instead, teachers of young children encounter a diverse group of individuals having very different personalities and temperamental characteristics (Keogh & Burnstein, 1988), some who have had prior day care or preschool experiences, and some who are entering a structured school setting for the first time. The cognitive and behavioral skills of children with less school-related experience may not be sufficient to meet the needs of the new in-school situation.

In a national survey of 3,000 kindergarten teachers, almost one-third reported that half of their students experienced difficulty working in groups and following directions in addition to lacking the necessary preacademic skills (Rimm-Kaufman, Pianta, & Cox, 2000). Also, 20 percent of the kindergartners were reported to experience deficits in other necessary social skills. In their review, Hemmeter, Ostrosky, and Fox (2006) found that key social skills as children enter school include the ability to form positive relationships with both adults and peers, to communicate their emotions, to attend to instruction, and to solve social problems. Citing the National Early Intervention Longitudinal Study, these authors concluded that in a preschool setting, as many as one-third of the children could experience significant problem behavior and that even more children may be at risk

Although some surmise that difficulty with such skills is a developmental stage for young children, research strongly indicates otherwise. For example, a national study conducted by Yale University found the rate of expulsion for three- and four-year-olds attending preschool programs was three times that of children in grades K through 12 (Gilliam, 2005). In addition, there is strong indication that without adequate intervention, poor social skills and behavior problems in the preschool and early elementary years persist into adolescence and adulthood (Caselman & Self, 2008; Choi & Kim, 2003; Dunlap et al., 2006; Elksnin & Elksnin, 2000; Entwisle, Alexander, & Olson, 2005; Whitted, 2011). For instance, such children may experience peer rejection, negative relationships with teachers, school failure, and violence, abuse, loneliness, and anxiety in adulthood (Technical Assistance Center on Social Emotional Intervention for Young Children, 2004).

An increasing number of children who enter the doors of preschools and kindergarten classrooms lack the basic social skills to interact positively with others, solve problems, follow directions, and participate in preacademic, academic, and social learning. Some children are lonely and respond by isolating themselves from their peers. Others display high levels of acting-out and aggressive behavior. Still others have difficulty following simple directions because of their inability to attend. Consider, for example, the following real-life scenarios.

> At recess time, Cory, age six, is often viewed by his kindergarten teacher on the sidelines of a group. He stands by himself and watches the ongoing play, not making any attempt to join in the activity. The teacher has encouraged Cory many times to play with the others and has even talked with him about what games he likes to play at recess, but Cory continues to be just an observer. His teacher feels discouraged.

> In one preschool classroom, Javier does mostly whatever he wants. When he wants something, like the markers, he leaves his area and just takes them. He doesn't seem to pay any attention to the directions given by the teacher. For example, every morning he leaves his assigned center after a minute or two and goes to another center, yelling at the student assigned to that activity to "just get away." Javier's teacher feels irritated.

> In another preschool classroom, Juan and Elizabeth, age four, both want all the Legos, even though there are enough to share. Elizabeth shouts out that all the Legos are hers and tells Juan to get away. Juan replies no and continues to build his Legos tower. Elizabeth angrily scoops away many of the Legos, pushes Juan on the shoulder, and knocks down his tower. The teacher feels frustrated and tells Elizabeth that she must take a time-out.

> Latecia, age 6, often gets in trouble for playing with little trinkets she keeps in her desk. When her first-grade teacher gives directions, Latecia rarely knows what she has been asked to do. Occasionally, Latecia will look at what another child is doing in an attempt to figure out what she should be working on. Very soon, however, she is engaged with another distraction. Latecia's teacher is annoyed.

> Rami, age six, appears to enjoy working by himself at the classroom learning center. One of his classmates wanders past the center where Rami is working and brushes against him. Rami turns and shouts at the peer, "You hit me! You wanna fight?" Most of the children in the class stop what they are doing and look toward the boys. The teacher stops working with other students and intervenes. Rami often seems to attribute negative motivations to his peers, and the class is often disrupted by his outbursts. His teacher feels hopeless to help him.

Behavioral concerns such as the ones illustrated in these examples have a profound impact not only on the individual child who is struggling behaviorally but also on the teacher, peers in the classroom, school leadership, and parents. What Cory, Javier, Elizabeth, Latecia, and Rami lack or are weak in are the skills, abilities, or behaviors needed to interact with others in appropriate ways; to react prosocially to common, everyday stressors; and to exhibit the school-related behaviors necessary to benefit from preacademic instruction. In other words, these children are deficient in prosocial skills, just as low achievers are deficient in academic readiness or academic skills. Children may not have acquired the specific skills needed, or they may not be able to perform the skills adequately. Other children may lack the motivation, fluency, or flexibility of skill use to be socially competent in their interactions with others. Some children may misperceive the intent of others' actions, words, or nonverbal behaviors. Still others may be able to react in prosocial ways under some circumstances but fail to perform in desirable ways when prosocial skill use is most critical.

Although many educational interventions have focused on decreasing undesirable social behaviors, educators and others have become increasingly aware that doing so is insufficient to bring about desired behavioral change. Furthermore, when such interventions to decrease undesirable behaviors are the only ones employed, children are often left even lonelier and more rejected and socially isolated. The recommended alternative is to engage in planned instruction and skill-focused strategies to actively teach young children behaviors that are acceptable and rewarding and that facilitate good interpersonal relationships and readiness to achieve academically. Pelco and Reed-Victor (2007), for example, have identified social skills needed beginning in kindergarten, including how to talk inside the school; wait one's turn; sit, stand, and move about the classroom and school; ask for help; take care of classroom materials; follow directions; and work independently.

WHAT IS SKILLSTREAMING?

Skillstreaming is an evidence-based strategy that involves systematically teaching social skills to address the needs of students who display aggression, immaturity, withdrawal, or other problem behaviors. For young children, social skills instruction focuses on ways to successfully navigate the school environment, follow teacher expectations, deal with peer and adult conflict, and cope with the many feelings typical of students in this age group. Skillstreaming focuses on four direct instruction principles of learning: modeling, role-playing, performance feedback, and generalization training. These learning procedures have been used to teach a variety of behaviors, from academic competencies to sports to daily living skills, and are applied in Skillstreaming to teach the child desirable social behaviors.

Before discussing what Skillstreaming is in more detail, it is important to point out what it is not: Skillstreaming is not an affective education strategy that focuses primarily on discussion of feelings. Although discussion is a part, Skillstreaming engages children in active learning through role-playing and practice, actions that are more developmentally appropriate for children at this young age. Skillstreaming will not address all children's needs in every situation at all times. Instead, it is a well-validated teaching procedure that should be included with other techniques, such as behavioral support planning, conflict resolution, parent involvement and education, and cooperative learning. Nor is Skillstreaming a procedure for teaching compliance skills, the focus of some skills-training programs. Although it will teach students the skills needed to follow school rules and routines better, this program is mainly intended to teach children the skills needed to solve problems that occur in their daily lives, to be assertive in handling situations that cause them stress or unhappiness, and to increase the chance that they will have satisfying relationships with both peers and adults.

A Skill-Deficit Model

The Skillstreaming model makes the assumption that the learner is weak in or lacks a behavioral skill or skills. This model includes learners who have not yet acquired the prosocial behavior, who may have knowledge of the behavior but are unable to perform it, who may perform the skill in some situations or under certain conditions but who are unable to use it when its use is indicated, or whose competing behaviors interfere with using the skill.

Researchers in the area of social skills training (e.g., Gresham, Sugai, & Horner, 2001; Gresham, 2002; and Gresham, Van, & Cook, 2006) advocate that practitioners consider the difference between a skill deficit (can't) and a performance deficit (won't). These authors explain that a child with a skill deficit lacks the knowledge of how to perform a skill. Other children may know how to perform a skill but lack the fluency in skill use necessary to execute the skill in a competent manner. Still other children may have a skill within their repertoires but fail to select the skill as appropriate in a given situation (skill flexibility). Others may experience competing problem behaviors, such as poor self-control, which inhibit their skill use. Still others may know how to carry out a skill but fail to do so because of the lack of positive reinforcement (a performance deficit). Research has also found that some children with increased social anxiety have a social information processing deficit (Crick & Dodge, 1994; Raine et al., 2006). In other words, these children experience errors in how they think about and respond to social cues.

In practice, acquisition (can't do), performance (won't do), fluency, and competing problem behaviors will be addressed within the context of a skill deficit. The assumption of skill deficit is helpful for several reasons. First, the belief that most young children do not know how to act productively in given situations lessens the frustration many adults experience when these children seem continually to react in the same inappropriate way despite concentrated efforts to eliminate problem behaviors through the application of negative consequences. With other skill acquisition, such as academic or athletic skills, it is widely accepted that direct instruction is needed. As with any teaching endeavor, and as the research on "brain-friendly" learning illustrates, new learning is more likely to take place when it occurs in an encouraging, supportive, and nonthreatening environment. When children experience fear or feel that they are being threatened—for example, when teachers or other adults engage in verbal reprimands—the brain "downshifts" (Brendtro, Brokenleg, & Van Bockern, 2002; Goleman, 1995; Jensen, 2000). The more primitive parts of the brain, which deal with emotions, take control. Thus, children react to the interaction in an emotional manner, often with a "flight or fight" response, and learning is improbable if not impossible.

The goal in all such cases becomes the active teaching of desirable skills. As one parent of a child with attention deficit/hyperactivity disorder remarked, "The worst thing that happened to my child at school was that he had a good day!" After the child had succeeded, the expectation was that if he could do it once, he could do it every day. Yet we know that for children with attention deficits, as well as for most children who experience behavioral difficulties, this is a faulty assumption. Providing direct instruction in prosocial skills will shift our energies toward teaching and away from expecting and consequating problem behavior. Children are far more likely to engage in learning

a skill when they are taught in a deliberate and concentrated manner than when they wait for rewards that may not be forthcoming. In addition, direct instruction will likely increase their motivation and performance consistency.

The skill-deficit assumption, then, allows adults to focus on proactive instruction instead of reacting to children's misbehavior as if it were done purposefully to create problems. In other words, it is recognized that it is more important to teach desirable skills than to punish children for inappropriate behaviors. This assumption, then, suggests that adults will be patient and encouraging while children learn these sometimes very difficult skills.

Planned, Systematic Instruction

During the last decade, most educators have realized that children need to be taught desirable behaviors in the same planned and systematic way that academic skills are taught. With increased emphasis on increasing student achievement, instruction in social skills and social-emotional learning is gaining acceptance (Docksai, 2010). Incidental learning (such as discussing alternatives or telling children what to do) is insufficient for children to learn alternative behaviors and perform them under stressful conditions, just as it is insufficient to tell children how to put letter sounds together and expect that they will be able to read. Further, for the learning of many academic skills, the correct response is always correct (e.g., beginning letter sounds, math computation). The learning of social skills, however, is more complex, with a variety of potentially correct responses. Whatever the reason for skill deficit or weakness, educators must establish and implement procedures to deliberately teach these skills, just as they would intervene to remediate academic or preacademic deficits.

A Way to Improve School Climate

Creating a welcoming and positive school climate is recognized as a critical factor in increasing academic learning. Historically, educational interventions dealing with student behavior problems have concentrated on strategies to diminish or extinguish behaviors of concern (e.g., time-out, loss of privileges). Although reinforcement strategies are effective in increasing positive behaviors, it is necessary to wait until a behavior is displayed before it can be rewarded. Thus, many students with infrequent appropriate behaviors rarely receive positive reinforcement; in most cases, they receive an abundance of negative feedback. Although negative procedures may be useful as part of a comprehensive behavior intervention plan, overemphasis may further discourage children with behavior problems. For these students, positive feelings about school and learning itself are unlikely. Creating a better balance of positive to negative consequences is necessary to foster a positive school climate.

Teaching prosocial skills provides the elementary school child with opportunities to be successful in both hypothetical and real-life situations and lends a sense of balance to behavior management programs. Although inappropriate behaviors will continue to need intervention, through Skillstreaming, students have the opportunity to build alternative socially acceptable behaviors to increase their choice opportunities. Teachers and others will also find that prompting students to use a previously learned social skill when problematic situations arise in the classroom or in other school settings will often stop the student's inappropriate actions in midstream and channel his or her energies in a more prosocial direction. Like reminding a student to use a reading strategy to master unknown vocabulary, when given in a helpful and encouraging manner, such prompting fosters a positive classroom and school climate.

A Way to Enhance Self-Esteem

A description of a child with difficult behaviors often includes the phrase "poor self-esteem." Counselors, teachers, and others often struggle to design interventions that improve the youth's positive feelings about himself or herself. One way of addressing this issue is to teach the student to be more competent. The traditional focus on academic competence recognizes that such competence contributes to the child's positive feelings about self in relation to achievement. Likewise, increasing competence in a variety of socially related skills will improve an individual's self-concept.

Although behavior management programs are useful, necessary, and very often effective in reducing problem behaviors, emphasis on such programs alone may reinforce the idea in students that adults are the dispensers of all rewards and punishments. The child may learn to believe that whatever he or she might do or however he or she might act, the positive or negative results of these actions will be determined by someone else in power—a teacher, parent, or other adult. Such a belief, referred to as an *external locus of control,* can foster feelings of helplessness. When students learn, for example, to handle conflict in ways that yield approval from others, they also learn a sense of responsibility and control. They more easily make the connection between their actions (e.g., use of a skill) and positive consequences. When students learn that they have the skills and ability to effect change, their self-esteem is likely to improve.

Remediation and Prevention

Skillstreaming is an approach effective in remediating social skills deficits in a wide range of children. The child with an identified attention deficit disorder, for example, may have a particular need to learn the skills of Ignoring (Skill 8), Following Directions (Skill 10), and Interrupting (Skill 12) to better adapt to the structure of the classroom. The child with a learning disability may need to learn the skill of Asking for Help (Skill 6), as well as skills to deal with frustration, such as Trying When It's Hard (Skill 11), to facilitate preacademic and academic learning. Another child may misperceive the intent of peers' actions and would benefit from skills such as

Reading Others (Skill 14) and Deciding How Someone Feels (Skill 25). Children with more severe disabilities, those with autism or cognitive disabilities, can be taught a variety of social skills to enhance independence and to make their lives more satisfying. Those with emotional or behavioral disorders—whether characterized by withdrawal, aggression, or immaturity—need to learn prosocial skills as well.

Although aggression and violence are very visible and perhaps cause more stress for peers, teachers, school administrators, parents, and the community, teaching prosocial skills to the withdrawn child or the child who reacts immaturely or inadequately is also important. Although many such children may not direct the distress of their social isolation outward or become aggressive toward others, they may later direct their aggression toward themselves through self-destructive behaviors.

Skillstreaming is also intended for the general education population—students whose behavior is not significantly problematic but who will increase their personal satisfaction and happiness by learning or improving upon prosocial skills. In an effort to prevent future interpersonal and academic problems, many preschool and kindergarten children may need help with the skills to form friendships, participate in problem solving, avoid distractions when engaged in learning activities, or deal productively with day-to-day stress. Such skill learning can assist children in developing the resiliency needed to deal with problems that may occur at a later age.

A Strategy to Help Prevent Violence and Aggression

As discussed in more detail later in this introduction, a great need exists to address violence and aggression in schools and other settings by teaching children and adolescents prosocial ways of resolving conflict, proactive problem solving, and the social skills necessary to enhance self-esteem and engender a sense of belonging. Ag-gressive children learn quickly and at an early age that they can get what they want by hitting, pushing, biting, and so forth. Because aggression is a remarkably stable behavior and is unlikely to change without intervention, alternatives to aggression need to be taught early. Skillstreaming is one method of doing just that.

SKILLS FOR KINDERGARTEN AND PRESCHOOL CHILDREN

Social skills, as defined by Gresham (1998a) are "socially acceptable learned behaviors enabling individuals to interact effectively with others and avoid or escape socially unacceptable behaviors exhibited by others" (p. 20). Caldarella and Merrell (1997) reviewed studies conducted using social skills rating scales or inventories and found five broad dimensions of social skills, including peer relation skills, self-management skills, academic skills, compliance skills, and assertion skills. Gresham et al. (2006) took a somewhat different perspective and have classified social skills into two categories: *replacement behaviors,* which are the skills that serve the same function or purpose as the problematic behavior, and *socially valid skills,* or those that include a set of competencies to enhance initiating and maintaining positive relationships, facilitate peer acceptance and friendships, contribute to satisfactory school adjustment, and allow students to cope and adapt to the social demands of the given environment.

The 40 skills in this book, designed to enhance the prosocial development of preschool and kindergarten children, are divided into six skill groups:

1. Beginning Social Skills, which are most easily learned by the young child and often are prerequisites to later skill acquisition and instruction

2. School-Related Skills, which enhance success primarily in the school or early childhood environment

3. Friendship-Making Skills, which encourage positive peer interaction

4. Dealing with Feelings, skills designed to foster awareness of the feelings of self and others

5. Alternatives to Aggression, skills that provide the child with prosocial choices in dealing with conflict

6. Dealing with Stress, skills that address the stressful situations young children frequently encounter

The skills in this curriculum, listed in Table 1, involve social behaviors believed to be related to peer acceptance (Dodge, 1983; Mize & Ladd, 1984), skills critical for school success, including self-control and cooperation (Cartledge & Milburn, 1980; Lane, Givner, & Pierson, 2004; Lane, Wehby, & Cooley, 2006), and social success (Chen, 2006; Fox & Boulton, 2003; Spivack & Shure, 1974; Warden & Mac-Kinnon, 2003), as well as those likely to enhance children's personal satisfaction (Goldstein & McGinnis, 1997). Additional prosocial skills have been selected to teach alternatives to the maladaptive behaviors often employed by unpopular or rejected children, such as poor cooperation (Coie & Kupersmidt, 1983; Meier, DiPerna, & Oster, 2006), anxiety (Buhremester, 1982), disruptive behaviors (Dodge, Coie, & Bralke, 1982), poor interpersonal problem solving (Chen, 2006) and verbal and physical aggression (Dodge et al., 1982). In addition, social skills include those related to academic performance, such as the ability to work in groups and respond appropriately to adult correction and other feedback, and building and maintaining friendships (Gresham, Sugai, & Horner, 2001).

The selection of social skills for instruction needs to be based on the child's individual characteristics (e.g., developmental level, cognitive and behavioral deficits) and on social criteria (e.g., cultural context, situational specificity, peer relationships, social validity) (Cartledge & Milburn, 1995; Gresham, Sugai, & Horner, 2001; Kauffman, 2005; Schoenfeld et al., 2008).

This list of prosocial behaviors is by no means all inclusive; instead, the goal is to provide teachers and others who recognize skill or performance deficits with detailed lesson plans to teach the behavioral skills typically needed. As the person who implements these plans observes concerns in the school and other social environments, and as parents and children express difficulties, new skills can and should be developed. More on this topic is included in chapter 4, "Refining Skill Use."

TEACHING PROSOCIAL SKILLS

Social skills deficits have been the target of considerable research scrutiny, and it is well accepted today that a child's lack of social competence relates to his or her later adjustment (Caselman & Self, 2008; Walker, Ramsey, & Gresham, 2004; Whitted, 2011). For most students, due to the length of time they spend in the school setting, the majority of socialization occurs in school (Schoenfeld, Rutherford, Gable, & Rock, 2008). A positive relationship between social skills and school success has been repeatedly demonstrated (Cartledge & Lo, 2006), and students who are socially competent have a greater likelihood of graduating (Caprara, Barbaranelli, Pastorelli, Bandura, & Zimbardo, 2000). Planned and direct instruction in social skills empowers students to get their needs met in desirable ways, helps them learn important social behaviors to deal effectively with increased social demands, and positively impacts their academic learning (Cartledge & Lo, 2006; Cook, Gresham, Kern, Barreras, & Crews, 2008; Docksai, 2010). For peers and teachers, social skills instruction will result in a more positive school climate and more time for teachers to spend on academic instruction instead of discipline, leading to a more rewarding learning and teaching experience.

What about children who go on to engage in serious violence during the teenage years? It appears that these youth do not give prior indication, either through a pattern of problematic behaviors or a high level of aggression, that

Table 1: Skillstreaming Curriculum for Preschool and Kindergarten Children

Group I: Beginning Social Skills

1. Listening
2. Using Nice Talk
3. Using Brave Talk
4. Saying Thank You
5. Rewarding Yourself
6. Asking for Help
7. Asking a Favor
8. Ignoring

Group II: School-Related Skills

9. Asking a Question
10. Following Directions
11. Trying When It's Hard
12. Interrupting

Group III: Friendship-Making Skills

13. Greeting Others
14. Reading Others
15. Joining In
16. Waiting Your Turn
17. Sharing
18. Offering Help
19. Asking Someone to Play
20. Playing a Game

Group IV: Dealing with Feelings

21. Knowing Your Feelings
22. Feeling Left Out
23. Asking to Talk
24. Dealing with Fear
25. Deciding How Someone Feels
26. Showing Affection

Group V: Alternatives to Aggression

27. Dealing with Teasing
28. Dealing with Feeling Mad
29. Deciding If It's Fair
30. Solving a Problem
31. Accepting Consequences

Group VI: Dealing with Stress

32. Relaxing
33. Dealing with Mistakes
34. Being Honest
35. Knowing When to Tell
36. Dealing with Losing
37. Wanting to Be First
38. Saying No
39. Accepting No
40. Deciding What to Do

From *Skillstreaming in Early Childhood: Teaching Prosocial Skills* (3rd ed.), © 2012 by E. McGinnis, Champaign, IL: Research Press (www.researchpress.com, 800-519-2707).

they will become violent. Therefore, the Public Health Service (2002) report of the Surgeon General's Office on youth violence, undertaken as a response to the Columbine High School tragedy, concludes: "Targeting prevention programs solely to young children with problem behavior misses over half of the children who will eventually become serious violent offenders, although universal prevention programs in childhood may be effective in preventing late onset (youth) violence" (chapter 3, p. 2). Instruction in prosocial skill use is considered to be an important component of such violence prevention programs.

Furthermore, we now know that even very young children can benefit from instruction in prosocial skills. For example, Dereli (2009) found that teaching social skills to six-year-olds was successful using modeling, imitation or role-playing, and positive reinforcement. Working with young children in Head Start classrooms, Hune and Nelson (2002) demonstrated that students could be taught to generate desirable resolutions to social problems. In their early work with preschoolers and kindergarten children, Spivack and Shure (1974) found that four- and five-year-olds can be successfully taught to identify alternative problem solutions, anticipate consequences, and use other problem-solving skills that enhance interpersonal adjustment. Young children are also able to recognize more subtle aspects of social interactions. Ladd, Kochenderfer, and Coleman (2000), for example, in their study of kindergarten boys and girls, found that children of this age are able to recognize differences in quality of friendships. McGlamery and Ball (2008) further cite evidence that children as young as three can understand mental states or emotions and can solve problems and draw conclusions about behavior by age four. According to Maccoby (1980) and others, these early years are the most critical for developing such prosocial behaviors as self-control and for organizing actions to achieve an external goal.

UNDERSTANDING VIOLENCE AND AGGRESSION

Although Skillstreaming is effective in changing the behavior of children and adolescents displaying a wide range of skill deficits, it is particularly effective in providing alternatives to aggression. Because aggression is such a problem among children and youth in schools and other settings, an overview of its causes and characteristics is important for teachers, support staff, administrators, and others involved in implementing Skillstreaming.

General factors associated with increased violence in schools and communities include frequent exposure to violence through the media, violent role models, health factors such as prenatal substance abuse, poverty, inadequate or abusive parenting, lack of social skills, discrimination, and lack of educational and job opportunities (National Association for the Education of Young Children, 1993). School demographics such as the school level (elementary, middle,

high school), neighborhood crime rate, and school location (city, urban fringe, rural) are additional factors impacting both crime and school disruptions (Nickerson & Martens, 2008).

Although a predisposition toward violent behavior may exist as a result of hereditary, hormonal, or biological factors (e.g., traumatic head injury), aggression is primarily a learned behavior. John Reid, clinical psychologist and director of the Oregon Social Learning Center in Eugene, has analyzed numerous studies suggesting that the two strongest predictors of violence and delinquency are ineffective, harsh, abusive, emotional discipline and lack of parental supervision (Bourland, 1995). Patterson, Reid, Jones, and Conger (1975) discuss these actions by describing a cycle of aggression that begins with coercive parenting. In this cycle, the parent reacts to the child in a hostile, threatening, or irritated manner. The parent is inconsistent in his or her discipline, at times providing very tight supervision and at other times providing almost no supervision at all. Discipline is characterized by yelling and corporal punishment. At times, the child will comply with the parent's coercion, providing a natural reward for the parent's disciplinary action. At other times, the child will act coercively in return—yelling, threatening, hitting, and so on.

As children so parented grow older, they deal with peer confrontations in a similar manner. If they want a toy, they take it. If they don't like something another child has said, they hit or kick. Other children (or these children's parents) react by not including aggressive youth, thus limiting the positive models from whom aggressive children can learn alternative behaviors and leading to social isolation. As aggressive children reach school age, they fulfill their need to have friends by seeking out peers who react similarly. Thus, the main characteristics of children who are the targets of coercive parenting are inadequate social skills and high levels of aggression both in and out of school.

A cycle similar to the one described by Patterson and colleagues (1975) in the home environment can often be seen in school. The teacher may yell at the child who refuses to follow directions in school. The one who verbally threatens to hit a peer may be threatened with punishment. The teacher's aggression (e.g., yelling, punishing) may further intensify the student's anger and problem behavior (Gemelli, 1996). Adults displaying such actions provide a powerful negative model for dealing with conflict, inadvertently teaching undesirable behaviors.

Aggressive children have been found to generate fewer alternative solutions when presented with problem situations, and their repertoires of solutions include fewer nonaggressive options (Camodeca, Goossens, Schuengel, & Terwogt, 2003). Instead, aggressive children offer more action-oriented solutions, such as pushing and fighting (Asarnow & Callan, 1985). Further, aggressive children anticipate that more positive outcomes and fewer negative outcomes will occur after an act of aggression (Hubbard, Dodge, Cillessen, Coie, & Schwartz, 2001).

Dodge, Lockman, Harnish, Bates, and Pettit (1997) and Crick and Dodge (1996) distinguish between two types of aggression: reactive and proactive. *Reactive aggression* is a response to frustration and the result of a child's diminished capacity for self-control. Aggressive behavior thus serves as a defense against a peer who is perceived as harmful. As stated by Guerra, Boxer, and Kim (2005), "An aggressive child is more likely to attend to aggression-promoting cues (e.g., being bumped into by a peer) and less likely to properly address prosocial cues (e.g., the peer subsequently apologizing" (p. 279). The child's perception of hostile intent results in a retaliatory response often accompanied with anger and high levels of social anxiety. *Proactive aggression* is a less emotional and more object-directed and organized response, likely driven by the expectation of receiving a reward. Proactive aggression, used to coerce or influence another, has been associated with criminal behavior (Raine et al., 2006).

Crick and Dodge (1994) hypothesize that reactive aggression is the result of a child's so-cial information processing deficit. In other words, there are errors in how a child thinks about and therefore responds to social cues. The child approaches social situations based on both biological capacity and as "a database of memories of past experiences" (p. 76). The child's response is dependent upon how these cues or events are processed. In this model of social information processing, the child's ongoing social experiences will contribute to his or her social knowledge in both quantitative and qualitative ways. Therefore, it is important to build the child's social knowledge by teaching alternative prosocial options.

INCLUDED IN THIS BOOK

This book provides a clear guide to understanding and using the Skillstreaming program with preschool and kindergarten children, organized into two parts. Part 1 includes chapters devoted to program content and implementation. Part 2 provides Skill Outlines and Homework Reports for each of the 40 skills in the curriculum.

Chapter 1, "Effective Skillstreaming Arrangements," describes the procedures necessary to plan and begin Skillstreaming at the preschool and kindergarten levels. Discussion concerns the specific arrangements to maximize the effectiveness of Skillstreaming instruction and the settings in which it occurs. In particular, we consider group leader selection and preparation; student selection and grouping; the role of support staff and parents in instruction; and specific instructional concerns such as skill selection, setting, materials, and instructional variations.

More than 30 years of research support the individual components of modeling, role-play (behavioral rehearsal), feedback, and generalization training, as well as the positive results when the four components are implemented together. Chapter 2, "Skillstreaming Teaching Procedures," examines these four core teaching procedures, along with the nine-step sequence constituting the Skillstreaming teaching method.

Chapter 3, "Sample Skillstreaming Session," offers an edited transcript of an introductory Skillstreaming session in a kindergarten classroom. This transcript depicts the leaders introducing students to the group's purpose and procedures and follows the Skillstreaming teaching procedures discussed in chapter 2. The skill used for instruction is Dealing with Teasing (Skill 27).

A challenge in intervention work is to match the intensity of the child's need to the type and amount of intervention. Chapter 4, "Refining Skill Use," describes factors that increase the effectiveness of Skillstreaming, as well as other skill-building strategies that may be incorporated for individuals with more intense behavioral concerns. Real-world use of this skill curriculum, especially in the face of difficult and challenging interpersonal circumstances, will require that trainees be skilled in employing skill sequences and combinations, also included in this chapter.

As evidence regarding Skillstreaming's effectiveness has accumulated, it has become clear that skill acquisition is a reliable finding. The main concern of any teaching effort is not how students perform in the teaching setting but how well they perform in their real lives. Chapter 5, "Teaching for Skill Generalization," examines approaches to enhance transfer and maintenance of skill learning.

Chapter 6, "Managing Behavior Problems," addresses issues in the group reflecting deficient motivation and heightened resistance and describes a framework of universal, targeted, and individual strategies for enhancing motivation and reducing resistance. Examination of individual strategies includes discussion of functional behavioral assessment (FBA) and steps in creating a behavior intervention plan (BIP).

Establishing positive relationships between families and the school is necessary to improve student behavior, as well as academic skills.

Although important at all age levels, positive working relationships with parents of the young child are critical. This is the subject of chapter 7, "Building Positive Relationships with Parents."

Finally, chapter 8, "Skillstreaming in the School Context" reviews issues surrounding school violence and discusses Skillstreaming as a viable schoolwide intervention for reducing aggression and other behavior problems in schools. Specifically examined are such topics as integrating Skillstreaming in the curriculum and the role of Skillstreaming as it relates to inclusion, multi-tiered systems of support, Positive Behavior Intervention and Supports (PBIS), and Response to Intervention (RTI).

Following these chapters, Part 2 presents Skillstreaming's 40 skills for the preschool and kindergarten child. Provided for each skill are a Skill Outline and two different Homework Reports. The Skill Outline includes the behavioral steps of the skill, notes for group leaders further explaining the steps, suggested situations for modeling displays, and related skill-supporting activities. Outlines and reports may be reproduced from this book or printed from the accompanying CD.

Three appendixes complete the book. Appendix A includes forms helpful in running the program in addition to the Skill Outlines and Homework Reports included in Part 2. These may be photocopied or printed from the CD at the back of this book. Recent research has pointed to the need to monitor the consistency and accuracy of program implementation. Appendix B therefore includes implementation checklists for leaders and those who supervise them, as well as for ensuring generalization integrity. Appendix C examines behavior management techniques based on behavior modification principles helpful in the Skillstreaming group and in general.

PART I

Skillstreaming Program Content and Implementation

CHAPTER 1

Effective Skillstreaming Arrangements

This chapter describes specific arrangements to organize and maximize the effectiveness of Skillstreaming instruction and the settings in which it occurs. Specifically discussed are topics relating to group leader selection and preparation; student selection and grouping; the role of support staff, program coordinator, and parents in instruction; instructional concerns such as skill selection, setting, and materials; and instructional variations.

GROUP LEADER SELECTION AND PREPARATION

Since Skillstreaming began, hundreds of persons with a wide variety of backgrounds and positions have been effective group leaders. Teachers, counselors, and psychologists in the schools; youth care workers in treatment facilities; and social workers in mental health and other community agencies are primary examples.

Regardless of the professional role of the leader, in any instructional group focusing on skill building, several competencies are necessary for effective instruction. These include general teaching skills, knowledge and understanding of Skillstreaming procedures, skills in managing behavior problems, a cultural understanding of group members, and motivation.

General Teaching Skills

In the Skillstreaming group, as in any learning environment, effective teaching skills are neces-

sary. The process involved in Skillstreaming—modeling, role-playing, performance feedback, and generalization—is the same sequence used when teaching a child any other skill, such as self-help skills (e.g., tying shoelaces) or academic behaviors (e.g., beginning reading or math skills). The competent classroom teacher, therefore, already possesses the necessary background to carry out Skillstreaming.

As in teaching any other skill or subject content, the teaching agenda, as described in chapter 2, is delivered in a clear and organized manner. Transitions from one activity to another are smooth, the lesson moves at an energetic pace, children are actively engaged, and the relevance of skills to children's real-life needs is emphasized. The teacher listens to what the children are saying, gives feedback to let the children know their views have been heard, and adjusts instruction according to the needs of the learners. Furthermore, the effective teacher believes in what he or she is teaching and demonstrates enthusiasm, thus conveying an excitement in learning.

Believing in the efficacy of the intervention contributes to the fidelity of implementation (implementing the Skillstreaming teaching agenda as designed). While some flexibility in Skillstreaming delivery is recommended to individualize the agenda to the particular needs of each student, for program success, the overall components must be implemented consistently and comprehensively. Group leader motivation may be increased by a thorough understanding of the rationale for Skillstreaming presented in this book and by mastering the program procedures.

Another quality of effective teaching, a component of group processing, is the ability to manage any behavior problems that may arise throughout the teaching process. One child may have difficulty paying attention; another child may want to talk about an unrelated topic; and still another child may wander about the room, reluctant to participate at all. The skilled teacher is able to respond to such events in a firm, helpful, and unobtrusive manner and to maintain the flow of instruction. Strategies for preventing and reducing the frequency or intensity of problematic behaviors that are nonresponsive to the general instructional procedures are presented in chapter 6.

In addition, teaching will be more effective if it occurs in an encouraging, positive classroom environment. Skill learning will also be more likely to endure and the skills more likely to be used in the child's real world by applying the strategies included in chapter 4 and by involving significant others (e.g., parents) in the child's learning (chapter 7).

Knowledge of Skillstreaming

In addition to general teaching skills, what specific knowledge is needed to make Skillstreaming instruction most effective? The following list describes the areas of preparation teachers or other leaders of Skillstreaming groups need, including skills and knowledge to implement procedures.

1. Knowledge of Skillstreaming background, goals, and procedures

2. Ability to orient participating children, support staff members, and parents to Skillstreaming

3. Ability to assess student needs and select skills relevant to children's real-life needs, emphasizing assertiveness and problem-solving skills

4. Ability to plan and present live modeling displays, including presentation of a coping model and verbal mediation techniques

5. Ability to initiate and sustain role-playing

6. Ability to present material in a sequential, clear, and detailed manner

7. Accuracy and sensitivity in providing encouragement and corrective feedback

8. Willingness to accept children's use of prosocial behaviors

9. Sensitivity to situations throughout the day in which skills could be used and prompting of appropriate skill use

Teachers and other group leaders may learn the background, goals, and procedures of Skillstreaming in a variety of ways, depending on their own learning styles. Some may read and study this Skillstreaming program book, then be ready to begin. Most other potential teachers of Skillstreaming will find that attending a workshop or training session, viewing the demonstration of real-life groups in operation presented in *The Skillstreaming Video* (Goldstein & McGinnis, 1988), or listening to others who have implemented the techniques successfully augments what they have read.

Although there is no right or wrong way to prepare to teach a Skillstreaming group, many adult learners respond most effectively to what might be called an apprenticeship training sequence. Reading this book, viewing the video, and attending a workshop are first steps in this sequence. A good next step is the opportunity to participate first in a mock Skillstreaming group led by experienced trainers and made up of leaders-to-be pretending to be students. After one or more such role-play opportunities, the potential group leader can observe an experienced leader conduct an actual group, then colead a group with the experienced leader, and, finally, lead the group while being observed by the experienced leader. This incremental training sequence, each of its steps adjustable in duration, has proven to be most satisfactory in training Skillstreaming group leaders.

In a school setting, for example, school social workers, psychologists, or counselors often carry out Skillstreaming groups, pulling individual children from various classrooms, or a counselor may co-teach Skillstreaming with the general education teacher in the classroom. A group of classroom teachers might request staff development training, which would first include participation in a mock Skillstreaming group. During planning time, individual teachers could observe and then participate as co-leader in an ongoing skills group. Support staff could then assist teachers in beginning groups in their own regular or special classroom settings. Some support staff and teachers together have decided to continue this team arrangement, with the teacher running the group alone only when the other leader must be absent.

Managing the Group

A variety of activities included in Skillstreaming will keep the enthusiastic attention of most preschool and kindergarten children within the recommended time frame (20 minutes for preschoolers and 25 minutes for kindergartners). It is helpful, however, to offer the children a special sticker (to be put on their clothing or on a classroom chart) or another small reward on completion of each session for behaviors such as participating, listening, providing feedback, and following classroom rules. If classroom rules have not been previously identified, they should be decided on prior to implementing Skillstreaming groups, discussed daily with the children to ensure understanding, and posted in the classroom. Rewarding such behaviors with small, material rewards, in addition to praising children's efforts, will help children feel positive about learning new prosocial behaviors.

Should behavioral concerns surface in the large group, a total-group management plan may be implemented. This type of plan might consist of dropping marbles in a jar when the group as a whole or specific youth show the desired behaviors, then providing a special activity for the entire group (e.g., extra recess) when the jar is full. Such plans may motivate the group to work cooperatively and may also increase the children's individual motivation. Children who have disabilities relating specifically to behavior, as well as others who frequently exhibit behavior problems, may need an even more structured plan to reinforce desirable group behaviors.

A frequent question from Skillstreaming training workshop participants is "Can one teacher alone successfully lead a Skillstreaming group?" The best answer to this question is "It depends." Whether or not an individual teacher will be successful depends on his or her skill in group management, as well as the skill deficiencies of the students. Though many Skillstreaming groups have been productively led by one teacher, we recommend that, whenever possible, two staff members work together, at least during the initial stages of instruction. To arrange and conduct a role-play between two children while at the same time overseeing the attention of other, easily distractible group members can be daunting. A much better arrangement involves two teachers (or one teacher and another adult, such as a paraprofessional, volunteer, or school support staff member). Most often the classroom teacher functions as the main teacher, leading the modeling and role-plays, while the other adult sits in the group, preferably next to the child who is most likely to have attention problems or to act disruptively. Facets of Skillstreaming that take place outside the training setting—implementing generalization techniques, for example—are most effectively accomplished by the classroom teacher throughout the school day, and, for this reason, the teacher must take the leadership role within the training setting.

Cultural Understanding

Skillstreaming group leaders need to demonstrate cultural proficiency. As defined by Robins,

Lindsey, Lindsey, and Terrell (2006), "Cultural proficiency is a way of being that allows individuals and organizations to interact effectively with people who differ from them" (p. 2). Which specific behaviors ideally define a given Skillstreaming skill? Which skills are optimal in any given setting? The answers will vary from culture to culture. Culture is defined by geography, ethnicity, nationality, social class, gender, sexual orientation, age, or some combination thereof. For Skillstreaming to be meaningful, it must be viewed and practiced within a multicultural context. The teacher must be aware of cultural differences so he or she can determine which behaviors are in actuality social skills deficits and which behaviors are a part of the child's culture and should either be appreciated as they are displayed or modified according to specific situations (Cartledge & Kourea, 2008; Cartledge & Milburn, 1996; Cartledge & Lo, 2006).

When teachers are members of or are only minimally familiar with different cultural groups, definitions and prescriptions may conflict. Learning goals may not be met. For example, youth may engage in verbal bantering that appears to observers from a different cultural orientation to be aggressive. Yet these behaviors may be common and acceptable in their culture. In such an instance, the behaviors themselves do not need to be changed; instead, instructional emphasis may need to focus on when and where such verbal exchanges are appropriate within the school context. Other examples of such differences include acceptability of assertiveness and nonverbal communication. For example, children from African American backgrounds tend to be more assertive, while individuals from Hispanic American, Native American, and Asian American backgrounds tend to be more passive, and Anglo students need more physical space between speakers than do the other groups (Elksnin & Elksnin, 2000).

In addition to addressing ethnic differences, Payne (1998) describes the culture of poverty. Referring to the hidden rules of generational poverty,

Payne states that poverty is more about other resources (emotional, mental, spiritual, physical, support systems, knowledge of middle-class hidden rules, role models) than it is about money. For example, hidden rules of poverty suggest a high value on relationships and strong beliefs in fate or destiny. Skillstreaming leaders need to understand poverty, as well as other cultures. Cartledge and Feng (1996) encourage teachers to "validate cultural background, making sure learners understand that certain situations will call for different responses, not that their ways of doing things are inferior" (p. 112). When we fail to address such cultural differences, students certainly will suffer. For instance, educators more frequently perceive African American students to have social difficulties (Harry & Klingner, 2006), and these students are more often identified for special education than are students from other groups (Donovan & Cross, 2002).

Classrooms in this country are increasingly characterized by different languages, cultures, and learning styles. With the increase in diversity, Perea (2004) has aptly observed that "there is no longer a single American culture to assimilate into" (p. 36). To reach all students, teachers and administrators will employ materials that are consistent with a diversity of backgrounds and learning styles (i.e., "appropriate") and that have been selected in consultation with persons representing the cultural groups concerned (i.e., "appreciative"). In discussing social skills interventions and what educators can do to interact with a culturally diverse student population, Cartledge and Johnson (1997) state:

> Social skill interventions are not to be viewed as a means for controlling students for the comfort of teachers or for homogenizing students so they conform to some middle-class prototype designated by the majority group in this society. Inherent in the concept of culturally-relevant social skill instruction is a reciprocal process where the educator: (a) learns to respect the learner's cultural background, (b) encourages the learner to appreciate the richness of this culture, (c) when needed, helps

the learner to acquire additional or alternative behaviors as demanded by the social situation, and (d) similarly employs and practices the taught behaviors. (p. 404)

Skillstreaming will be most effective when it reflects awareness of issues associated with skill strengths and differences versus skill deficits, differential teaching strategies and instructional methods, student channels of accessibility and communication styles, stereotyping of and by culturally different student populations, and culturally associated characteristics of target students. Culturally proficient instructional strategies may include multiple response techniques, appropriate pacing, establishing a community of learners, using models from the learner's cultural group, incorporating the learner's language into the instructional scripts, and involving parents in support of the instruction (Cartledge & Kourea, 2008). To deliver the program in a manner appreciative of and responsive to cultural factors, teacher knowledge, skill, and sensitivity are required.

Motivation

The decision to learn and teach this particular approach is typically motivated by the potential group leader's desire to enhance his or her own teaching or intervention skill to better serve children. Teachers and other professionals who work with children with behavioral problems typically do so to make a difference. In addition, implementing Skillstreaming can motivate both classroom teachers and administrators to employ the program because with fewer behavior problems, they will be allowed more time to focus on teaching and learning.

STUDENT SELECTION AND GROUPING

Student Selection

Student selection involves a twofold assessment task: First, if not all of the children in the class will be included, the task is to identify those who can benefit from direct instruction in skill building. The second part of the assessment task is to determine students' levels of proficiency in necessary skills. The selection process for young children may involve a number of assessment strategies, including sociometrics, behavior rating scales (teacher, parent, child), naturalistic observation, rubrics, and skill checklists. These last three strategies are the most user friendly and the least obtrusive and are the ones that lead most directly from assessment to instruction. It is important to remember, however, that assessment results are most useful when more than one type of evaluation procedure is used (i.e., the assessment is multimodal) and when children's strengths and deficits are assessed in a variety of situations and settings and by a variety of individuals—for example, peers, adults, parents (i.e., it is multisource).

In most Skillstreaming programs, assessment typically involves each child's teacher and parent, as well as the child. It is common, however, for a discrepancy between adult and child ratings to occur. Whether such a discrepancy reflects overconfidence, denial, blaming others, lack of ability to assess one's own skills, or some other process in the child's or adult's perception, it is important to get the perspective of each child on his or her own skill strengths and weaknesses, either through verbal interaction or via a skills checklist. Teaching the skills the student believes necessary has proven to be a major motivational strategy.

Direct Observation

Direct, or naturalistic, observation involves observing what the child does at particular times or in particular situations. Such observations, easily implemented by a classroom teacher, might involve taking frequency counts (e.g., how often a child deals with being teased or reacts to frustration in a particular manner), recording duration (e.g., how long it takes for a student to decide on something to do or the length of a crying episode), or making anecdotal records (e.g., what specific behaviors are of concern and their antecedents and consequences). Direct observation is especially valuable if the person or persons who are planning to serve as group leaders (teachers, youth care workers, etc.) are the same persons who are with the child all day and routinely see the child in interactions with others. In such circumstances, the behavioral observations can be frequent, take place in the child's natural environment, and reflect skill competence across diverse settings and situations.

Direct observation is one method that is also advocated in assessing the goal or purpose of the child's behavior, as in a functional behavioral assessment. Seeking to determine the student's motivation for engaging in a given maladaptive behavior will better help the adults who work with the child develop alternative, prosocial behavior plans, strategies, and skills to serve the same function for that child.

Skill Checklists

Skill checklists are designed to assess various individuals' perceptions of a student's skill proficiency. Checklists for teachers and other school staff, parents, and students are included in Appendix A. The Teacher/Staff Checklist is completed by a teacher or another person in the school environment who is familiar with the child's behaviors in a variety of situations. The rater is asked to gauge the frequency of the particular student's use of each of the 40 Skillstreaming skills. The checklist also provides an opportunity for the rater to identify situations in which skill use is particularly problematic, information that will be useful for later modeling scenarios. In situations in which whole-class instruction in Skillstreaming will be provided, the checklist may be used in two ways. First, a checklist may be completed for target students, those who demonstrate a high level of problematic behavior. Second, checklists completed for all students can provide a picture of overall student behavior or the skills in which the majority of students in the classroom struggle. Both approaches provide additional guidance for skill instruction.

The Parent Checklist assesses the parent's perceptions of the child's skill needs in the home and neighborhood. Like the Teacher/Staff Checklist, this rating scale allows the parent to respond to descriptions of the 40 prosocial skills in terms of the frequency of skill use. Information relative to the child's skill use outside of the school setting may be very useful; however, some discretion in requesting a parent to complete this checklist is necessary. The complete checklist may be given, or specific questions on the checklist may be selected to assess the child's strengths and weaknesses in skill areas that are of concern. Others may wish to use the checklist in an interview format with the parent. In whatever manner the Parent Checklist is used, it solicits valuable information regarding the child's skill competence and serves to increase parent involvement.

When used with the Child Response Record, also in Appendix A, the Child Checklist assesses children's own perceptions of the skills they feel they want or need to learn. Most appropriate for children ages five and older, the checklist is designed to be read to the individual child or to small groups of children in four separate evaluation sessions. This checklist helps children identify what types of behaviors they will be working on and will help increase their motivation if they see the skills as ones that have relevance to their lives.

Rubrics

Rubrics are rules or guides by which students' performance or a product is judged. The use of rubrics as an evaluation tool related to academic skills, content, and behaviors has become accepted practice in education. Using rubrics related to the acquisition of social skills is particularly useful for the following reasons:

1. Because of the qualitative nature of social skills, rubrics portray a better composite of skill acquisition, performance, and fluency than do more traditional social skills assessment measures. Rubrics offer descriptions of quality that are not necessarily included

in other performance evaluations (Schmoker, 1999).

2. Proficiency in using selected social skills does not necessarily equate with social competence. Rubrics allow for a more comprehensive picture of a child's social interaction.

3. By providing a clear target or objective, rubrics encourage the Skillstreaming leader to include the more subtle aspects of social performance in instruction, aspects beyond the rote learning of individual skills.

4. Rubrics convey a clear description of social expectations to teachers, parents, and students.

5. Rubrics permit assessment of a sequence from a lower quality to a higher quality of performance.

Rubrics describing levels of performance offer a fixed scale and identify specific characteristics that describe performance at each point on the scale (Marzano, Pickering, & McTighe, 1993) and provide a clear description of what is to be taught. Rubrics also provide useful, quantitative data on clear, carefully selected qualitative criteria. A rubric for assessing the social performance of preschool and kindergarten children is presented in Appendix A.

Student Grouping

Once selected for participation, children are grouped on the basis of two criteria. The first criterion is shared skill deficiency. It is useful to group students who share similar skill deficiencies or patterns of deficits. By doing so, leaders will provide more intense skill instruction in the areas those children most need. The Grouping Chart (Appendix A) is designed to summarize scores on the 40 social skills for entire classes, units, or other groups of children; it can readily be used to identify shared skill deficiencies.

The second grouping criterion concerns the generalization-enhancing principle of identical elements. This principle, discussed in greater detail in chapter 5, holds that the greater the similarity between the teaching setting and the real-world or application setting, the greater the likelihood that the child will actually perform the skill outside of the instructional setting. This principle is operationalized by teaching Skillstreaming to all children in a particular class, living unit, or neighborhood group. Classroom-based instruction is especially effective because of this important generalization principle, as well as because teachers are available to prompt skill use when appropriate situations in the classroom occur. When instruction is carried out in this manner, it functions as a universal intervention, reaching all students who may benefit. Some students may need more intense interventions (e.g., increased instructional time, additional interventions), and in such cases Skillstreaming in a whole-class model will be only a part of the behavior change plan. Including all children in the group or class in Skillstreaming may also help those who may develop behavior problems later on and who could benefit from skill instruction but who teachers or others have not at the present time identified as having skill needs.

SUPPORT STAFF AND PROGRAM COORDINATOR ROLES

Support Staff

The effort to teach prosocial behavior should not go forward in isolation; teachers and their students are a part of a school, a center, or another larger setting. Ways to select and prepare staff members who will serve as Skillstreaming group leaders have been described. What about the rest of the staff? They also have a meaningful role to play in this effort, even if they will not be serving as group leaders.

The goal of changing the behaviors of aggressive, withdrawn, or immature students often succeeds only at a certain time and in a certain place. That is, the program works, but only at or shortly after the time of instruction and only in the place of instruction. Thus, a program may make a child behave in more desirable ways during and immediately following the weeks of teaching, in the classroom where it took place. But a few weeks later—or in the school hallways, outside on the playground, on a field trip, at home, or elsewhere outside the classroom—the child's behavior may be as problematic as ever.

This temporary success followed by a relapse to the old, negative pattern of behavior is a failure of generalization. Generalization failures are much more the rule than the exception with many children. During Skillstreaming instruction, students receive a great deal of support, encouragement, and reward for their efforts. However, between group sessions or after instruction ends, many students receive little support for skill use.

The common failure of generalization is not surprising. However, this outcome can be minimized. Newly learned and thus fragile skills need not fade away after Skillstreaming instruction. Chapter 5 details ways to improve generalization outcomes. Briefly, however, if attempts to use such skills in the real world are met with success (i.e., support, enthusiasm, encouragement, reward), children will be much more likely to continue using the skills. Teachers, school staff, community members, parents, friends, counselors, peers, school administrators, and others who work directly with children are in an ideal position to promote continued skill use. All of these individuals can be powerful "transfer coaches," helping to make sure the Skillstreaming curriculum turns into a long-term or even permanent gain. Following are some specific ways these individuals can assist.

Learning the Program

All school or agency staff should become highly familiar with their institution's Skillstreaming program—its goals, methods, group leadership, and, especially, the skills themselves. Memos, faculty meetings, attendance at Skillstreaming workshops, hall corridor "Skill of the Week" posters, and other means should be regularly employed. In these ways, the transfer coach's prompting, encouraging, reassuring, and re-warding behaviors will more accurately target student skill needs.

Prompting

Under the pressure of real-life situations, both in and out of school, children may forget all or part of the skills they learned earlier. If their anxiety is not too great or their forgetting too complete, all they may need to perform a skill correctly is prompting. Prompting involves reminding children what to do (the skill), how to do it (the steps), when to do it (now or at another "good time"), where to do it (and where not to), and why the skill is useful (the positive outcomes expected). For example, the lunchroom supervisor may prompt a student to ignore teasing, in the school hallways the principal may suggest that a student deal with not being first in line, and in the library the librarian may prompt a student to ask a question or offer help to a classmate. The school playground offers many opportunities for children to practice friendship-making skills and alternatives to aggression; playground supervisors need to take an active role in prompting skill use in such environments.

Encouraging

Offering encouragement to children assumes they know a skill but are reluctant to use it. Encouragement may be necessary, therefore, when the problem is primarily a lack of motivation rather than a lack of knowledge or ability. Encouragement can often best be given by gently urging children to try using what they know, by showing enthusiasm for their skill use, and by communicating optimism about the likely positive outcome of skill use.

Reassuring

For particularly anxious students, skill generalization attempts will be more likely to occur if the threat of failure is reduced. Reassurance is an effective threat reduction technique. "You can do it" and "I'll be there to help if you need it" are examples of the kinds of reassuring statements the transfer coach can provide.

Rewarding

The most important contribution the transfer coach can make for skill generalization is to provide (or help someone else provide) rewards for correct skill use. Rewards may take the form of approval, praise, or compliments, or they may consist of special privileges, points, tokens, recognition, or other reinforcers built into a classroom's or school's management system. For example, one school successfully enhanced skill generalization by having all staff in the school distribute "Gotcha Cards" whenever they observed a student using a prosocial skill. All such rewards will increase the likelihood of continued skill use in new settings and at later times.

The most powerful reward that can be offered, however, is the success of the skill itself. For example, if after a student practices Accepting Consequences (Skill 31) and a real-life interaction goes very well, that reward (the successful interaction) will help the skill transfer and endure more than any external reward can. The same conclusion, that success increases generalization, applies to all of the Skillstreaming skills.

It is important for all adults and peers to react with behaviors that signal awareness of effective skill use. If transfer and maintenance become schoolwide goals—supported by staff, administrators, students, and parents—and all make a concerted effort toward this end, fragile skills will become lasting skills, and Skillstreaming will have been successful.

Program Coordinator

Even if teachers, students, and support staff are prepared and motivated to begin a Skillstreaming program, the participation of one more professional helps ensure a successful outcome. Many effective programs involve the appointment of a program coordinator or master teacher. It is unfortunately common for Skillstreaming programs to begin with appropriate organization, good intentions, and adequate enthusiasm, only to wind up being discarded a few months later because of a lack of oversight. The barrage of other responsibilities often placed on teachers and other frontline staff makes intervention programs more likely to fail in the absence of such guidance.

The program coordinator should be well versed in both Skillstreaming and program management. His or her responsibilities may include providing staff development, observing sessions, monitoring schoolwide progress, setting up specific generalization-increasing efforts, motivating staff, facilitating the gathering and distribution of materials, and handling the many other details on which program success depends.

PARENT INVOLVEMENT

Parents can and should be an integral part of the Skillstreaming program. Initially, informing parents of program goals will help them better understand and support these instructional efforts. Young children often select role-plays and homework assignments that depict problems at home, and children are likely to report to parents the new ways they are learning to handle such problems. Because situations that occur at home are included in program instruction, parents need to understand the purpose of the program and the manner in which such situations are being discussed. Potential misunderstandings can be averted if parents are aware of the purpose of the program, its procedures, and ways they may be involved in an ongoing manner.

Approaching skill instruction as a cooperative effort between parents and teachers will likely enhance communication and improve the relationship between home and school. Additionally, when children see that the skills they have learned at school are accepted and rewarded at home, they are more likely to use the newly learned behaviors in a variety of situations and environments, thus enhancing the success of teaching efforts. Because of the importance of involving parents and facilitating their participation in the Skillstreaming program, chapter 7 is devoted to this effort.

SPECIFIC INSTRUCTIONAL CONCERNS

Program planners and the teachers or others who carry out Skillstreaming instruction will need to consider the following mechanics of implementation.

Prerequisite Skills

The behavioral skills outlined in Part 2 are designed for children three to six years of age and for older children if their social and cognitive development warrants. Although most children in this age group will be successful in learning the skills when provided Skillstreaming instruction, the teacher will need to consider a few prerequisites. Specifically, children selected should be able to (a) attend to an ongoing activity for a short period of time (15 to 20 minutes); (b) follow simple directions; and (c) understand basic language concepts such as same, different, or, and not (Spivack & Shure, 1974). Deficiencies in these competencies will need to be remediated by maturation or direct teacher efforts prior to these children's involvement in Skillstreaming instruction. However, young children who possess some of the prerequisites but who, for example, have difficulty attending for this time period in a group setting may benefit from skills instruction conducted on an individual basis. Likewise, children with deficits in language or communication skills may be included in the group instruction but with special attention and instruction being given in areas such as understanding concepts and sequencing.

Skill Selection and Negotiation

We recommend that the group leader initiate instruction with the Beginning Social Skills (Group I). Several of the skills included in this group serve as behavioral steps for later skills or address important facets of skill performance, such as the way in which a skill is performed.

Other skills in this group are frequently needed and will likely bring a positive outcome, thus validating the success of skills teaching for children and teachers alike.

Once the children have learned the Group I skills, other skills should be selected on the basis of the needs and problems the children experience. Although some will be eager to discuss areas of skill need for themselves or their peers (e.g., "Sam says I'm a baby, and I hit him"), it is often up to the teacher to plan group discussions that will facilitate the sharing of skill need. In addition, the children's responses on the Child Checklist (Appendix A) will provide information about the skills children feel they need and want to learn. Because the needs of the group may vary, one or more skills may be selected from each of the remaining five skill groups, with the sequence of instruction depending on the most critical needs of the majority of the children in the class or group. Allowing the children to identify their own areas of skill need and to use skills in ways that benefit them will help promote effective and enduring learning and will increase their desire to learn other skills.

Skills that are important to others in the child's environment, such as parents and other teachers, are considered next. Selection of skills valued in the home and neighborhood can be made easier by considering parents' responses on the Parent Checklist (Appendix A). Considering parent input in the selection decision may also help identify skills that, although beneficial in the school setting, may actually be contradictory to the expectations of the home and neighborhood. The teaching challenge then, in addition to teaching the skill itself, becomes to emphasize skill flexibility—in other words adjusting skill use to different people and different situations. Parent input will guide the teacher in emphasizing the specific settings in which a given skill will most likely be useful.

The teacher can select additional skills for instruction by observing difficulties the children are experiencing in following school routines, interacting with their peers, and dealing with situations involving stress or conflict. The Teacher/Staff Checklist (Appendix A) can be useful in identifying these problematic skill areas. Selecting skills needed in day-to-day school-related problem situations allows the teacher to coach or prompt the child through the skill at the very time skill use is indicated. This powerful strategy, termed instructed generalization or capturing teachable moments, greatly enhances skill learning and performance.

Teaching the prosocial skills valued by the children's parents and teachers (and, in some cases, by peers) increases the likelihood that natural rewards will be forthcoming in the real-world environment. Such rewards are likely to help children maintain their use of the skills once direct teaching is withdrawn.

Introduction of New Skills

To reduce the possible interference of new learning with previously learned material, the teacher should introduce a second skill only when the child can recall the steps of the first skill, has had an opportunity to role-play it, and has shown some initial generalization of learning outside the teaching setting. Therefore, it may be necessary to spend four or five sessions on one skill. In the case of more complicated skills, two or three weeks, or even longer, may be needed before proceeding to another skill. Periodic review of previously learned skills reinforces these skills and encourages their use in new situations, provides systematic fading of the teaching to enhance generalization, and prevents boredom that may occur with concentration on only one skill for the time required for sufficient learning.

Instructional Setting

Ideally, the instructional setting for Skillstreaming will be the classroom, day care or preschool room, or other location where the child spends the majority of instructional and play time. Research provides two very important reasons in support of this recommendation. First, because the child's peers in this setting will also have received instruction, the child will be more likely to receive encouragement and assistance in actually using the skills. Second, because generalization from the teaching setting to the application setting does not occur automatically, teaching the skills in the environment in which the child will most often need the skills (i.e., the natural environment) promotes learning and skill maintenance. Alternative and typically less structured school areas—such as hallways, the playground, the school cafeteria, and the school bus—are good places to carry out instructional and practice sessions. When a given skill applies in an easily accessible school environment, modeling and role-playing should occur in that setting.

Occasionally, it may be necessary to provide skills instruction in another, more artificial environment, such as a counselor's office or a special education resource room. Although this type of instructional setting is less likely to promote long-term learning, teaching can and should be done if the child needs additional coaching to learn the skill. Such settings are not recommended either for ongoing instruction or as the only setting for skills teaching.

A special space should be provided in the classroom for the initial instruction of each skill. This most often is an area of the classroom where the children can sit cross-legged on the floor in a semicircle, a configuration that allows all children to view the modeling displays and role-plays. As with other types of group instruction, accommodations may need to be made to minimize problem behavior that may occur at this age level. These accommodations include having children sit in a clearly defined space (using tape on the floor or individual carpet samples), at a distance from a "best friend," and the like. Once the children can perform the skill in this somewhat artificial instructional setting, skills instruction can and should occur in other natural classroom settings (e.g., at tables or desks, play areas, or learning centers).

Time Factors

Frequency and Length of Sessions

At the preschool and kindergarten levels, skills-training sessions should be held on a daily basis whenever possible. Approximately 20 minutes for preschoolers and 25 minutes for kindergarten children should be planned for each session, with the time of the sessions adjusted on the basis of the children's attention span, interest, and maturity. Many teachers have found it most beneficial to conduct a 15-minute session early in the day (e.g., immediately following the classroom opening activities) and another 10-minute session later on (e.g., following recess or lunch). Holding the Skillstreaming session early will give the children more opportunity to practice the newly learned behaviors throughout the remainder of the day. Additional time can be planned for supplemental activities related to skill performance, such as those suggested in the Skill Outlines in Part 2 of this book. Continued skill use will also be facilitated if an additional five minutes at the end of the day is allotted for teacher and students to chart the skills they have practiced throughout the day. This and other generalization-enhancing procedures are discussed in chapter 5.

Throughout the school day, in both structured and unstructured settings, the teacher may prompt, encourage, reassure, and reward children for using the behavioral skills. When a situation suggesting instruction in Skillstreaming arises, the teacher may choose to provide additional group or individual sessions. From this viewpoint, Skillstreaming is an ongoing effort, with initial instruction occurring at the time set for the group and additional learning and generalization-enhancing procedures taking place throughout the school day.

Program Duration

When Skillstreaming groups first began in the 1970s, many practitioners implemented skills instruction for a few weeks, covering skills that appeared critical in the child's social development. More recently, it has been accepted that such instruction needs to be an ongoing part of the curriculum for young children in both general and special education programs. The 40 social skills included in Part 2 of this book may be taught repeatedly throughout successive school months or years as the child's proficiency, flexibility, and use of the behaviors become more refined. Teachers or other group leaders may then progress to more advanced skills, such as those included in *Skillstreaming the Elementary School Child* (McGinnis, 2012).

Materials

Other than the substantial cost of staff time, Skillstreaming is not an expensive program to implement. Necessary checklists and other program forms are provided in Appendix A and may be reproduced as needed. These materials may also be printed from the CD that accompanies this book.

A whiteboard or easel pad, skill cards listing the skill steps, and skill-step posters to hang in the classroom and school are also needed. Skill cards may be of the preprinted variety available from Research Press (see the example in Figure 1), or group leaders may make these cards themselves. (Skill posters are also available from the publisher.)

Other materials to enhance the effectiveness of Skillstreaming instruction already exist in most classrooms. For example, if a game or particular toy is an important part of the role-play, the actual object should be used whenever possible. The use of such real-life materials is based on the important principle of identical elements, discussed in chapter 5. Briefly, this rule states that the greater the similarities between the teaching and application settings, the greater the likelihood that children will transfer skills from one setting to the other. For this reason, items the children normally have access to should be used in both modeling displays and role-plays.

Figure 1: Sample Skill Card

SKILL 26

26

Showing Affection

1. Decide if you have nice feelings.

2. Choose.

    a. Say it.

    b. Hug.

    c. Do something.

3. When?

4. Do it.

INSTRUCTIONAL VARIATIONS

Historically, applications of Skillstreaming have been directed toward children and adolescents selected from a larger classroom group. There are advantages to doing so, as well as other gains to be achieved from providing instruction to the whole class. Therefore, instruction may be carried out in large or small groups and occasionally, in special circumstances, with individual children.

Large-Group Instruction

For two main reasons, it is best that all of the children in a given preschool or kindergarten class be involved in Skillstreaming instruction. First, teaching the whole group may prevent children

from developing maladaptive patterns of behavior that may over time become more well established and thus more difficult to change. There is value in providing all children with skill strategies and prosocial behaviors on a preventive basis to enable them to handle future skill-relevant difficulties. Second, providing instruction to the entire class involves the use of socially competent peers as models for those children with skill deficits or weaknesses. If the situation is handled with sensitivity, including skilled peers gives the skill-deficient child a unique advantage. Because the effectiveness of modeling is enhanced when the model is similar to the observer in age and other characteristics, children who are adept in a skill may be more effective models than the classroom teacher. In addition, children who are more competent in skill performance can function effectively as coactors in the role-plays.

General instruction, modeling displays, and the first several role-plays can be successfully carried out in a group of 20 or more children. Subsequent role-plays, sufficient to allow all children the opportunity to try out the skill under direct teacher guidance, are often carried out in two or more smaller groups, with an adult leader assigned to each group. With fewer children in a role-play group, more opportunity exists for each child to assume the role of the main actor and to receive constructive suggestions, encouragement, and reinforcement. The more practice a child has with a particular skill, the more likely he or she will be to apply that skill over time and in other environments.

Briefly, then, the whole group meets first to generate skill-relevant situations, present the skill, discuss the skill, and conduct the modeling and one or two role-plays. It is important not to stop the instruction of the given skill at this point, however. Skillstreaming is an experiential activity, and the role-playing is vital for learning. Role-plays, feedback, and homework must therefore be done in smaller groups.

When working with large groups of children, teachers have elicited assistance from other adults in the school (e.g., volunteers, school administrators, older children who act as peer helpers, even custodians). Some preschool, day care, or special education teachers may likely work with co-teachers or paraprofessionals, but kindergarten teachers may not have such help and may be faced with instructing the large group in all aspects of Skillstreaming. In this circumstance, it is particularly important that the teacher gain the attention and involvement of as many children as possible.

Teachers can encourage involvement by assigning group-helper roles, such as pointing out the skill steps on a skill poster as they are being role-played; encouraging children who are not active participants in the role-play to watch for the enactment of specific skill steps; and walking around these observers as much as possible while still maintaining verbal involvement in the role-play. Others have found success by using several older students as coactors in role-plays or by asking an older peer helper to watch for and provide feedback on particular skill steps.

Still others choose to teach Skillstreaming within the classroom, in a fashion similar to traditional reading groups. In this variation, the teacher introduces the skill and presents the modeling display and one or two role-plays to the whole group but conducts subsequent role-plays, feedback sessions, and assignment of homework in small groups. Thus, the teacher is able to spend time with students who need extra practice in role-playing to learn the skill.

Small-Group Instruction

Under certain circumstances, preschool and kindergarten children may be assigned to smaller groups according to common skill needs. This will likely mean that participating children will not be from the same classroom. Because role-playing is more effective when the teaching setting closely resembles the real-life environment, it is useful to include children whose social environments and peer groups are similar. Selecting participants from a common peer group will not

only make the role-play more realistic, but will also increase the likelihood that the children will attempt the skill with peers in the classroom or neighborhood.

The ideal small group consists of eight or fewer students, depending on student needs. If students exhibit particularly problematic behaviors, a more appropriate group size may be three or four students. If a smaller number is necessary due to members' aggression or out-of-control behavior, additional students may be added (perhaps at the rate of one new member per week) once the smaller group is operating successfully.

Small-group instruction is often carried out by a school counselor or other school support person. This type of setting and instruction is most beneficial if it provides added opportunities for skill learning and practice to those children who are in critical need of mastering the skills. Following this type of small-group instruction, it is most helpful if the children participate in whole-class instruction as well.

Individual Instruction

Although Skillstreaming is primarily designed to be carried out in a group setting, in special cases, modifications can be made to include one-to-one instruction. The child who needs additional help in learning a specific skill, who withdraws from group involvement, or who lacks the prerequisite skills for the group setting benefits from this type of instruction. For example, the child who bullies others can assume a leadership role in subsequent groups by first learning the skill via coaching and assisting the teacher in the modeling displays. When carried out individually, the Skillstreaming procedures remain the same, but the adult—or the child's peer if this is feasible—serves as the coactor in each role-play and provides the feedback, except for that elicited from the target child. Although individual instruction is a useful way of providing skills instruction to some children, the main objective should be to include all youth in a Skillstreaming group as soon as possible.

CHAPTER 2

Skillstreaming Teaching Procedures

More than 30 years of research support the individual components of modeling, role-play (behavioral rehearsal), feedback, and generalization, as well as the positive results when the four components are implemented together. These four core teaching procedures of Skillstreaming are described here, along with the sequence of steps illustrating how these procedures are incorporated into instruction. The importance of closely following these procedures for program integrity is discussed last.

CORE TEACHING PROCEDURES

Modeling

Modeling is defined as learning by imitation. Research has demonstrated that a wide array of behaviors can be learned, strengthened, weakened, or facilitated through modeling. These include acting aggressively, helping others, behaving independently, interacting socially, displaying dependency, exhibiting certain speech patterns, and behaving empathically, among others. It is clear that modeling can be an important tool in teaching new behaviors.

Three types of learning by modeling have been identified: *Observational learning* refers to the learning of behaviors a person has never performed before. Children are great imitators. Even very young children learn new behaviors by observing others (mostly peers), whether these are styles of dressing, ways of talking, play activities

(e.g., house, school), or other positive or negative behaviors.

Inhibitory and *disinhibitory effects* involve the strengthening or weakening of behaviors previously performed only rarely by a person because of a history of punishment or other negative reactions. Modeling offered by peers is, again, a major source of inhibitory and disinhibitory effects, and it frequently results in children's succumbing to peer pressure. Children who know how to be altruistic and caring may inhibit such behaviors in the presence of models who are behaving more egocentrically and being rewarded for their egocentric behavior. Aggressive models may have a disinhibitory effect: If a child sees another go unpunished for aggression, the observing youth may engage in aggressive behavior as well.

Behavioral facilitation refers to the performance of previously learned behaviors that are neither new nor a source of potential negative reactions from others. One person buys something he or she seems to enjoy, so a friend buys one, too. A child deals with a confrontational peer in an effective manner, then a classmate approaches a similar problem the same way. These are examples of behavioral facilitation effects.

Although modeling is powerful, it is also true that most people observe dozens and perhaps hundreds of behaviors that they do not then engage in themselves. Television, radio, magazines and newspapers, and the Internet expose people to very polished, professional modeling displays of someone's buying one product or another, but observers do not later buy the product. People observe expensively produced instructional videos, but they may not learn the skills depicted. Children may see many behaviors enacted by peers in a given school day but copy only a few or none. Clearly, people learn by modeling under some circumstances but not others.

Modeling Enhancers

Research on modeling has successfully identified modeling enhancers, or conditions that increase the effectiveness of modeling. These modeling enhancers are characteristics of the model, the modeling display, or the observer (the learner). These variables affect learning, as does use of a coping model.

Model characteristics

More effective modeling will occur when the model (the person to be imitated) (a) seems to be highly skilled or expert; (b) is of high status; (c) controls rewards desired by the observer; (d) is of the same sex, approximate age, and social status as the observer; (e) is friendly and helpful; and, of particular importance, (f) is rewarded for the behavior. That is, we are all more likely to imitate expert or powerful yet pleasant people who receive rewards for what they are doing, especially when the particular rewards involved are things we, too, desire.

Modeling display characteristics

More effective modeling will occur when the modeling display shows the behaviors to be imitated (a) in a clear and detailed manner; (b) in the order from least to most difficult behaviors; (c) with enough repetition to make overlearning likely; (d) with as little irrelevant detail as possible; and (e) performed by several different models rather than a single one.

Observer (learner) characteristics

More effective modeling will occur when the person observing the model is (a) told to imitate the model; (b) similar to the model in background or attitude toward the skill; (c) friendly toward or likes the model; and, most important, (d) rewarded for performing the modeled behaviors.

Coping model

Modeling is more effective when a coping model, or a model who has some difficulty achieving the goal of competent skill performance, is presented (Bandura, 1977). When demonstrating Dealing with Feeling Mad (Skill 28) or Saying No (Skill 38), for example, it is important to show some emotion and to struggle a little with modeling. This struggle must be demonstrated in a low-key manner and in an acceptable way so it does not detract from the modeling display. However, if young children perceive that the skill is "easy" and can be performed without any feeling, they may be less likely to try the skill when caught up in the emotion of a real-life event. Depicting coping models will further enhance children's ability to identify with the model and will likely give them more courage to try the skill themselves.

Stages of Modeling

The effects of these modeling enhancers, as well as of modeling itself, can be better understood by considering the three stages of learning through modeling.

Attention

Children cannot learn from watching a model unless they pay attention to the modeling display and, in particular, to the specific behaviors being modeled. Students are better able to attend to the modeling if the display eliminates irrelevant detail, minimizes the complexity of the modeled material, makes the display vivid, and implements the modeling enhancers previously described.

Retention

To later reproduce the behaviors observed, the child must remember or retain them. Because the behaviors of the modeling display itself are no longer present, retention must occur by memory. Memory is aided if the observer classifies the displayed behaviors. Another name for such classification is *covert rehearsal* (i.e., reviewing in one's mind the performance of the behaviors modeled). Research has shown, however, that an even more important aid to retention is overt rehearsal (i.e., behavioral rehearsal). Such practice of the specific behavioral steps in a skill is critical for learning and, indeed, is the second major procedure of Skillstreaming—role-playing. It should be noted at this point, however, that the likelihood of retention by either covert or overt rehearsal is greatly aided by rewards provided to both the model and the observer.

Reproduction

Researchers in the area of learning have distinguished between learning (acquiring or gaining knowledge) and performance. If a person has paid attention to the modeling display and has remembered the behaviors shown, it may be said that the person has learned. However, the main interest is not so much that the person can produce the behaviors observed but whether he or she does produce them. As with retention, the likelihood that a person will actually perform a learned behavior greatly depends on the expectation of a reward for doing so.

Verbal Mediation or "Thinking Aloud"

Saying aloud what would normally be thought to oneself silently, or verbal mediation, is a valuable and necessary part of both modeling and role-playing. Saying the steps aloud as the models or role-players are enacting the behaviors demonstrates the cognitive processes underlying skill performance, helps curb impulsivity, and facilitates both initial learning and generalization of the skill (Camp & Bash, 1981,

1985). For example, in Joining In (Skill 15), the model might say, "I want to ask if I can play, but I'm afraid they might say no. But I'm going to try. OK, the first step is to watch." Likewise, in Knowing When to Tell (Skill 35), the model would recite the skill steps in the context of the situation—for example, "Those kids are teasing Jessie. They shouldn't do that. It's a problem, but should I tell? What's the first step?" This type of accompanying narration increases the effectiveness of the modeling display (Bandura, 1977), draws the attention of the observers to the specific skill steps, and may facilitate generalization of the skill (Stokes & Baer, 1977). Verbal mediation also helps to demonstrate a coping model. For example, in Waiting Your Turn (Skill 16), the model might say aloud, "It's hard to wait, but I can do it." Many young children will need to be taught the process of thinking aloud by having them practice while they are engaged in other types of activities (e.g., "Which picture goes with the dog? Look at all of them. Is it the chair? No. Keep looking").

Role-Playing

Role-playing has been defined as when an individual is asked to demonstrate specific behaviors not typical for him or her or to respond to certain situations with behaviors within his or her repertoire (Mann, 1956). Learning appears to be improved when the learner has the opportunity and is encouraged to practice, rehearse, or role-play the behaviors and is rewarded for doing so. The use of role-playing to help a person change behavior or attitudes has been a popular and useful approach for many years. However, as with modeling, behavior or attitude change through role-playing will occur and be more lasting only if certain conditions are met. If the role-player has enough information about the content of the role-play to enact it and if sufficient attention is paid to the factors that enhance role-play effectiveness, it is more likely that behavior or attitude change will occur. Specific role-play enhancers include (a) choice on the part of the trainee regarding whether to take part in the role-play; (b) public commitment to the behavior; (c) improvisation in enacting the role-played behaviors; and (d) reward, approval, or reinforcement for performing the behaviors. The role-players should also be reminded to think out loud what they would normally think silently. Thinking aloud helps the students stay focused on the skill steps during the role play, helps organize their thoughts, and helps observers better understand why steps and choices are made.

Seeing the modeling display teaches students what to do, but repeated practice in a variety of contexts is needed to increase skill fluency. However, in most attempts to help a person change behavior, neither modeling alone nor role-playing alone is enough. Combining the two is an improvement, for then the learner knows both what to do and how to do it. But even this combination is insufficient, for the learner still needs to know why he should behave in new ways. That is, a motivational or incentive component must be added. Performance feedback is this component.

Performance Feedback

Performance feedback is defined as providing the learner with information on how well he or she has done during role-playing. It may take such forms as constructive suggestions for improvement, coaching, reteaching, material rewards, and, especially, social reinforcement such as praise and approval. Social reinforcement (i.e., praise, approval, and encouragement) has been shown to be an especially potent influence on behavior change. In addition, positive feedback from peers has been shown to increase peer acceptance, as well as appropriate behavior (Jones, Young, & Freeman, 2000; Moroz & Jones, 2002; Skinner, Cashwell, & Skinner, 2000). Peer feedback has been shown to have positive effects on prosocial behavior. For example, Moroz and Jones (2002) implemented a positive peer reporting program that taught students to describe

and provide praise to socially isolated classmates during structured sessions. Results showed a decrease in negative behaviors and an increase in positive social interactions in the classroom. Jones, Young, and Friman (2000) also instructed peers in giving positive feedback to delinquent, socially rejected adolescents. This protocol included looking at the learner, smiling, saying a positive thing the learner did or said, and giving verbal praise. Their results indicated improved peer acceptance for the target youth. Younger children have also been successfully taught how to recognize socially appropriate behavior and to tell teachers when peers behaved in socially appropriate ways (to "tootle" versus "tattle"; Skinner et al., 2000). Results of these studies suggest involving peers in the endeavor to improve the social behaviors of skill- deficient children.

Because peer feedback has been found to be instrumental in improving the behavior of target youth, this is an important element in Skillstreaming. To be most effective, group leaders should follow these guidelines:

1. Provide reinforcement only after role-plays that follow the behavioral steps.
2. Provide reinforcement at the earliest appropriate opportunity after role-plays that follow the behavioral steps.
3. Always provide reinforcement to the coactor for being helpful, cooperative, and so forth.
4. Vary the specific content of the reinforcements offered (e.g., praise particular aspects of the performance, such as tone of voice, posture, phrasing).
5. Provide enough role-playing activity for each group member to have sufficient opportunity to be reinforced.
6. Provide reinforcement in an amount consistent with the quality of the given role-play.
7. Provide no reinforcement when the role-play departs significantly from the behavioral steps (except for "trying" in the first session

or two; instead, coach the learner in following the skill steps).

8. Provide reinforcement for an individual learner's improvement over previous performance.

Generalization

As noted previously, the main interest of any intervention program and where most programs fail is not student performance during the instruction but, instead, to what degree the student uses newly learned skills in natural settings and contexts and experiences improved quality of life. The goal of Skillstreaming is successful social functioning in school, at home, or in other places. Generalization training assists the learner in identifying where and when skill use is desired or necessary. Chapter 5 includes a variety of generalization strategies to enhance continued use of skills over time and in different settings.

STEPS IN THE SKILLSTREAMING SESSION

Carrying out the core Skillstreaming teaching procedures—modeling, role-playing, performance feedback, and generalization—involves leading the group through the following nine steps:

▶ Step 1: Define the skill

▶ Step 2: Model the skill

▶ Step 3: Establish student skill need

▶ Step 4: Select the first role-player

▶ Step 5: Set up the role-play

▶ Step 6: Conduct the role-play

▶ Step 7: Provide performance feedback

▶ Step 8: Select the next role-player

▶ Step 9: Assign skill homework

The following text describes these steps and illustrates the Skillstreaming procedure in operation. Table 2 provides a detailed summary of the steps for ongoing reference.

Step 1: Define the Skill

Most young children are likely to be more motivated to learn the behaviors presented in Skillstreaming instruction when they feel they need to learn a particular behavioral skill. For example, if a preschooler often feels that he is the brunt of teasing from peers, the child will be more highly motivated to learn Dealing with Teasing (Skill 27) than another skill not as immediately relevant. Information regarding relevant skills can be obtained by referring to the children's responses on the Child Checklist (Appendix A), as well as by discussing with the group the day-to-day problems they encounter.

In a brief discussion activity, the teacher or other group leader presents the skill. The goal is for students to understand the skill in a general way. The presentation and discussion should be relatively brief because the attention span of this age group is short. The following types of questions will help stimulate appropriate discussion:

▶ "Who finds it hard to wait for a turn while playing a game?" "Why is this important to learn?" (Waiting Your Turn, Skill 16)

▶ "What does sharing mean?" "Is it hard for you to share a toy with someone else?" (Sharing, Skill 17)

▶ "Who can tell me what a mistake is?" "Who feels really mad after making a mistake?" (Dealing with Mistakes, Skill 33)

The skill is typically defined in only a few minutes of discussion when children are prompted with such questions.

The specific behavioral steps to achieve the skill are presented next and discussed briefly. The teacher should ensure that the participants understand the vocabulary included in the skill and have a general understanding of what they will be learning. Children should receive a skill card (see Figure 1), and/or the skill and corresponding steps should be presented on a poster or written on a whiteboard or easel pad and displayed for the group.

Table 2: Skillstreaming Session Outline

Step 1: Define the skill

1. Choose skills relevant to the needs of the children as they perceive them.

2. Discuss each skill step and any other relevant information pertaining to each step.

3. Use skill cards and/or poster or whiteboard or easel pad on which the skill and steps are written so all group members can easily see the steps and illustrations.

Step 2: Model the skill

1. Use at least two examples for each skill demonstration.

2. Select situations relevant to the children's real-life circumstances.

3. Use modeling displays that demonstrate all the behavioral steps of the skill in the correct sequence.

4. Use modeling displays that depict only one skill at a time. (All extraneous content should be eliminated.)

5. Show the use of a coping model.

6. Have the model "think aloud" steps that ordinarily would be thought silently.

7. Depict only positive outcomes.

8. Reinforce the model who has used the skill correctly by using praise or encouraging self-reward.

Step 3: Establish student skill need

1. Elicit from the children specific situations in which the skill could be used or is needed.

2. List the names of the group members and record the theme of the role plays.

Step 4: Select the first role-player

1. Select as the main actor a child who describes a situation in his or her own life in which skill use is needed or will be helpful.

2. Provide encouragement and reinforcement for the child's willingness to participate as the main actor.

Step 5: Set up the role-play

1. Have the main actor choose a coactor who reminds him or her most of the other person involved in the problem.

2. Present relevant information surrounding the real event (i.e., describe the physical setting and events preceding the problem).

3. Use props when appropriate.

4. Review skill steps and direct the main actor to look at the skill card or the skill steps on display.

5. Assign the other group participants to watch for specific skill steps.

Step 6: Conduct the role-play

1. Instruct the main actor to "think out loud."

2. As needed, assist the main actor (e.g., point to each behavioral step as the role-play is carried out; have the co-leader sit among the group members, directing their attention to the role-play).

Step 7: Provide performance feedback

1. Seek feedback from the coactor, observers, leader(s), and main actor, in turn.

2. Provide reinforcement for successful role-plays at the earliest appropriate opportunity.

3. Provide reinforcement to the coactor for being helpful and cooperative.

4. Praise particular aspects of performance (e.g., "You used a brave voice to say that").

5. Provide reinforcement in an amount consistent with the quality of the role-play.

Step 8: Select the next role-player

Ask, "Who would like to go next?"

Step 9: Assign skill homework

1. Assign homework to the main actor if he or she has successfully role-played the skill.

2. Give the main actor the appropriate Homework Report.

3. Discuss with the main actor when, where, and with whom he or she will use the skill in real life.

From *Skillstreaming in Early Childhood: Teaching Prosocial Skills* (3rd ed.), © 2012 by E. McGinnis, Champaign, IL: Research Press (www.researchpress.com, 800-519-2707).

It is important for the teacher to avoid giving a lecture when defining the skill. Although part of a teacher's job is to talk and explain, Skillstreaming must be carried out as an experiential activity, and defining the skill must be carried out with dispatch.

Step 2: Model the Skill

Before the session, leaders should plan their modeling displays, including at least two examples for each skill demonstration. If a skill is used in more than one group session, it is wise to develop two new modeling displays. The display should show situations relevant to children's real-life circumstances, and the leader enacting the behavioral steps of the skill should be portrayed as a child reasonably similar in age, socioeconomic background, verbal ability, and other characteristics salient to the children in the Skillstreaming group. Modeling displays should demonstrate all the behavioral steps of the skill in the correct sequence, should use a coping model, and should show positive outcomes. Finally, modeling displays should depict only one skill at a time, with no extraneous content, and the model using the skill well should always be reinforced.

To encourage students to attend to the skill portrayals, skill cards, which list the name of the skill being taught and its behavioral steps, are distributed prior to the modeling displays (see Figure 1). A skill poster outlining the skill steps may be used instead of or in addition to skill cards. Students are asked to watch and listen closely as the modeling unfolds. Particular care should be given to helping students identify the behavioral steps as they are being modeled. The teacher can do this by pointing to the steps in the course of the modeling. As the model follows the behavioral steps, he or she "thinks out loud" what would normally be thought silently. At the conclusion of each modeling vignette, group members are asked, "Did I follow the first step?" "How do you know I did this?" The model may also provide self-reinforcement, such as "Yes, I followed all of the steps. I think I did a good job!"

To summarize, modeling displays should relate to the group's real-world concerns, and leaders should take care to incorporate the following guidelines:

1. Use at least two examples for each skill demonstration. If a skill is used in more than one group session, develop two new modeling displays.

2. Select situations relevant to students' real-life circumstances.

3. The model (i.e., the person enacting the behavioral steps of the skill) should be portrayed as a child reasonably similar to the group members in age, socioeconomic background, verbal ability, and other characteristics.

4. A coping model should be portrayed with skills that typically elicit strong emotion.

5. The model should "think aloud" what would normally be thought to oneself as the modeling display unfolds.

6. Modeling displays should depict positive outcomes. In addition, the model who is using the skill well should always be reinforced.

7. Modeling displays should depict all the behavioral steps of the skill in the correct sequence without extraneous or distracting content.

8. Modeling displays should depict only one skill at a time.

The Skill Outlines included in Part 2 of this book suggest a number of possible modeling situations in school, home, and peer settings.

Step 3: Establish Student Skill Need

Behavioral rehearsal is the purpose of the role-play. Before group members begin role-playing, it is important to identify each child's current and future need for the skill. Reenactment of a past problem or circumstances is less relevant than current and future need unless the student predicts that such circumstances are likely to reoccur in the future. Current skill needs will probably have been established earlier as part of the skill selection and grouping process through use of the skill checklists. Nonetheless, a discussion within the class or group is needed to establish relevant and realistic role-plays. Each student is in turn asked to briefly describe where, when, and with whom he or she would find it helpful to use the skill just modeled. Instruction with a large group requires that those children who will be role-playing give such information during each session. More than one or two sessions will be needed for all students to offer this information and be the main actor in a role-play of the target skill.

To make effective use of this information, it is often valuable to list the names of the group members on the whiteboard or easel pad at the front of the room and to record next to each name the general theme of the role-play. With children at this young age, especially when Skillstreaming is new, the teacher or other group leader may need to ask leading questions to prompt the generation of skill situations. Such questions could include "I notice that many kids have difficulty ignoring when at the listening center. How many of you think you need to practice this skill at the listening center?"

Step 4: Select the First Role-Player

All members of the Skillstreaming group will be expected to role-play each skill taught; therefore, in most cases it is not of great concern who does so first. Typically, teachers ask for volunteers to begin the series of role-plays. If for any reason there are children who appear to be reluctant to role-play a particular skill on a particular day, it is not necessary to ask them to be one of the first. Observing others can be reassuring and may help them ease their way into the activity.

In general, young children should be encouraged, reassured, and reminded to use the skill to meet their own needs rather than penalized, threatened, or otherwise coerced into partici-

pation. When confronted with a reluctant participant, many teachers of young children have found that coaching the child through the role-play on a one-to-one basis outside of the group or allowing the student to participate in another manner before role-playing (e.g., point to the behavioral steps or pictures as a peer's role-play unfolds) will be sufficient for the child to join in a role-play at a later time.

Step 5: Set Up the Role-Play

Following the discussion and listing of situations in which the skill is needed, a main actor is selected. The main actor chooses a second person (the coactor) to play the role of the other person (e.g., teacher, peer, parent) with whom he or she will use the skill in real life. The main actor should be encouraged to select as the coactor someone who resembles the significant other in as many ways as possible—in other words, someone who reminds the main actor most of the actual person.

The teacher then elicits from the main actor any additional information needed to set the stage for the role-play. To make role-playing as realistic as possible, the teacher should obtain information as to where the problem will likely occur, what typically happens before the problem situation, and what attitude or manner the coactor should display. Props may be used if available and appropriate.

Step 6: Conduct the Role-Play

At this point the teacher should remind group members of their roles:

▶ Main actor: Follow the behavioral steps and "think aloud" what would normally be thought silently.

▶ Coactor: Stay in the role of the other person.

▶ Other students: Watch carefully for the portrayal of the behavioral steps.

It is useful to assign separate behavioral steps to the observers, have them watch for the display of these steps, and then report on step use during the subsequent feedback session. For the first several role-plays, observers can be coached as to what kinds of cues to observe (e.g., body language, words chosen, tone of voice, facial expression).

The role-players are then instructed to begin. At this point, it is the teacher's responsibility to remind the main actor to "think out loud" and provide any help or coaching needed to keep the role-play going according to the behavioral steps. If the role-play is clearly going astray, the scene can be stopped, needed instruction provided, and the role-play resumed. It is helpful for the teacher (or co-leader if one is available) to be positioned near the skill poster and point to each of the steps as they are enacted. This will help the main actor, as well as the observers and coactor, follow the steps in order.

Role-playing should be continued until all group members have had an opportunity to participate as the main actor or until the attention of the group is waning. Sometimes giving everyone a chance will require two or more sessions for a given skill. As noted, each session should begin with two modeling vignettes for the selected skill, even if the skill is not new to the group. It is important to note that, although the framework (behavioral steps) of each role-play remains the same, the content can and should change from role-play to role-play. For example, even though several children may have difficulty with being teased on the playground, the situations in which they are teased, as well as the person who is the teaser, will be different. It is important for each child to role-play within the context of the real-life situation.

Other strategies may be used to support a role-play. For example, role reversal is often useful. If a main actor has a difficult time perceiving the coactor's point of view, having the two exchange roles and resume the role-play can be most helpful. On occasion, the group leader can also assume the coactor role in an effort to give students the opportunity to handle types of reactions not otherwise role-played during the session. It may be critical to have a difficult adult role realistically portrayed, for instance. The leader as a coactor may also encourage less verbal or more hesitant students. Finally, the leader as coactor also may be indicated with particular skills (e.g., Dealing with Teasing, Skill 27), which otherwise would require the student coactor to engage in inappropriate or attention-getting behaviors.

Step 7: Provide Performance Feedback

A brief period of feedback follows each role-play. Feedback lets the main actor find out how well he or she followed the behavioral steps, offers an evaluation of the impact of the role-play on the coactor, and gives the main actor encouragement to try out the behavior in real life. Feedback is presented in the following order:

1. The coactor is asked to react first (e.g., "How did it feel when she said that to you?").

2. Next, the observers comment on whether or not the skill steps they were assigned to watch for were followed and on other relevant aspects of the role-play. When asking for this feedback, it is helpful to ask questions such as "Did _____ follow the first step? Did he stop and think about what could happen? How do you know he did this?" Many children will likely explain that they heard the main actor talking about his thinking (thinking aloud).

3. Then the teacher or co-leader comments in particular on how well the behavioral steps were followed and provides social reinforcement (praise, approval, encouragement) for close following of the skill steps.

4. After listening to the feedback from the coactor, observers, and group leaders, the main actor is asked to make comments regarding the role-play and, if appropriate, to respond to the comments of others. In this way the main actor can learn to evaluate the effectiveness of his or her skill performance in light of others' viewpoints.

The teacher should provide enough role-playing activity for each group member to have sufficient opportunity to be reinforced. The teacher should not provide reinforcement when the role-play departs significantly from the behavioral steps (except for "trying"). However, he or she may provide reinforcement for an individual student's improvement over previous performances and reteach the skill if necessary.

In all aspects of feedback, group leaders must maintain the behavioral focus of Skillstreaming. Leader comments must point to the presence or absence of specific, concrete behaviors and not take the form of general evaluative comments or generalizations. Feedback may be positive or negative in content. Positive feedback should always be given first; otherwise, the child may be concentrating on the negative comments and not hear the other feedback. Negative feedback should be constructive in nature, offering suggestions for what might improve skill enactment. The group leader will need to model constructive comments before allowing young students to give this type of feedback to their peers.

Whenever possible, children who fail to follow the behavioral steps in the role-play should be given the opportunity to repeat the steps after receiving corrective, constructive criticism. At times, as a further feedback procedure, we have videorecorded entire role-plays. Giving students the opportunity to observe themselves can be an effective aid, enabling them to reflect on their own behavior.

Because a primary goal of Skillstreaming is skill flexibility, role-play enactment that departs somewhat from the behavioral steps may not be "wrong." That is, a different approach to the skill may actually be effective in some situations. Teachers should stress that they are trying to teach effective choices and that learning the behavioral steps as shown will give children more choices for dealing with problems.

Step 8: Select the Next Role-Player

The next student is selected to serve as the main actor, and the sequence just described is repeated until all members of the Skillstreaming group or class are reliably demonstrating proficiency in using the skill. As noted previously, for young children, opportunities for all to role-play successfully may require several Skillstreaming sessions on each skill.

Step 9: Assign Skill Homework

Skill homework constitutes an essential part of the generalization component of Skillstreaming. At the end of each session, group members who completed a successful role-play (those in which the behavioral steps have been followed) are asked to try the skill in their own real-life setting. It is most helpful to begin with relatively simple homework assignments (e.g., situations that occur in the school environment, situations without a high level of stress or emotion) and, as mastery is achieved, work up to more complex assignments. This sequence provides the teacher with an opportunity to reinforce each approximation toward competent performance. The child should not be expected to perform the skill perfectly when first using it in real-life contexts. Reinforcement should be given as the child's performance comes closer to the ideal. Successful experiences when beginning to use the skill in the real world (i.e., successful completion of homework) and rewards received for doing so are critical in encouraging the student to attempt further use of the skill.

Two levels of homework are suggested. The first is used until the teacher is reasonably certain the child has a good understanding of the expected performance of the skill. The child can then be instructed to practice the skill by completing the second level of homework. Part 2 of this book provides Homework Reports of both types for each skill.

Homework Report 1

At this beginning level, the child thinks of a situation either at home or school in which he or she would like to or needs to practice the skill. When Skillstreaming is still fairly new to the group, the teacher may need to provide strong guidance in selecting these situations. It is especially helpful if the situation chosen is the same one the child has role-played successfully. As shown on the sample Homework Report 1 (Figure 2), the teacher lists the child's name and the date the assignment is made. Together, the teacher and the child decide on the person with whom the child will try the skill and when the attempt will be made (e.g., during free play, outside at home after school). After the child actually tries the skill, the child evaluates how well he or she followed the steps by coloring in one of the three faces on the form. Because many young children may not be able to make accurate self-evaluations when they first begin this procedure, the teacher should discuss the child's reasons for the choice. In addition, it must be made clear to the child that this evaluation pertains to how well the skill steps were followed rather than how well the skill worked. If desired, the teacher may use the blank Homework Report 1 form in Appendix A, providing assistance as needed to have the child list and illustrate the skill steps. Having the child do so is a good way to enhance skill learning.

Homework Report 2

The child who has been successful with Homework Report 1 is ready to attempt monitoring his or her own skill use. As the sample in Figure 3 shows, throughout the course of the day, the child colors a happy face whenever the skill is practiced. As appropriate, the teacher may assist the child in writing the behavioral skill steps and drawing illustrations for the target skill on the blank Homework Report 2 included in Appendix A.

Using the Homework Reports

The first part of each Skillstreaming session after the first is devoted to presenting and discussing the children's homework assignments, which the teacher has previously reviewed on an individual basis. This individual review is suggested so that a child who may have been unsuccessful can be spared the possible embarrassment of sharing this failure publicly. When possible, the teacher may point out one aspect of the homework that was positive and ask the child to share this step. Students with challenging behaviors often receive too little praise; therefore, when children have made an effort to complete their homework assignments, the teacher should provide social reinforcement for this achievement (e.g., "You showed courage in trying this skill! This was a good try!"). A child who repeatedly fails to complete the homework is likely to need further skill instruction, an opportunity to complete homework in a school setting that will allow the teacher to prompt the child, or more potent reinforcers (i.e., tangible rewards).

Group Rewards, Self-Monitoring Forms, Reinforcers, and Awards

Self-monitoring forms like the one shown in Figure 4 can help children follow through with skill practice, as can group reward forms (see the example in Figure 5). Skill tickets and notes like the examples in Figure 6 (p. 45) and Figure 7 (p. 46) can likewise motivate continued skill use. Appendix A includes a variety of different self-recording forms and awards. Suggestions for using such materials to enhance skill generalization are given in chapter 5.

IMPLEMENTATION INTEGRITY

Recently, increased attention has been drawn to implementing interventions with integrity. *Implementation integrity*—also called implementation fidelity, treatment integrity, and procedural reliability—is defined by Lane, Menzies, Barton-Arwood, Doukas, & Munton (2005) as "the extent to which the intervention plan is implemented as originally designed" (p. 22) and is concerned with both the consistency and accuracy of implementation (Gresham, Sugai, & Horner,

Skill 15: Joining In

Name ___Cory___ Date ___10/10___

SKILL STEPS

1. Move closer.

2. Watch.

3. Ask.

Who?

Juan

When? Recess

How I did

40

Skill 28: Dealing with Feeling Mad

Name_____*Elizabeth*_____Date_____10/10_____

SKILL STEPS

1. Stop and think.

2. Choose.

   a. Turtle.

   b. Relax.

   c. Ask to talk.

3. Do it.

I did it!

Figure 4: Sample Self-Monitoring Form 1

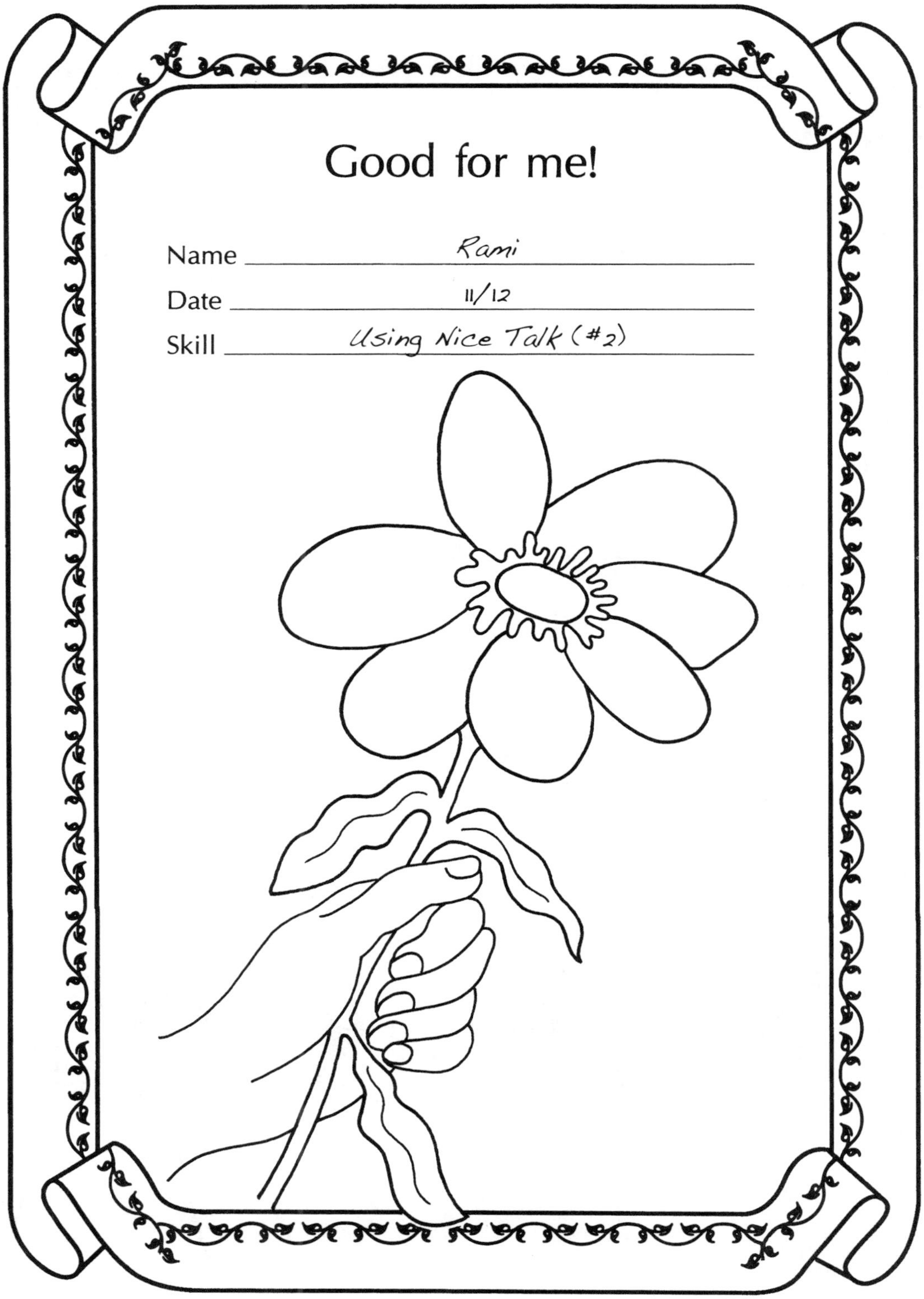

Good for me!

Name Rami

Date 11/12

Skill Using Nice Talk (#2)

2001). Sanetti and Kratochwill (2009) go beyond this standard definition, stating, "Treatment integrity is the extent to which essential intervention components are delivered in a comprehensive and consistent manner by an interventionist trained to deliver the intervention" (p. 448). This concept involves the following matters (Gresham, 2009; Sanetti & Kratochwill, 2008):

► Competence of the interventionist: What is the skill level of the interventionist? Does the interventionist believe in the strategy, or is he or she required by another to do this?

► Quality of intervention delivery: How well was the intervention implemented?

► Quantity of the intervention: How much of the intervention was delivered?

► Process of intervention delivery: For example, were all components of the intervention included?

Although acknowledged as a critical factor in assessing the usefulness of interventions, implementation integrity is rarely measured (Gresham, 2009; Gresham, MacMillan, Beebe-Frankenberger, & Bocian, 2000) and instead is often just assumed (Cochrane & Laux, 2007). We expect that the intervention will be implemented as originally planned; when change occurs, we assume the changes were due to the intervention. When there is no change, we assume this was due to an inappropriate or ineffective intervention (Gresham & Gansle, 1993). Instead of drawing one of these faulty conclusions, it is quite probable that the intervention in applied settings (e.g., school, clinic) was changed in some way (Gresham, 2005). Therefore, it is important that this concept be addressed when implementing Skillstreaming as an intervention to change the problematic behavior of children.

Measuring implementation integrity is necessary to derive accurate conclusions regarding the effectiveness of the intervention and to help understand outcomes such as the behavior change of the target individuals (Lane et al.,

2005; Wood, Umbreit, Liaupsin, & Gresham, 2007). Stated another way, "intervention is effective only to the degree to which it is reliably measured." (Kulli, 2008, p. 145). In order to know if Skillstreaming or any other intervention is producing the desired behavior change, monitoring the quality and quantity of the instruction, as well as the motivation of the interventionist, must occur.

Sanetti and Kratochwill (2009) offer several observations helpful in addressing treatment integrity:

► Typically, most intervention components are not equally important.

► Rigid implementation may not be most desirable, and flexibility may be needed.

► Evaluation and documentation are needed to assess the successfulness of multi-tiered models.

► For some interventions, there may be a threshold beyond which increased use does not provide a meaningful effect.

► As requirements change for research proposals and publications, attention to treatment integrity may increase.

Ways to measure implementation integrity include both direct and indirect methods. Direct methods include direct observation and video observation. Indirect methods include self-reports, permanent products, interviews, and component checklists, with component checklists being the most common strategy. Jung, Gomez, Baird, and Keramidas (2008) recommend a process that is most useful for Skillstreaming purposes. Their instructions state:

"(a) provide a short checklist identifying the critical features of the strategy; (b) provide concrete examples of how this objective is addressed using the strategy; (c) model use of the selected strategy, and (d) offer to watch other team members using the selected strategy and provide feedback." (p. 31)

Figure 6: Sample Skill Ticket

In addition to implementing the intervention with integrity, it is important that the intervention be appropriate to meet the needs of the youth. Therefore, some flexibility in implementation may be required (Maag, 2006; Sanetti & Kratochwill, 2009). Relative to Skillstreaming, this flexibility includes selecting modeling and role-play scenarios to address the needs of group members and changing the language of the skill steps to reflect cultural factors and individual needs of the participants. For example, Sanetti and Kratochwill (2009) emphasize that "deviations may add effective strategies or make the intervention contextually relevant" (p. 451). These authors suggest that we emphasize "flexibility with fidelity" and distinguish between intervention adaptation (intentional adaptation of the intervention to meet individual needs of the recipient (such as context and culture) and intervention drift (unplanned, gradual changing of the intervention).

Both the Leader's Checklist and the Observer's Checklist, included in Appendix B, are used to ensure implementation integrity. The Leader's Checklist is completed by leaders at the completion of each session when first beginning groups. When leaders are consistently implementing all of the steps, this checklist may then be used every two or three weeks. This checklist may also serve as a planning guide to coach leaders through a Skillstreaming session. The Observer's Checklist is designed for use by a skilled trainer of group leaders, who observes newly trained group leaders to provide feedback to improve performance in implementing Skillstreaming instruction. This observation checklist should be used frequently when the trainer first begins his or her instruction of group leaders. This feedback to is most valuable to leaders early on to ensure procedures are being implemented as intended. Leaders have also used this form to observe one another, thereby providing feedback to enhance their own skills. In general, if integrity ratings fall below 80–90 percent, a review of intervention steps and procedures should occur (Lane et al., 2005).

Name _____Latecia_____

Date _____10/10_____

Message _Today Latecia used the skill Trying_
When It's Hard. She put together
a very difficult puzzle. Terrific job!
                                    Mr. Rodriguez

CHAPTER 3

Sample Skillstreaming Session

This chapter presents an edited transcript of an introductory Skillstreaming session with children in a kindergarten classroom. This transcript depicts the leaders introducing students to what will happen in the group and follows the Skillstreaming teaching procedures discussed in chapter 2. The skill used for instruction is Dealing with Teasing (Skill 27).

The goal of the introductory session for preschool and kindergarten children is to acquaint them with the concept of social skills, illustrate the activities that will be performed, and emphasize that, in this group, they will learn the things they want and need to learn. The following text suggests a typical format for this session. The teacher uses a white board or easel pad to illustrate the Skillstreaming procedure and record students' homework situations, as well as a skill step poster and skill cards on which steps are written.

INTRODUCTION TO SKILLSTREAMING

Introductions

Introduce yourself and the other leader if the children do not know you. Ask the children to say their names if you or the other leader do not know the children or if the children do not know each other.

Explanation of Prosocial Skills and Group Purpose

Teacher: First of all, I'm going to tell you what we'll be learning the first thing in the morning every day. We're going to learn the things that you need and want to learn about getting along with friends and adults. How many of you like to play games? *(Children respond with "Me," "I do," or raised hands.)*

Well, we're going to learn how to take turns so everybody has more fun in games. Taking turns is a social skill. Now, who likes to get in trouble? *(Children respond with "Not me," shaking their heads no.)* No, getting in trouble isn't much fun, is it? So we'll also learn ways to stay out of trouble, like what to do when you're mad or upset. And we'll all learn to be better friends with one another. These are all kinds of *social skills.* Do you think you'd like to learn these skills? *(Children respond in the affirmative.)*

Overview of Skillstreaming Procedures

Teacher: First, we'll show you how to do a skill. *(Modeling)* Then you'll get to try it.

(Role-playing) And we'll talk about how well you did. *(Performance feedback)* Then you'll get to practice it. *(Generalization)*

The teacher demonstrates an example of learning another type of skill (in this case, a self-help skill).

Teacher: Let's say I want to learn how to tie my shoes. How am I going to learn to tie my shoes? *(Children respond with "Oh, you know," "Can't you tie your shoes?" etc.)*

(Holding up a large tennis shoe) I need to learn how to tie my shoe. How will I learn this?

Jordan: Here, I'll show you.

Teacher: Terrific, Jordan. I'm going to need someone to show me how. I'm going to need to watch someone else. *(Writes "1. Watch" and draws two large eyes on the easel pad.)* That's the first part of learning a skill. What should I do next?

Rami: You do it.

Teacher: You're absolutely right! I'm going to try it. *(Writes "2. Try" and draws a stick figure showing motion.)* Now, what if it's hard for me—what if I need some help?

Marcus: Jordan will tie it for you.

Teacher: OK, that's one good way, Marcus. That would be kind of Jordan, and I'd certainly get my shoe tied. But would I learn how to tie it myself? *(The group responds, "No.")*

So what I need, then, is someone to tell me what I'm doing that's right and where I've messed up. Would that help me learn? *("Yes" and "Yeah" can be heard from the group. The teacher writes "3. Listen" and draws two large ears on the easel pad.)*

Then once I've had someone tell me how to do it better, I'll need lots of practice, right? *(Writes "4. Practice" on the easel pad.)* This is the same way we'll learn social skills.

Explanation of Reinforcement System and Discussion of Group Rules

Teacher: *(Pulling a package from a bag)* Here I have lots of dinosaur stickers. Who likes dinosaurs? *(Group responds, "I do!")* Well, for everyone who follows our classroom rules during social skills class and tries to learn the skills we're working on, I'll have a sticker for you to wear on your shirt at the end of the group.

Some groups or individual children may need a plan that gives positive reinforcement on a more frequent basis. If the children do not know one another, a brief discussion of basic rules for group participation is in order. Otherwise, already established classroom rules will generally suffice.

Conclusion

Teacher: We'll have fun learning these new social skills, and we'll help each other learn them. We may also have some special visitors come to the class—we'll have to wait and see!

Subsequent sessions begin with review of students' homework reports.

SKILL INSTRUCTION

Step 1: Define the skill

Teacher: Today we're going to learn a very important skill. It's called Dealing with Teasing. What does the word *teasing* mean?

Enrique: Somebody tries to get you mad.

Marcus: They say mean things.

Ayul: They make fun of you, and you cry.

Cory: Or you hit them.

Savannah: My sister, she calls me "little creep." So I tell my mom.

Teacher: Those are good examples of teasing. Someone saying something mean, calling you a name, or in some way making fun of you are all examples of teasing. Some of you said you want to cry or hit the person who is teasing you, right? *(The children respond with nods and affirmative words.)* So when you are teased, you can feel sad or angry, right? *(Children respond.)* Well, it's OK to feel sad or angry when you're teased, but what will happen if you hit someone?

Ayul: You get yelled at.

Cory: I have to do a time-out.

Enrique: I miss recess.

Teacher: OK, then. Let's work on Dealing with Teasing so you don't have to cry or get into trouble by fighting back. Here are the steps to Dealing with Teasing.

At this point, the teacher shows and reads the skill step poster with corresponding pictures. The teacher then hands out a skill card to each student and explains that the cards list the same steps as the chart.

Skill 27: Dealing with Teasing

1. Stop and think.

2. Say, "Please stop."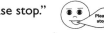

3. Walk away.

Teacher: These three steps, in this order, make up a good way to deal with being teased. The first step is to tell yourself to stop so that you don't hit the person and get in trouble or cry. If you cry, the person will probably keep teasing you, right? *(Students respond.)* Yes, the person will know the teasing works—that it makes you very sad.

With the second step, saying, "Please stop," it's important to use a brave voice. Remember when we practiced Using Brave Talk (Skill 3)? The third step is walking away. Remember to walk away in a brave way, too.

Step 2: Model the Skill

Teacher: Julia, our peer helper, is here today to help with modeling the skill of Dealing with Teasing. We'll show you how to follow each of the steps. While we show you, what is your job? *(Points to the word* watch *and the picture of the eyes.)* Right! Your job is to watch as Julia, first, stops and thinks about the problem. Then Julia will ask me to please stop. Then she'll walk away. Are you ready, Julia? *(Julia nods.)* We're on the playground, and Julia is playing by herself. I'll tease her, and we'll watch Julia follow the steps.

(Julia is holding a ball and tossing it gently; the teacher walks past her.) Hey, little creep. What's a creep like you doing with that ball?

Julia: First I need to tell myself to stop and think. If I cry, she'll keep teasing me. If I hit her, I'll just get in trouble. I need to tell her to stop in a brave voice. *(Turns toward the teacher.)* Please stop. *(Turns away.)* Then I need to walk away. *(Walks away from the teacher.)*

Teacher: Did Julia follow the steps of the skill? Did she first stop and think? *(Children respond.)* Yes, you knew she did because she talked herself through it. Did she follow the second step? Did she say, "Please stop"? *(Children respond.)* And did she follow the last step? Did she walk away? *(Children respond.)* How did Julia do? Did she follow all three steps? *("Yes," etc.)* Good job! Thank you, Julia. Now we'll show you another example.

Julia and the teacher model another example.

Step 3: Establish Student Skill Need

Teacher: Let's think of some times when you are really teased and it's difficult for you to deal with. I'll write your names on the board and your situation beside your name. Who can think of a time when you are teased, and it's a problem?

Marcus: When I play football with my friends. They laugh at me.

Savannah: My sister calls me names.

Cory: On the bus, going home, the big kids call me shrimp, and I'm not doing anything to have them call me that.

Ayul: A girl says I look funny.

The listing continues as each child identifies a situation for skill use and are recorded on chart paper by the co-leader.

Step 4: Select the First Role-Player

Teacher: You all came up with really good examples of when you need to use the skill. Who would like to role-play or try the skill first? OK, Ayul. The girl who teases you really seems to be a problem for you.

Step 5: Set Up the Role-Play

Teacher: Ayul, could you tell us a little more about what happens?

Ayul: When I walk home, this bigger girl, I don't know her name, but she says I look stupid. She says I have fat lips. *(Starts to cry.)*

Teacher: Ayul, this skill will help you get her to stop, OK? Will you work with us to learn how to handle this so she'll stop? *(Ayul nods.)* Great! Let's start. I tell you what, Ayul. How about I pretend first to be the girl who teases you? *(Ayul agrees.)*

I think we have a good idea of what happens. *(To the group)* Before we start with the role-play, I'm going to ask each of you to watch the role-play carefully. I want each of you to watch for a certain step.

Enrique, John, and Hannah, will you watch to see if Ayul does the first step? See if she stops and thinks?

Jordan, Rami, and Joel, will you watch for the second step? See if Ayul says, "Please stop"?

And Savannah, Cory, and Marcus, will you watch for the third step? Will you watch for Ayul to walk away?

Step 6: Conduct the Role-Play

Teacher: Ayul, look at your skill card with the skill steps. The pictures will help you remember. First, you'll say something like "I have to stop and think." This is to give you some time. Then you'll say, "Please stop," in a brave way. The third step is to walk away. Remember, we'll help you if you want. Are you ready? *(Ayul nods.)*

Okay, Ayul, you're walking home from school. Here's your backpack.

This chair will be at the corner where the older girl teases you. *(Ayul puts on her backpack and starts to walk across the room.)*

(In a taunting voice) Hey, you, funny-looking girl. You sure look funny.

Ayul: *(Stops.)*

Teacher: The first step is to stop and think. Ayul, say it out loud so we know you're thinking this.

Ayul: I have to stop and think. I won't be sad.

Teacher: Good. Now, what's the next step? You can look at your card.

Ayul: *(Turning to the teacher)* Please stop.

Teacher: Good. Next, what will you do?

Ayul: *(Looking at her card, Ayul walks off with her head held high.)*

Teacher: Good for you, Ayul!

Ayul: *(Smiles.)*

Step 7: Provide Performance Feedback

Order of feedback is coactor, observers, teacher, main actor. In this case, the teacher as coactor comments both first and last.

Teacher: Ayul, if I were the girl teasing you, I think I'd pick on someone else instead. I don't think I got you upset! Let's check out what the group saw. *(Puts her arm around Ayul.)* Did Ayul do the first step? Did she stop and think? *(The children nod.)* How do you know?

John: Ayul said stop and think.

Teacher: Good watching! We heard her think this out loud! Did Ayul follow the second step? Did she say, "Please stop"?

Joel: Yeah.

Teacher: Yes, she did. Did she say this in a brave way? *(The children nod.)* Yes, she wasn't shy or angry. Good. And the third step?

Marcus: She walked away.

Teacher: Thank you, Marcus. She did walk away. You all did a terrific job watching! Ayul, how did it feel to use this skill?

Ayul: Good.

Teacher: Was it hard to do?

Ayul: Kinda.

Teacher: Sure. Dealing with teasing is difficult! Ayul, you're off to a great start in really using this skill on your way home from school! Good for you—you did it!

Ayul, after the group, we'll plan out a homework assignment, a time when you can try out the skill, OK? *(Ayul agrees.)*

Step 8: Select the Next Role-Player

Teacher: Who would like to try the skill next?

The process continues until all have had a chance to role-play the skill.

Step 9: Assign Skill Homework

As described for Ayul, the teacher provides each child who role-plays with a homework report, helps the child identify a time to try out the skill, and coaches the child through the process.

Teacher: Ayul, let's plan your homework assignment. Here is the homework report that we'll use. I've filled the date in for you. Go ahead and write your name. The steps for and pictures for Dealing with Teasing are right here so you can see them. So, now we're ready to plan with whom and when you will try out this skill. Who often teases you?

Ayul: The big girl . . . I don't know her name.

Teacher: OK, then. Will you draw a picture of this girl on your homework report?

Ayul follows these directions.

Teacher: Great! Now, when will you follow the skill steps? When will you: 1. Stop and think; 2. Say, "Please stop"; and 3. Walk away?

Ayul: After school on my way home.

Teacher: Good. Will you draw a picture of this time? Ayul draws a picture of herself walking home.

Look at the three faces on the homework report. After you use the skill of Dealing with Teasing with the big girl when you walk home from school, you'll get to color in one of the faces. If you did all the steps, you'll color the happy face. If you forgot a step, you'll color the straight-line face. This means you tried the skill but forgot a step. If you don't do the skill at all, then you'll color the sad face. Do you think you can try the skill today if the big girl teases you?

Ayul: *(Nods yes.)*

To increase the likelihood that Ayul will be successful in using the skill with the real-life provocation, the teacher will coach Ayul again before she actually tries the skill.

Teacher: Your situation isn't an easy one. Let's practice one more time before you try this, OK? *(Ayul agrees.)*

CHAPTER 4
Refining Skill Use

Although Skillstreaming is a psychoeducational derived primarily from social learning theory, cognitive-behavioral interventions such as problem solving, accurate perceptions of social situations, anger control, and verbal mediation are embedded in its instructional format and enhance its effectiveness. This chapter briefly examines the role of these approaches in Skillstreaming, as well as that of strategies to increase a child's social performance, including reducing competing problem behaviors, supportive modeling, empathy, nonverbal behaviors, and skill shifting/skill combinations.

COGNITIVE-BEHAVIORAL STRATEGIES

Kaplan and Carter (2005) explain the concept of cognition relative to behavioral intervention strategies to include cognitive processes, cognitive structures, and inner speech. *Cognitive processes* involve "more the way we think as opposed to what we think" (p. 381). Gresham (2005) further explains this concept:

> Cognitive-behavioral theory is based on the premise that thoughts, emotions and actions are inextricably linked and that changing one of these necessarily produces changes in the others. These reciprocal relationships between thoughts, emotions, and actions serve as the fundamental basis of all cognitive-behavioral intervention strategies. (p. 213)

Therefore, cognitive structures can be modified through strategies such as teaching problem solving, impulse control, and self-mediation. Smith, Lochman, and Daunic (2005) further cite support for using these strategies to prevent and remediate patterns of aggressive and disruptive behavior. For example, many aggressive youth perceive negative intentions of others, even when actions clearly appear accidental in nature, whereas more socially competent youth do not. Incorporating elements of the cognitive-behavioral approach will promote the self-control needed by many young children to change their typical manner of reacting, thus better enabling them to change their typical manner of reacting, recall skill steps, and generalize the skills they learn. Knowledge of the following areas—problem solving, anger/impulse control, and verbal mediation-- will guide group leaders in enhancing Skillstreaming instruction.

Problem Solving

As Ladd and Mize (1983) point out, children and adolescents may be deficient in such problem-solving competencies as identifying the appropriate goal for a social interaction, identifying the desirable behaviors or strategies for reaching a goal, and understanding the context in which specific behaviors are appropriate. Young children may perceive the goal of playing a game with peers as winning instead of having fun, for example. The strategies selected will therefore differ (e.g., cheating to win versus fair play). Cartledge and Feng (1996) state that a purpose of problem-solving instruction is "to teach people how to think through and resolve interpersonal conflicts using a four-step process: (a) identifying and defining the problem, (b) generating a variety of solutions, (c) identifying potential consequences, and (d) implementing and evaluating a solution." Solving a Problem (Skill 30) presents the specific steps for using this process in a social context. However, the cognitive aspect suggests that the general skill of problem solving might be used in conjunction with other skills. Therefore, problem solving may be applied broadly as well as taught as one skill of many. The teacher's challenge, then, is to structure the application of skill use to a variety of situations encountered in children's everyday lives.

Anger/Impulse Control

Many students may know the desired and expected behavior and may, in fact, be likely to behave in this manner in many situations. However, when angry, anxious, or otherwise upset, they are unable to see beyond the emotion-producing event. Before many students will be able to recall the steps of a specific skill, they must use strategies to stop themselves from reacting in a perhaps well-established pattern of aggression or other unproductive behavior. Such impulse control procedures are often referred to as coping skills or self-regulation strategies.

In contrast to the direct facilitation of prosocial behavior in Skillstreaming, anger control training, developed by Feindler (Feindler, 1979, 1995; Feindler & Ecton, 1986), facilitates such skill behavior indirectly, by teaching ways to inhibit anger and loss of self-control. In this method, youth are taught how to respond to provocations to anger by (a) identifying their external and internal anger triggers; (b) identifying their own physiological/kinesthetic cues signifying anger; (c) using anger reducers to lower arousal via deep breathing, counting backwards, imagining a peaceful scene, or contemplating the long-term consequences of anger-associated behavior; (d) using reminders, or self-statements that are in opposition to triggers; and (e) self-

evaluating, or judging how adequately anger control worked and rewarding oneself when it has worked well.

Two programs that pair Skillstreaming with an anger control component include Aggression Replacement Training and the EQUIP Program. Aggression Replacement Training (Glick & Gibbs, 2010; Goldstein, Glick, & Gibbs, 1986, 1998) includes Skillstreaming, anger control training, and a moral reasoning component. The EQUIP Program (Gibbs, Potter, & Goldstein, 1995) employs these three components within the context of a positive peer helping milieu. The Prepare Curriculum (Goldstein, 1989, 1999b) combines Skillstreaming with anger control training, empathy training, problem-solving training, and other competencies.

The majority of Skillstreaming skills used under stressful conditions include an anger or impulse control strategy--counting to five or taking three deep breaths, for example. Emphasizing these methods, taking additional time to teach them and reinforce their use, or using the anger control training process just described will increase the likelihood of success in students' real-life skill use.

Verbal Mediation

As discussed in chapter 2, verbal mediation, or saying aloud what would normally be said to oneself silently, is a valuable and necessary part of both modeling and role-playing. Saying the steps aloud as the models or role players enact the behaviors demonstrates the cognitive processes underlying skill performance, facilitates learning, and may be employed to demonstrate a coping model.

Verbal mediation techniques have been used to teach impulse control in hyperactive children (Kendall & Braswell, 1985), anger control in adolescents (Goldstein et al., 1998), impulse control in aggressive youth (Camp & Bash, 1981), academic behaviors through self-instruction training (Meichenbaum, 1977), and coping strategies for students who experience depression (Maag &

Swearer, 2005). By practicing talking themselves through a skill or saying aloud ways to control the impulse to react in an undesirable way, students learn to regulate their actions until these actions become nearly automatic. As stated by Camp and Bash (1985):

> A good deal of evidence suggests that adequate development of verbal mediation activity is associated with (1) internalization of the inhibitory function of language, which serves to block impulsive and associative responding in both cognitive and social situations, and (2) utilization of linguistic tools in learning, problem-solving, and forethought. (p. 7)

Many young children will need to be taught the process of thinking aloud by practicing while they are engaged in other types of activities (e.g., completing academic tasks, doing classroom chores). Maag and Swearer (2005) offer factors to increase the effectiveness of verbal mediation, including the following:

1. Initially, self-instruction should be limited to three words or a short phrase or sentence.

2. The student should verbalize the exact wording of the phrase.

3. The phrase should refer to increasing or decreasing a specific behavior as opposed to being a vague statement.

4. The student should be reinforced for using self-instruction.

FACTORS IN SUCCESSFUL SKILL USE

In addition to strategies relating to the cognitive-behavioral approach, factors that impact successful skill use include skill fluency, social perceptions, reduction of competing behaviors, nonverbal behaviors, empathy, and supportive modeling.

Skill Fluency

Fluency in performing selected social skills is largely achieved through the generalization prin-

ciple of overlearning. Just like any other skill, such as learning to read or playing a sport, prosocial skill performance is often somewhat artificial and rote in the initial stages of learning. The more practice students have in using the skill in a variety of different situations and settings, and with different co-actors, the more fluent and natural the performance will become. A positive relationship between the amount of social skills training and successful performance has been found (Gresham, Van, & Cook, 2006; McIntosh, Vaughn, & Zaragoza, 1991). When skill fluency is at issue, more intense and frequent skill training is called for.

Perceptions of Social Situations

Processing Social Information

A model for processing social information useful in refining the skill use of young children is presented by Dodge (1983) and his colleagues. This model includes (a) encoding relevant information, (b) applying meanings, (c) accessing a response, (d) evaluating a response, and (e) enacting a response.

Encoding relevant information

Relative to a social interaction, children must first attend to cues that are appropriate to the interaction. Some children may focus on all of the cues in an interaction, thus having difficulty determining which cues to single out for response. Aggressive children often focus on the cues that appear to them to be aggressive ones. Others may ignore salient social cues—for example, failing to recognize boredom in one's listener when dominating a conversation (Gresham & Elliott, 1990).

Further noted by Gresham and Elliott, "Some children are deficient in a social skill because certain social cues which would prompt socially appropriate behavior are absent" (p. 29). Typical social cues may be absent, for example, when a child is playing with a group of familiar peers.

Applying meanings

One's perception of intent influences one's behavior (Dodge, Murphy, & Birchsbaum, 1984). Meaning is given to the social cue in relation to the individual child's emotional needs or goals. For example, children who often act aggressively may interpret the intent of an action as hostile.

Accessing a response

Children typically do what they know or what is familiar to them. It is far easier for children to access a behavior and follow through on its performance when they have mastery of that behavior. Aggressive children, for instance, access more aggressive and less effective ways to solve problems with others (Guerra & Slaby, 1989). The focus of social skills training is to increase these children's repertoire of choices.

Evaluating a response

The capacity to evaluate the potential consequences of an action is associated with social competence. Aggressive youth, for example, identify fewer negative consequences for aggression and view their aggressive choices more positively than do others (Cartledge & Milburn, 1995). In addition, children who are aggressive often believe that their aggression will bring rewards, not negative consequences, including being treated less aversively by others (Perry, Perry, & Rasmussen, 1986).

Enacting a response

The performance of a behavior or skill is relative to the child's proficiency in performing that skill, as well as to his or her motivation to do so. Social performance, then, involves the enactment of a sequence of behaviors in relevant and appropriate ways within a context.

Social Perceptions and Behavioral Flexibility

Even if a student becomes proficient in a given skill, the student may misread the context in which the prosocial skill is desirable or acceptable. Although the procedures to teach social skills are the same as those in teaching academics, the teaching of social skills is more complex due to the reciprocal nature of social interactions. With academic instruction, it is often the case that there is one, and only one, correct response. Furthermore, that correct response is always correct. Social skills performance, on the other hand, is influenced by culture, setting, and group dynamics (Scott & Nelson, 1998).

A major emphasis in psychology concerns the importance of the situation or setting, as perceived by the individual, in determining behavior. Morrison and Bellack (1981), for example, state that individuals must not only possess the ability to enact given behavioral skills, they must also know when and how these responses should be applied. These authors further state that in order to use this knowledge, individuals must have the "ability to accurately 'read' the social environment" (p. 70). This ability, they suggest, includes awareness of the norms and conventions in operation at a given time as well as understanding of the message given by the other person.

Students can be taught to read the context (situation and setting) of the social situation accurately and adjust their behavior accordingly. Therefore, emphasis must be placed not only on skill performance, but also on such questions as the following: "What is the behavior expected in this setting?" "Which skill should I use with this person, considering his or her role?" and "What signs are there that this is a good time to use the skill?" Attending to such questions while teaching behavioral skills will likely result in more successful skill use and guide students in developing the flexibility needed to adjust skill use across settings, situations, and people.

The work of Dodge (1985) and Spivack and Shure (1974) suggests that children should be able to respond to the following questions throughout their skill performance:

▶ Why should I use the skill?

▶ With whom should I use the skill?

- ▶ Where should I use the skill?
- ▶ When should I use the skill?
- ▶ How should I perform the skill?

Although many of these issues are addressed in the skills themselves as particular behavioral steps and in the four components of Skillstreaming (modeling, role-playing, performance feedback, and transfer training), additional emphasis can be achieved through group discussion, supplementary role-play practice, and related activities.

Why should I use the skill?

Children will be more likely to learn a new behavior or skill if they are motivated to do so. Understanding how prosocial skill performance will help them meet their needs—get the favor they want or need, stay out of trouble, and so forth—is valuable in enhancing motivation. Therefore, as teachers and other group leaders introduce each skill, they must point out the specific and direct benefits to be gained.

With whom should I use the skill?

To perform the skill competently, the child must learn to assess and interpret the verbal and nonverbal cues of the person or persons to whom the skill performance is directed. For example, it is sometimes the case that a child who is learning Joining In (Skill 15) fails to assess the receptivity of the target peer group. If the group appears to be avoiding the skill-deficient child (e.g., continuing to move the activity away, refusing to make eye contact, or even shouting at the child to go away), the child will need to learn how to attend to such cues and interpret their meaning. The teacher can help by guiding the child in selecting another person or group to approach or by urging the child to use a related back-up skill with the first group. Likewise, although Saying No (Skill 38) may help avoid trouble when directed toward a friend, the outcome may be quite different if the skill is tried with a parent who is directing the child to get ready for school. Such

parameters of skill use may not be easily identified by many young children, and discussions and perhaps role-plays of this issue will need to be an integral part of instruction.

Where should I use the skill?

The skill-deficient child will need help in evaluating the setting in which he or she intends to use the skill. A child's using Asking Someone to Play (Skill 19), for instance, may be desirable during classroom free play or during outside recess but would not be desirable while grocery shopping with a parent. Although adults may assume that most children automatically make this type of determination, this has not proven to be the case. Instead, varied settings in which the skill will likely be successful or unsuccessful should be addressed through group discussion and multiple role-plays.

When should I use the skill?

When a skill should be used is often a question for the preschool or kindergarten child. It is not unusual, for example, for the child to use Asking a Question (Skill 9) while the teacher is giving directions or while a parent is involved in an interaction with another person. Therefore, discussions related to the timing of skill use need to be included with each skill.

How should I perform the skill?

The manner in which a child performs a skill can determine its effectiveness. For example, a child who uses Asking a Favor (Skill 7) in an angry manner will likely find that the favor is not granted. Likewise, the child who employs the steps of Dealing with Teasing (Skill 27) but who is obviously upset at being provoked may not find that the skill yields a positive outcome. Two behavioral skills to be taught early on therefore deal solely with the manner in which a skill is delivered: Using Nice Talk (Skill 2), to encourage the child to employ a friendly manner, and Using Brave Talk (Skill 3), to encourage the child to make an assertive response.

Reduction of Competing Problem Behaviors

Gresham (1998a) explains that the problem behavior may be more efficient for the child than a more socially acceptable behavior. In other words, the outcome the child desires is easier to obtain through using the problem behavior than through using an alternative, more socially acceptable behavior or skill. The problem behavior is also likely to be reliable as well, consistently leading to reinforcement for the individual. For example, when Joey wants to play with a toy another preschooler is playing with, he typically just grabs the toy away. By the time the peer complains and a teacher intervenes, Joey has played enough with the toy and is off doing something else. Nonetheless, grabbing the toy works for Joey. Grabbing is reliable (it works most of the time), and it's efficient (it works quickly and he doesn't have to wait to play with the toy). A goal, then, is to reduce the reliability and efficiency of the problem behavior--in other words, to make sure the problematic behavior doesn't work for the child. For children whose emotional responses (e.g., anger, fear, frustration) inhibit or prevent skill performance, Elliott and Gresham (1991) suggest that instruction in the prosocial skill be paired with strategies to reduce the interfering problem behavior. Therefore, in the example above, the function of Joey's problematic behavior is likely to gain the toy. Joey's plan includes positive reinforcement for asking for help in obtaining the toy (using a skill), but also consequences (a brief time-out or loss of the privilege of being in the toy area) if he grabs the toy from a peer. Preschoolers whose problematic behavior is more intense or resistant to such change procedures will benefit from more comprehensive behavior change strategies such as those included in chapter 6.

Nonverbal Behaviors

Nonverbal communicators such as body posture and movements, facial expressions, and voice tone and volume give others messages either consistent with or contradictory to verbal content. Consider, for example, a child who is told by a playground supervisor to leave the playground for not following the rules. Often it is not the breaking of the rule per se that results in the playground expulsion but the child' response to the rule. When questioned, the supervisor may report that the child was defiant or failed to show remorse (e.g., "She acted like it wasn't her fault" or "He didn't look sorry!"). Understanding the influence of nonverbal language is an important factor in learning prosocial behaviors. Fox and Boulton (2003) for example, researched behaviors that discriminated between victims and nonvictims of bullying. They found that 50 percent of the behaviors that best predicted victimization were nonverbal behaviors, including looking scared, standing in a way that suggests weakness, and looking like an unhappy person.

Nowicki and Duke (1992) identify six areas of nonverbal communication:

1. Paralanguage (voice tone, speech rate, variation of speech, nonverbal sounds)
2. Facial expressions
3. Postures and gestures
4. Interpersonal distance (space) and touch (intimate, personal, social, and public zones)
5. Rhythm and time (e.g., being on time, spending time with friends)
6. Objectics (hygiene, style of dress)

In brief, skill-deficient students will need to be made more aware of the ways in which nonverbal communicators send clear and definite messages.

Empathy

Very young children possess the capacity to show empathy. Denham (1998), citing the work of Zahn-Waxler and Radke-Yarrow (1982, 1990), states that "children as young as two years of age are able to broadly interpret others' emotional states, to experience these feeling states in response to others' predicament, and attempt to alleviate discomfort in others" (p. 34). Chronically aggressive or other skill-deficient youth have been shown to display a pattern of personality traits high in egocentricity and low in concern for others (Slavin, 1980).

Expression of empathic understanding can serve both as an inhibitor of negative behaviors and as a facilitator of positive actions. Results of a number of studies inquiring into the interpersonal consequences of empathic responding show that empathy is a consistently potent promoter of interpersonal attraction, dyadic openness, conflict resolution, and individual growth (Goldstein & Michaels, 1985). In addition, Grizenko et al. (2000) found more lasting improvement from social skills instruction when social perspective taking was added. In other words, children who are able to show empathy are far less likely to act out aggressively toward others, are more accepted and sought after in social situations, are more able to participate in resolving interpersonal disputes, and are more satisfied with themselves.

Some helpful methods of encouraging empathy include (a) instructing children in skills such as Deciding How Someone Feels (Skill 25); (b) providing opportunities for role reversal during role-plays, followed by actors' expression of feelings; (c) providing opportunities for observers to take the perspective of others (e.g., that of the main actor) during feedback sessions; and (d) encouraging empathy toward others through the modeling and discussion of appreciation for individual differences.

Supportive Modeling

Typically, aggressive children are exposed to highly aggressive models. Peers, parents, and siblings are often chronically aggressive individuals themselves (Knight & West, 1975; Loeber & Dishion, 1983; Robins, West, & Herjanic, 1975). At the same time, relatively few prosocial models that might help counteract the effects of aggressive modeling exist for these youth to observe and imitate. When prosocial models are available, they apparently can make a tremendous difference in social development. Werner and Smith (1982), in their longitudinal study of aggressive and nonaggressive youth *Vulnerable but Invincible,* clearly demonstrated that youth growing up in a community characterized by high crime, high unemployment, high secondary school dropout rates, and high levels of aggressive modeling were able to develop into effective, satisfied, prosocially oriented individuals if they had sustained exposure to at least one significant prosocial model—be it parent, relative, teacher, coach, neighbor, or peer.

The classroom teacher can be a powerful model for students. Needless to say, a powerful negative effect can be exerted on students if the teacher models prosocial skill deficiencies. Throughout the course of the school day, the teacher should make a sustained effort to model desirable, prosocial behaviors and to use the behavioral steps for selected skills when it is appropriate to do so. When frustrated or angry with an individual student's behavior, for example, the teacher can greatly affect student learning by modeling the steps of Dealing with Feeling Mad (Skill 28) in a clear and deliberate manner.

SKILL SHIFTING, COMBINATIONS, ADAPTATION, AND DEVELOPMENT

Skill shifting refers to the selection and performance of an alternative skill when one skill is not successful for the child. Although the Skillstreaming setting is designed to provide for successful skill performance, it is obvious that in real life even a highly competent performance may fail to bring about the desired outcome. This failure may be the result of inaccurate assessment of the receptivity of the other individuals involved or of aspects of the setting, such as the degree of structure imposed. Despite the uncontrollability of the world outside the Skillstreaming setting, it is important to reward the child for his or her attempts and, whenever possible, to offer opportunities for repeated practice in making other prosocial skill choices when initial choices fail. Thus, group instruction should help the child discern when a skill is unsuccessful, when an alternative skill should be tried, and which specific skill should be attempted. For example, if Samantha attempts the skill of Joining In (Skill 15) on the playground during recess and finds the attempt unsuccessful, she may need to shift to another skill, such as Feeling Left Out (Skill 22) or Deciding What to Do (Skill 40).

When such lack of success in using a skill seems to permeate the child's attempts in real life, a combination of skills should be taught. In the previous example, if using the skill of Joining In consistently fails to bring about a desired response, Samantha will likely need to use a skill combination (e.g., Joining In and Deciding What to Do) to find satisfaction in both attempting the skill and enjoying herself during recess.

Skill shifting and skill combinations are initially very challenging for the young child. However, as Skillstreaming instruction becomes a regular part of the school routine, and as student skill proficiency increases, efforts to include these instructional strategies will enhance successful skill use.

Sometimes circumstances suggest the adaptation of skills and even the development of new skills. In other circumstances, it may be appropriate to retain a given skill but alter one or more of its behavioral steps. Steps may be simplified as the skills and needs of the students suggest. For example, a child who repeatedly becomes out of control when losing may learn only two of the behavioral steps constituting Skill 36, Dealing with Losing.

1. Say, "Everybody can't win."
2. Say, "Maybe I'll win next time."

And although Asking a Question (Skill 9) is intended to encompass asking permission as well, the teacher who finds frequent problems pertaining to asking may choose to adapt this skill to address asking permission.

Developing a new skill might be helpful when students are continually disruptive when moving into the group setting, for example. The perceptive teacher, recognizing that transitions are difficult for this particular group of students, could present the following skill to address the concern.

Coming to Group
1. Put materials away.
2. Look up to show the teacher you are ready.
3. Wait quietly until your name is called.

In another example, Melisa Genaux, a behavioral expert in the area of autism, developed a specific skill for the students with Asperger's syndrome, who have behavioral difficulty when their routines change.

Changes in Routine/It's Not What I Thought Would Happen Skill
1. Stop.
2. Take a deep breath.
3. Count to 5.
4. Say, "OK."
5. Follow the direction.

In adapting existing skills and developing new ones, group leaders will need to use their knowledge of the needs and abilities of the specific group.

CHAPTER 5

Teaching for Skill Generalization

Historically, therapeutic interventions have reflected a core belief in personality change as both the target and outcome of effective intervention; thus, environmental influences on behavior were largely ignored. It has been assumed that the positive changes believed to have taken place within the individual's personality would enable the individual to deal effectively with problematic events wherever and whenever they might occur. That is, transfer and maintenance would occur automatically.

Research on psychotherapy initiated in the 1950s and expanded in the 1960s and 1970s sought to ascertain whether gains at the end of the formal intervention had in fact generalized across settings and/or time. Stokes and Baer (1977) described this time as one in which transfer and maintenance were hoped for and noted if they did occur ("train and hope"). The overwhelming result of these investigations was that, much more often than not, transfer and maintenance of intervention gains did not occur. Treatment and training did not persist automatically, nor did learning necessarily transfer (Goldstein & Kanfer, 1979; Keeley, Shemberg, & Carbonell, 1976). This failure, revealed by evidence accumulated during the train-and-hope phase, led to a third phase—the development, evaluation, and use of procedures explicitly designed to enhance transfer and maintenance of intervention gains.

As the social skills movement in general and Skillstreaming in particular have matured and

evidence regarding Skillstreaming's effectiveness has accumulated, it has become clear that skill acquisition is a reliable finding across both training methods and populations. However, generalization is another matter. Both generalization to new settings (transfer) and over time (maintenance) have been reported in only a minority of cases. The main concern of any teaching effort is not how students perform in the teaching setting, but how well they perform in their real lives. Therefore, generalization is often considered the most important goal in social skills instruction (Gresham, 1998a, 1998b). Approaches to enhance transfer and maintenance are listed in Table 3 and discussed in the following pages.

Beyond these strategies, many concerned with the social development of children and adolescents hypothesize that social skills often fail to generalize due to the presence of stronger, competing problem behaviors. Children may fail to use a newly learned skill not just because reinforcement in their real lives does not occur or because the Skillstreaming leader has not attended to the generalization principles adequately during the instruction. As Gresham, Sugai, and Horner (2001) note, "One reason . . . that socially skilled behaviors may fail to generalize is because the newly taught behavior is masked or overpowered by older and stronger competing behaviors" (p. 340). Although failure of generalization is surely to occur if

---

Table 3: Transfer- and Maintenance-Enhancing Procedures

Transfer

Before Instruction

Entrapment (including relevant peers in the instruction)

During Instruction

1. Provision of general principles (general case programming)
2. Overlearning (maximizing response availability)
3. Stimulus variability (training sufficient exemplars, training loosely)
4. Identical elements (programming common stimuli)

After Instruction

5. Instructed generalization
6. Mediated generalization (self-reinforcement, self-monitoring)

Maintenance

During the Skillstreaming Intervention

1. Thinning reinforcement (increase intermittency, unpredictability)
2. Delaying reinforcement
3. Fading prompts
4. Providing booster sessions
5. Preparing for real-life nonreinforcement

Beyond the Skillstreaming Intervention

6. Programming for reinforcement in the natural environment
7. Using natural reinforcers

---

generalization strategies are not put in place, some students may experience intense emotions, such as anger or anxiety, or in other ways have difficulties in self-regulating their emotions or behaviors. For these youth, Skillstreaming efforts must include additional strategies to refine skill use (chapter 4) and reduce problem behaviors (chapter 6).

The Generalization Integrity Checklist, included in Appendix B, guides Skillstreaming instructors in the use of generalization principles and strategies and helps ensure that the fidelity of Skillstreaming generalization is addressed. This tool is for use by group leaders to evaluate how they incorporate generalization into their training before, during, and after carrying out Skillstreaming instructional procedures. The checklist may also be used by Skillstreaming master trainers as they work with and observe novice group leaders.

TRANSFER-ENHANCING PROCEDURES

Efforts to maximize transfer have resulted in considerable success. A variety of useful techniques have been developed, evaluated, and put into practice. As suggested by Kame'enui and Simmons (1990), the techniques described are generally separated into procedures to implement before, during, and after instruction.

Before Instruction

Skillstreaming employs the principle of transfer enhancement by including as group members the same people the child interacts with on a regular basis outside of the group (McIntosh & Mackay, 2008; Walker, Ramsey, & Gresham, 2004). Including the peer group allows peers to reward the target student for skill use (Maag, 2006). This concept is referred to as *entrapment,* or providing natural reinforcement by peers for the student's performance of a desirable social behavior (McConnell, 1987). Thus, if possible, in the school setting all members of a Skillstreaming group should be from the same class or unit. For the same reason, in residential, agency, or institutional settings, teaching groups are most often constructed to directly parallel the facility's unit, cottage, or ward structure. Participation in the same group presents an excellent opportunity to teach children positive alternatives for dealing with their real-life difficulties.

During Instruction

Provision of General Principles

Generalization may be facilitated by providing the child with the general mediating principles that govern satisfactory performance on both the original and the transfer task. The child can be given the rules, strategies, or organizing principles that lead to successful performance. The general finding that understanding the principles underlying successful performance can enhance transfer to new tasks and contexts has been reported in a number of domains of psychological research, including studies of labeling, rules, advance organizers, and learning sets. It is a robust finding, with empirical support in both laboratory and psychoeducational settings.

No matter how competently Skillstreaming leaders seek to create in the role-play setting the "feel" of the real-life setting in which the child will need to use the skill and no matter how well the coactor in a given role play matches the actual qualities the real target person possesses, there will always be differences between role-play and real world. Even when the child has role-played the skill a number of times, the demands of the actual situation will depart in some respects from the demands portrayed in the role-play. And the real parent, real peer, or real teacher is likely to respond at least somewhat differently than the child's role-play partner. When the child has a good grasp of the principles underlying a situation (demands, expected behaviors, norms, purposes, rules) and the principles underlying the skill (why these steps, in this order, toward which ends), successful transfer of skill performance becomes more likely.

Overlearning

Transfer of training is enhanced by procedures that maximize overlearning or response availability: The likelihood that a response will be available is clearly a function of its prior use. We repeat and repeat foreign language phrases we are trying to learn, we insist that our child spend an hour per day in piano practice, and we devote considerable time practicing to make a golf swing smooth and automatic. These are simply expressions of the response-availability notion—that is, the more we have practiced responses (especially correct ones), the easier it will be to use them in other contexts or at later times. It has been well established that, other things being equal, the response emitted most frequently in the past is more likely to be emitted on subsequent occasions. However, it is not sheer practice of attempts at effective behaviors that is of most benefit to transfer but practice of *successful* attempts. Overlearning involves extending learning over more trials than would be necessary merely to produce initial changes in the individual's behavior. In all too many instances, one or two successes at a given task are taken as evidence to move on to the next task or level of the original task. This is an error in terms of transfer via overlearning. To maximize transfer, the guiding rule should not be "practice makes perfect" (implying that one simply practices until one gets it right and then moves on) but "practice of perfect" (implying numerous overlearning trials of correct responses after the initial success).

Some children who have just received good feedback from group members and leaders about their role-play (all steps followed and well portrayed) may object to the request that they role-play the skill a second or third time. Although valid concerns exist about the consequences of boredom when teaching a group of potentially restless children, the value of skill repetition cannot be overstressed. Often, leaders, not children, are most bored by the repetition. To assuage student concerns, leaders can point to the value for professional athletes of warm-ups, shoot-arounds, batting practice, and other repetitive practice. Such practice makes core skills nearly automatic and frees the player to concentrate on strategy.

In many real-life contexts, people and events actually work against the child's use of prosocial behaviors. It is therefore appropriate for a Skillstreaming group to spend two, three, or even more sessions role-playing a single skill. To reduce the possible interference of new learning on previously learned materials, a second skill should be introduced only when a child can recall the steps of the first skill, has had opportunities to role-play it, and has shown some initial transfer outside of the group teaching setting (e.g., has successfully completed a homework assignment).

Stimulus Variability

The previous section addressed enhancement of transfer by means of practice and repetition—that is, by the sheer number of correct skill responses the child makes. Transfer is also enhanced by the variability or range of situations to which the individual responds. Teaching related to even two situations is better than teaching related to one. As Kazdin (1975) summarizes:

> One way to program response maintenance and transfer of training is to develop the target behavior in a variety of situations and in the presence of several individuals. If the response is associated with a range of settings, individuals, and other cues, it is less likely to be lost when the situations change. (p. 21)

Epps, Thompson, and Lane (1985) discuss stimulus variability for transfer enhancement as it might operate in school contexts under the rubrics "train sufficient examples" and "train loosely." They observe that generalization of new skills or behaviors can also be facilitated by training students under a wide variety of conditions. Manipulating the number of leaders, settings, and response classes involved in the intervention promotes generalization by exposing students to a variety of situations. If, for example, students are asked to role-play a given skill correctly three times, each attempt should involve a different coactor, a different setting, and, especially, a different need for the same skill.

Identical Elements

In perhaps the earliest experimental work dealing with transfer enhancement, Thorndike and Wood-

worth (1901) concluded that, when one habit had a facilitative effect on another, it was to the degree that the habits shared identical elements. Ellis (1965) and Osgood (1953) later emphasized the importance for transfer of similarity between characteristics of the training and application tasks. As Osgood (1953) noted, "The greater the similarity between practice and test stimuli, the greater the amount of positive transfer" (p. 213).

In Skillstreaming, the principle of identical elements is implemented by procedures that increase the "real-lifeness" of the stimuli (places, people, events, etc.) to which the leader is helping the child learn to respond with effective, satisfying behaviors. Two broad strategies exist for attaining such high levels of correspondence between in-group and extra-group stimuli. The first concerns the location in which Skillstreaming takes place. Typically, groups remain in the school or institution and by use of props and imagination recreate the feel of the real-world context in which the child plans to use the skill. Because skills learned in context are more likely to generalize (Gresham, Sugai, & Horner, 2001) whenever possible, however, the Skillstreaming group leaves the formal teaching setting and meets in the actual locations in which the problem behaviors occur: "Fight on the playground? Let's have our session there"; "Playing alone during free play in the gym? Let's move there"; "Argument with a peer in the recess line? Today's group will meet in the hallway."

After Instruction

Instructed Generalization

One of the group leaders should be the person with whom the students regularly interact (e.g., a classroom teacher). This group leader's experience with group members aids in identifying needed skills and allows for prompting and coaching of student skill use as situations arise during the day (Pelco & Reed-Victor, 2007). As McIntosh and Mackay (2008) state, "The person teaching the [social skills] lessons should be the person who supervises the generalization setting" (p. 19). The Skillstreaming group leader may additionally imbed instruction within naturally occurring events, such as academic skill classes (Smith & Gilles, 2003). This powerful strategy, termed *instructed generalization* or *capturing teachable moments,* greatly enhances both skill learning and generalization.

Mediated Generalization

The one certain commonality present in both teaching and real-life settings is the target child. Mediated generalization—mediated by the child, not by others—is an approach to transfer enhancement that relies on instructing the individual in a series of self-regulation competencies (Neilans & Israel, 1981). Operationally, it consists of instructing the child in self-recording (self-monitoring), self-reinforcement, self-punishment, and self-instruction. Two of these mediation strategies—self-reinforcement and self-monitoring—are particularly useful for the preschool and kindergarten child.

Self-reinforcement

Often, environmental support is insufficient to maintain newly learned skills. In fact, as mentioned earlier, many real-life environments actually discourage children's efforts to behave prosocially. For this reason, we have found it useful to include self-reinforcement and self-monitoring procedures. Many young children are far more motivated to use newly learned skills when they, rather than an outside observer, monitor and report or record their use of a skill.

Leaders should encourage children's continued use of a learned skill by ongoing reinforcement and monitoring of skill use. Self-monitoring provides an intrinsically reinforcing function. It may consist of verbally reporting skill use and may include self-recording. For example, if a student follows all the steps of a particular skill especially well, self-reinforcement might take the form of saying something positive (e.g., "Good for me" or "I did a good job"). Teachers can help encourage the child by having her rehearse self-rewarding statements following completion of homework assignments or after spontaneous skill use.

Self-monitoring

Self-monitoring involves the child's noting when a skill has been performed and documenting his own skill performance. For example, the child may place a sticker or star on a card or color a space or happy face when he performs the skill. The sample self-monitoring form (shown in Figure 8) is associated with one such plan. In using this form, the teacher identifies the skill for practice, and the child colors a spot on the giraffe each time the skill is performed. When all the spots have been colored, the child is allowed to keep the picture of the giraffe as a reinforcer. A stronger reinforcer (e.g., an additional tangible reward or special privilege) may be provided, particularly if the child has been successful in achieving repeated skill performance to remediate an especially problematic behavior. This type of plan lends itself best to skills that can be performed in view of the teacher, especially for preschoolers, who may not accurately report their own behavior. Examples of other self-monitoring forms are included in Appendix A or may be created as needed.

MAINTENANCE-ENHANCING PROCEDURES

Maintenance of behaviors developed through skills training approaches is primarily a matter of reinforcement during the original teaching and in the child's natural environment. The strategies first discussed can be accomplished during the Skillstreaming intervention; the last two apply to generalization after the intervention is over.

During the Skillstreaming Intervention

Thinning Reinforcement

A rich, continuous reinforcement schedule is optimal for the establishment of new behaviors. Maintenance of learned behaviors will be enhanced if the reinforcement is gradually thinned. Thinning of reinforcement proceeds best by moving from a continuous (every trial) schedule,

I reached
my goal!

Name _____ Marcus _____

Date _____ 10/15 _____

Skill _____ Asking for Help (#6) _____

to some form of intermittent schedule, to the level of sparse and infrequent reinforcement characteristic of the natural environment. In fact, the goal of the thinning process is to make the reinforcement schedule indistinguishable from that typically found in real-world contexts. For example, a child would initially receive a reward for each time she uses a skill (as recorded on Homework Report 1), then the reinforcement would gradually be thinned and the child would receive the reward (perhaps a larger or more desirable reward) for two or more skill performances (as recorded on a self-monitoring form).

Delaying Reinforcement

Resistance to extinction is also enhanced by delaying reinforcement. During the early stages of learning a new skill, immediate reinforcement contingent on display of the behavior or skill is necessary. Once the skill has become a part of the child's behavioral repertoire, reinforcement should be delayed, more closely approximating the reinforcing conditions in the natural environment.

Delay of reinforcement may be implemented by (a) increasing the size or complexity of the responses required before reinforcement is provided; (b) adding a time delay between the response and the delivery of reinforcement; and (c) in token systems, increasing the interval between the receipt of tokens and the opportunity to spend them and/or requiring more tokens in exchange for a given reinforcer (Sulzer-Azaroff & Mayer, 1991). For example, the child may initially be rewarded for performing the skill in real life (e.g., choose from the prize box), then he may instead receive a token or ticket for each performance. When a given number of tickets are earned, the child may exchange these for a reward (e.g., make a choice from a box with bigger prizes) or a special privilege at the end of the day (e.g., free play). Later on, an increased number of tickets may be required to earn an even larger reward (e.g., lunch with the teacher).

Fading Prompts

Prompting may involve describing the specific types of situations in the real world in which students should use a given skill (i.e., instructed generalization). Children can be encouraged to use a particular skill or verbally prompted in a variety of real-life settings. Historically, teachers have used this principle of generalization by prompting students during "teachable moments," or times the skill is actually needed. When potential problems arise in the classroom, the teacher can elicit a prosocial response by suggesting a particular skill. For example, Jake, who often became disruptive in the classroom, had completed his workbook page and was sitting quietly at his desk. Rather than waiting for Jake to become disruptive, the teacher suggested that he use Deciding What to Do (Skill 40). This proactive approach turns naturally occurring problem situations into realistic learning opportunities, thus providing more opportunities for practice. Furthermore, it helps create a positive environment for learning ways to deal with interpersonal problems.

Another way of prompting skill use is to provide written prompts in the form of leader-created cue cards or cue sheets. Cue cards and sheets list the skill's behavioral steps and include spaces for the child to check off each step either as the step is enacted or after all steps are completed. The child may tape a card of this type to the work area if it is a skill that is to be used in the classroom, or keep it in a pocket or folder if it is for use in another setting (e.g., on the school bus, on the playground, at home). For example, Ayul needed to practice Joining In (Skill 15) on the playground. The cue card Ayul's teacher made for her is shown in Figure 9.

Displaying a poster of a given skill will help children remember to practice it. Placed wherever it is most appropriate, the skill poster gives the name of the skill and lists and illustrates its behavioral steps. If the children have been instructed in the skills of Asking Someone to Play (Skill 19) and Playing a Game (Skill 20), for example, displaying posters for these skills in the area of the classroom used for free play may remind the children of these particular skills and skill steps.

The gradual removal of such suggestions, reminders, coaching, or instruction may enhance maintenance. Fading of prompts is a means of moving away from artificial control (the teacher's) to more natural self-control of desirable behaviors. As is true for all the enhancement techniques examined here, fading of prompts should be carefully planned and systematically implemented.

Providing Booster Sessions

Periodically, it may be necessary to reinstate instruction for certain prosocial behaviors to continue in the natural environment. Booster sessions between teacher and student, either on a preplanned schedule or as needed, have proven valuable (Feindler & Ecton, 1986; Karoly & Steffen, 1980; Walker et al., 2004). When the teacher notices that skills previously taught are not used on a consistent basis, these sessions may also be carried out with the group as a whole. In such cases, the skill is retaught via the same methods as initially presented (modeling, role-playing, performance feedback, and generalization). Because the instruction is a review of the skill, the session will likely move more quickly than initial skill instruction.

Preparing for Real-Life Nonreinforcement

Both teacher and child may take steps to maximize the likelihood that reinforcement for appropriate behaviors will occur in the natural environment. Because on a number of occasions, reinforcement will not be forthcoming, it is important for the child to be prepared for this eventuality. As described previously in this chapter, self-reinforcement is one option when desirable behaviors are performed correctly but are unrewarded by external sources.

Graduated homework assignments

The student may also be prepared for nonreinforcement in the natural environment by completing graduated homework assignments. It may become clear as Skillstreaming homework is discussed that the real-life figure is too difficult a target—too harsh, too unresponsive, or simply too unlikely to provide reinforcement. When this is the case, with the newly learned skill still fragile, teachers may redirect the homework assignment toward two or three more benevolent target figures. When the child finally does use the skill correctly with the original target figure and receives no reinforcement, these previously reinforced trials help minimize the likelihood that the behavior will be extinguished.

Group reward plans

In this procedure, the teacher or the children decide on a target skill. Most often, this skill will be one recently taught in the Skillstreaming group or one that the children need an extra reminder to use throughout the day. Each time any child (or teacher) performs the skill, a block is colored in on

Figure 9: Ayul's Cue Card

a group reward form (for a sample, see Figure 5, in chapter 2). When all of the blocks have been colored, the entire group earns a special reward, such as a popcorn party, an extra recess period, or a favorite story. Using plans in which all group members work together to achieve a common goal helps to create a cooperative spirit in the classroom and will often result in children's reminding one another to use the skill when a situation suggests its use.

Skill tickets

To encourage the continued use of prosocial skills in the preschool or kindergarten setting, token reinforcers such as the skill ticket shown in Figure 6 (chapter 2) may be given throughout the school day when individual children use any prosocial skill. Tickets can be accumulated until a given number are earned, then redeemed for a special activity or reward. If necessary, these tickets may also be given in the Skillstreaming group itself to encourage following group rules, role-playing, and completing homework assignments. Such tokens should always be paired with verbal praise. It is also important that each child's name appear on these tickets and that a special place be provided in which to store them.

Skill notes

Teachers typically send notes home to parents pertaining to preacademic or behavioral achievements. Skill notes such as the one illustrated in Figure 7 (chapter 2) can be completed and sent home with a child who has demonstrated skill use in the classroom or in another school environment. If parents are unlikely to read the note or provide praise for skill use, it will be important that the child take the note to another person in the school setting (e.g., principal, librarian, other teacher) before taking the note home. Again, the purpose of such notes is to provide the child with additional reinforcement for prosocial skill use and to communicate to others which specific skills are being emphasized at school.

Awards

Children are more likely to continue their attempts to use a prosocial skill if they are rewarded by significant others in their environment. The teacher, principal, and/or parents may give awards. The teacher award is a type of material reinforcer to be given after children have attained proficiency in some or all of the skills included in one of the six main skill groups. Figure 10 illustrates an award given for achievement in Dealing with Feelings (Group IV). These awards may be displayed in the classroom on a bulletin board reserved for this purpose and then taken home by the child to show to parents.

Whenever a teacher or another person in the school environment observes a child using a prosocial skill, the child may be sent to the principal's or director's office to receive a Principal Award, along with words of praise and encouragement (for a sample, see Figure 11). Such reinforcement from a person in authority may provide a strong reinforcer to the child to continue to use prosocial behaviors.

The parent award, illustrated in Figure 12, is designed to be used by parents who have been involved in a Skillstreaming training session and who will likely notice prosocial skill use in the home setting. The Parent Award identifies the prosocial skill parents should watch for and includes a space so parents can sign the award and return it to school with the child once the skill is observed. The awards can then be displayed in the classroom as appropriate. This method provides additional reinforcement to the child as he or she attempts skill use outside of the classroom.

Additional awards for teachers, principals, and parents are included in Appendix A.

Goal setting

Setting individual goals is a form of self-management that can have a powerful effect on learning. The preschool or kindergarten child has the capacity to participate in identifying a specific social goal toward which to direct learning efforts. In many

Friendship Award

Name _____ Cory _____

Date _____ 4/27 _____

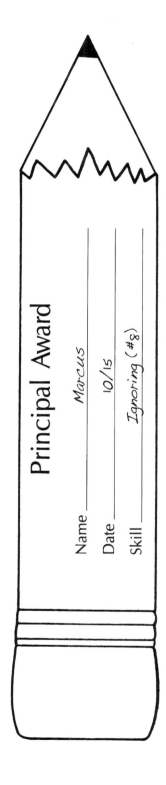

Principal Award

Name _Marcus_

Date _10/15_

Skill _Ignoring (#8)_

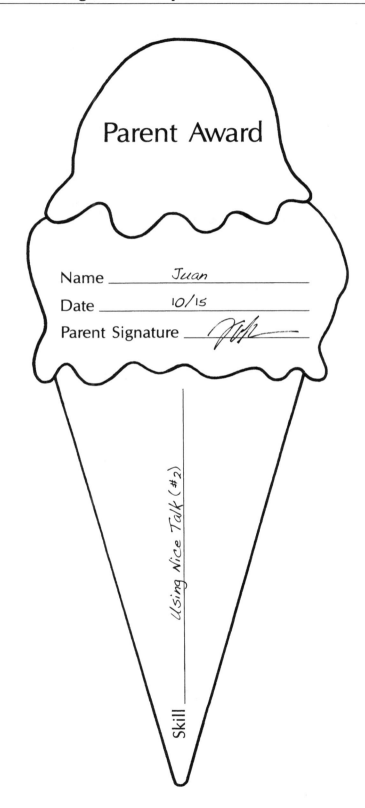

Parent Award

Name _____Juan_____

Date _____10/15_____

Parent Signature _____

Using Nice Talk (#2)

Skill

Figure 13: Savannah's Goal-Setting Card

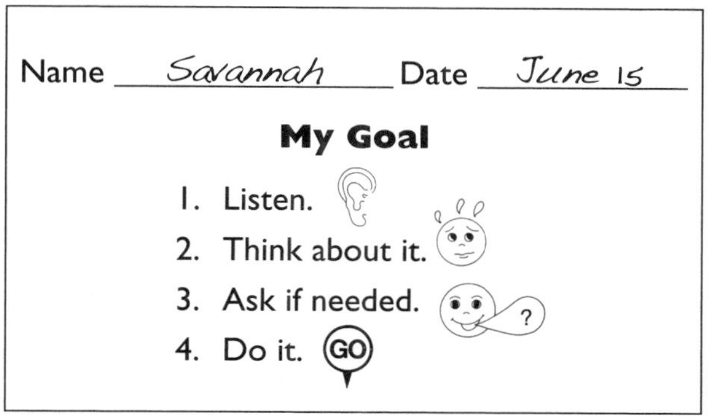

Name _Savannah_   Date _June 15_

My Goal

1. Listen.
2. Think about it.
3. Ask if needed.
4. Do it. GO

classrooms, individual social goals are posted in the child's work area. Figure 13 shows a teacher-made goal-setting card that might be used in this way. In other classrooms, skill steps are written on a blank name tag and worn by the child. Then when the child performs the social skill, a sticker or star is placed directly on the tag, thus allowing the child to receive ongoing feedback on specific goal performance. The display of individual student goals helps the child and also reminds the adults in the learning environment to prompt the child to meet the goal.

Graham, Harris, and Reid (1992) offer guidelines for the most effective use of goal setting:

1. Specificity. Goals should be defined in specific versus more global terms (e.g., offer to share with one person during free play versus cooperate).

2. Difficulty. The goal defined should be challenging to the child but one that he or she can attain with reasonable effort. For example, a child who is often the recipient of teasing from peers may not initially be successful in Dealing with Teasing (Skill 27) on the playground at recess. Instead, a more achievable goal for the child may be to use the skill Asking for Help (Skill 6) or Ignoring (Skill 8) during free play in the classroom, where the teacher is available for ongoing support and guidance.

3. Proximity. The goal selected should be achievable within a reasonable time (the next hour, the same day, the same evening). This is particularly important for the young child.

In addition, the child should be prompted or reminded of his or her individual goal shortly before the opportunity to use the skill presents itself and should receive feedback and positive reinforcement as soon as the goal has been achieved.

Social skills games

A variety of games can be developed and used to enhance skill learning. Group games require students to practice a variety of social skills (e.g., joining in, sharing, being a good sport). Types of games that lend themselves well to Skillstreaming include board games and role-playing games. Cartledge and Milburn (1980) make several points worth considering when using social skills games:

1. The connection between performing a skill in the game setting and in real life must be made explicit.

2. The winner (if there is one) should be determined on the basis of performance rather than chance.

3. If rewards are used, they should be given for appropriate (skilled) participation rather than winning.

4. Participants should not be "out" in a game without provisions for being allowed to participate again within a short period of time.

5. If teaming is required, skill-deficient children should be included on the same team as skill-competent children.

Skill folders

All students in the Skillstreaming group or classroom should keep a prosocial skills folder. This is simply a way of organizing materials—skill cards, homework assignments, awards, self-monitoring forms, and the like. Children will then have a readily available record of the behavioral steps of the skills they have practiced in the past. To enhance the likelihood that these prosocial behaviors will also be used outside the instructional setting, the teacher may send the child's skills folder home on a regular basis. When parents communicate that the child demonstrates prosocial behaviors at home, parent awards can be inserted.

Beyond the Skillstreaming Intervention

The generalization-enhancing techniques examined thus far are directed toward the child. But maintenance and generalization of appropriate behaviors also may be enhanced by efforts directed toward others, especially those in the child's natural environment who function as the main providers of reinforcement.

Programming for Reinforcement in the Natural Environment

The child's interpersonal world includes a variety of people—parents, siblings, peers, teachers, neighbors, and others. By their responsiveness or unresponsiveness to the child's newly learned skills, to a large extent these people control the destiny of these behaviors. We all react to what the important people in our lives think or feel about our behavior. What they reward we are more likely to continue doing. What they are indifferent or hostile to will tend to fall into disuse.

The involvement of educators, agency and institutional staff, parents, and peers is critical in children's acquisition and maintenance of prosocial skills. Parents in particular can enhance the likelihood that prosocial skills, once learned, will be maintained. (Chapter 7 offers a rationale and detailed procedures for involving parents in this very important work.)

Using Natural Reinforcers

A final and especially valuable approach to maintenance enhancement is the use of reinforcers that occur naturally in the child's environment. As Stokes and Baer (1977) observe:

> Perhaps the most dependable of all generalization programming mechanisms is the one that hardly deserves the name: the transfer of behavioral control from the teacher-experimenter to stable, natural contingencies that can be trusted to operate in the environment to which the subject will return, or already occupies. To a considerable extent, this goal is accomplished by choosing behaviors to teach that normally will meet maintaining reinforcement after the teaching. (p. 353)

Alberto and Troutman (2006) suggest a four-step process to facilitate the use of natural reinforcers:

1. Observe which specific behaviors are regularly reinforced and how they are reinforced in the major settings that constitute the student's natural environment.

2. Instruct the student in a selected number of naturally reinforced behaviors (e.g., certain social skills, grooming behaviors).

3. Teach the student how to recruit or request reinforcement (e.g., by tactfully asking peers or others for approval or recognition).

4. Because its presence in certain gestures or facial expressions may be quite subtle, teach the student how to recognize reinforcement when it is offered.

CHAPTER 6

Managing Behavior Problems

Problems can and do occur in the Skillstreaming group, just as they may in any group teaching endeavor. Some young children may prefer to engage in an unrelated activity and are therefore not motivated to participate. Others may actively resist involvement in group instruction. Still others may fail to see why the skills are important in their everyday lives. Their resistive behavior may interfere not only with their own skill acquisition but also with the learning of others in the group.

Once a management problem has been identified, the task becomes to select and implement one or more techniques to foster more desirable behavior. Just as one type of reinforcer may be rewarding for one child but not for another, a particular management strategy is likely to be more effective for one child than for another. Therefore, teachers and other group leaders should consider a range of strategies when conducting Skillstreaming groups and individualize these methods, first using the least intrusive techniques.

This chapter describes a variety of management techniques for use with typical problem behaviors encountered during Skillstreaming instruction. Suggested strategies are described in the following three tiers: Universal strategies are those used to manage the group as a whole, targeted strategies are for some students who exhibit moderate behavior problems, and individual strategies are for students with significant problem behaviors.

UNIVERSAL STRATEGIES

Learning Climate

The atmosphere of the Skillstreaming group, and the classroom in general, should be positive and encouraging. In other words, the teacher should openly notice the children following group rules, making prosocial choices, and "being good" rather than focus on catching them breaking rules. A benefit of this approach is that when teachers see a child behaving appropriately and state approval of that behavior publicly, other children engaging in unacceptable behavior are likely to stop problem behaviors and engage in the behaviors that received teacher approval (Kounin, 1970). Effectively managing ongoing classroom activities, creating structure and routines, and defining and enforcing behavioral expectations through classroom or group rules are ways of establishing an encouraging and supportive setting for learning. Teachers and other group leaders should also take time to establish positive relationships with the children, families, and other colleagues. Positive, encouraging relationships will provide motivation for all involved to work together and to risk learning the sometimes very challenging skills.

Physical Structure

The physical environment can structure the learning setting. Most preschool and kindergarten classrooms have areas designed for a variety of free-play activities and learning activities (e.g., learning centers). To minimize potential behavior problems during teaching, the area in which Skillstreaming instruction is carried out needs to be large enough so children can participate in role-plays without disrupting other group participants. Chairs or carpet samples for the children to sit on can help create physical distance between the children. To reduce distractions, enticing activities such as sand or water tables should be moved out of the group's view. Visuals are typically necessary with this age group; therefore the group rules or behavioral guidelines should be posted and reviewed prior to each instructional session as a reminder for the entire group to use positive behavior.

In the classroom in general, allowing space for traffic can minimize disruption of ongoing activities as children move from one area to another. Enhancing the physical structure of the group setting or classroom with strategies like those just described can minimize and avert many behavior problems; the structure can then be gradually lessened as the children become more familiar with working together.

Schedules and Routines

The teacher should provide a structure by creating a daily schedule of events. Within this schedule, the teacher sets the time for group instruction in Skillstreaming and plans opportunities to practice the prosocial skills the children have learned in the formal group setting. For example, if the skill is Waiting Your Turn (Skill 16), activities in which the children will need to take their turns, such as completing a puzzle as a group or drawing a group picture, can be planned. Most preschool and kindergarten teachers find it helpful to follow the same general schedule each day. Although special activities may occasionally alter the schedule, young children often feel more secure when they have a predictable daily routine. Providing a schedule of the school day in picture format and reviewing the schedule at the beginning of the school day can help avert many of the problems associated with changes in schedule.

Structure in the form of routine is important within the Skillstreaming sessions as well. Although most young children quickly learn the pattern of Skillstreaming activities, it is helpful at the beginning of each session to let children know what activities will be taking place (e.g., "We'll show you the skill of Waiting Your Turn, then some of you will get a chance to try it"). Informing the children of the specific activities they will be participating in will help prepare them for learning.

Rules and Procedures

Communicating classroom expectations is a critical aspect of providing effective structure. This is most clearly and easily done by establishing group rules for acceptable behavior. Such rules should be reasonable ones that tell the children what to do rather than forbid unacceptable behaviors. Establishing clearly defined rules in the early stages of group work may prevent many behavior problems and allows teachers to redirect the children in an encouraging and supportive manner. Teachers in supportive classrooms teach rules and procedures as explicitly as they teach academic content. Effective teachers integrate their rules and procedures—as well as consequences for not following them—into their classroom routines.

A number of effective "rules for the use of rules" exist in the behavior management literature (Greenwood, Hops, Delquadri, & Guild, 1974; Sarason, Glaser, & Fargo, 1972; Walker, 1979), including the following:

1. Define and communicate rules for student behavior in clear, specific, and, especially, behavioral terms. It is better (more concrete and behavioral) to say, "Raise your hand be-

fore asking a question" than "Be considerate of others." A statement such as "Be kind or considerate of others" is a good goal, but it is too abstract. Instead, student behaviors should be clearly defined and phrased in a manner that students will understand, such as "Wait until another person has finished talking before you begin" and "Leave toys and other objects at your desk."

2. It is more effective to tell students what to do than what not to do. For example, if it is necessary to address aggression, instead of "No pushing or shoving," the rule should be phrased as "Keep hands and feet to yourself." Other positive examples include "Talk over disagreements" instead of "No fighting" and "Work quietly" instead of "Don't talk out of turn."

3. Rules should be communicated in a manner that will help students remember them. Depending on the age group and rule difficulty, memorization aids may include keeping rules short and few in number (four or five rules is a workable number to use in most preschool and kindergarten classrooms), repeating the rules several times, and posting the rules in written and picture form in the classroom, as well as sending them home to parents. Rules should be reviewed at the beginning of each Skillstreaming session until all children remember them. Periodic review of rules may also be needed.

4. Following the rules is more likely when students have had a role in rule development, modification, and implementation. However, often school and classroom rules are established by a committee of adults without student participation. Allowing the group to participate encourages the children's commitment to abide by the rules. Students can be asked to think of behaviors they feel they need to work together. Often students will state many rules that group leaders themselves would have identified. At times,

more specific guidance may be needed, ideally in the form of leading questions, such as "Would everyone have a chance to be heard if everyone talked at once?" or "How might you let the leader know that you have something you want to say?"

In addition to the preceding ideas, further effective rules for rules are that (a) they be developed before group instruction begins; (b) they be fair, reasonable, and within students' capacity to follow; (c) that all members of the group understand them; and (d) they be applied consistently and fairly to all group members.

Rules are guidelines governing appropriate and inappropriate student behaviors; procedures are what students need to know and follow to meet their own personal needs and perform routine instructional and classroom housekeeping activities. As is the case for rules, classroom procedures need to be explicitly taught; one cannot assume that students will know them without instruction. Unlike rules, which need to be taught "up front," procedures (e.g., for obtaining help, leaving the room, using rest room passes, sharpening pencils, handing in class work) usually can be explained as the need arises. However, procedures also will need to be clearly stated, closely monitored, consistently followed, retaught when necessary, and consequated when not followed.

Supportive Interventions

Young children will more readily learn the Skillstreaming curriculum when it is presented in an encouraging and supportive environment. The previous section described considerations related to planning and structuring such a learning environment. The following interventions are designed to support children's desirable behaviors in an unobtrusive manner within the actual teaching sequence. These interventions include group teaching techniques, enhancing motivation, modifying antecedents, precorrection and specific praise, offering choices, simplifying, prompting, surface management techniques, behavioral redirection, and relationship-based techniques.

Group Teaching Techniques

What do teachers actually do to support positive behaviors in the learning setting? According to Kounin (1970), first, the teacher knows what is going on. Such *with-it-ness* is communicated to the class in a number of ways, including swift and consistent recognition and, when necessary, consequating of low-level behaviors likely to grow into disruptiveness or more serious aggression. Closely connected to such attentiveness is *overlapping,* the ability to manage simultaneously two or more classroom events, whether instructional or disciplinary. *Smoothness,* the ability to transition from one activity to another without "downtime," is a third facilitative teacher behavior. Downtime is a time for students to become bored and act out; avoiding or minimizing downtime significantly deters such behaviors.

Another way to minimize boredom is by instructing with momentum, maintaining a steady progress or movement throughout a particular lesson, class, or school day. A group focus, the ability to keep the entire class involved in a given instructional activity, also diminishes the likelihood of student aggression. Finally, an especially significant contributor to a supportive learning environment is the teacher's communication of optimistic expectations. Students live up to (and, unfortunately, also down to) what important people in their lives expect of them. The teacher who expects a child to be a "slow learner" or a "behavior problem" because of his or her past record, a sibling's past poor performance, or the neighborhood the student comes from will likely be rewarded with low performance or behavior problems. By contrast, the teacher who lets the student know he or she can achieve and will have the teacher's help along the way is likely to motivate the student to be more successful and less disruptive. The message is, expect the best of your students—you may well get it!

Consistent application of rules and procedures provides clear expectations for student behavior and establishes that the teacher is in charge of the classroom. Yet such consistency is difficult to maintain over time. Teachers become tired, overworked, and distracted. When this occurs, students are quick to get the message that perhaps "just this once" can become more than once. Then the boundary between what is and is not acceptable is no longer clear. Young children test the limits to reestablish the boundary, and, as this happens, the foundation for a supportive learning environment begins to erode.

Supportive environments are predictable environments. As noted previously, a well thought out and fairly and consistently enforced set of school rules or guidelines strongly helps establish such predictability. Consistent enforcement means that all staff are aware of and enforce rules in agreed-upon ways. But the demands of fairness and consistency may be contradictory at times. Consistency requires rule enforcement for all applicable occasions; fairness may require taking special circumstances into account and not enforcing a given rule in some instances.

Enhancing Motivation

Two types of motivators are typically employed to increase a child's use of desired behaviors: extrinsic and intrinsic. Extrinsic motivators are tangible rewards provided contingent upon performance of a desired skill or behavior. Such rewards take many forms, but at this point, most practitioners agree that the use of a combination of external and internal motivators is the most effective motivational strategy. Tangible motivators are widely used in schools and other settings serving children and youth. The stars and stickers of the preschool and kindergarten years take the form of points and special privileges and activities in the later grades. Extrinsic rewards appear to be especially useful in eliciting initial involvement in learning unfamiliar skills. It has been the experience of many teachers of Skillstreaming, however, that using only external rewards—whether in the form of tangible reinforcers or other incentives—is insufficient to sustain learning. In Skillstreaming, the skills themselves are intrinsically motivating, especially those skills the children choose themselves and use successfully in real-world settings. When children have the opportunity to select the skills they feel they need, they are more motivated to participate. When such student-selected—and, perhaps to a somewhat lesser degree, teacher-selected—skills yield positive outcomes in interactions with family, peers, or significant others, motivation is further enhanced.

In addition to regularly allowing children to select the skills for instruction, a second tactic to augment intrinsic motivation is helpful: communicating to the children, both during the initial structuring of the Skillstreaming group and periodically as the sessions unfold, that the goal of Skillstreaming is to teach alternatives, not substitutes. Many children who participate have been reprimanded and punished many times for behaviors their parents, teachers, or others deem inappropriate. In one way or another, they have been told, "Stop doing that and do this instead" (e.g., "Stop talking and listen" or "Stop hitting and talk out the problem"). When teachers encounter preacademic or academic skill deficits in young children, they quickly understand the need to teach the child the necessary skills. For example, if a child has learned an inappropriate response (such as giving the sound of long *o* when shown the letter *a*), it is understood that additional instruction in that specific skill must occur. At this point, the child must both unlearn the inappropriate response and learn the correct response. The same is true when dealing with children's undesirable behaviors. The most successful means of decreasing a child's inappropriate behavior is to expand the child's behavioral repertoire, or range of possible responses. For example, if the child loses at a game with a peer and the only response to losing he or she has learned, practiced, and been rewarded for is

hitting, the child will hit again. The child has, in effect, no choices. If Skillstreaming teaches the child that a response to losing may also be talking about feelings or making a coping statement (e.g., "Everybody can't win"), at least some of the time the child may use one of the more desirable responses instead of aggression.

Modifying Antecedents

Addressing antecedents, or what happens before problem behaviors to elicit them, is an effective way to minimize these behavior problems. As discussed in the introduction, children come to the structured preschool or kindergarten setting with a variety of skills, abilities, and prior experiences. Jones and Jones (1998) address modifications of antecedents related to academic achievement, including adjusting time, the learning environment, content (type, difficulty, amount, or sequence), and organization. Such modifications of academic task antecedents are appropriate in the Skillstreaming process as well.

Children's abilities to handle particular group participation tasks will vary. Some may have difficulty following a series of instructions or understanding the meaning of specific concepts included in the directions. For these children, it would be helpful to present fewer instructions at a time or to repeat instructions, rephrasing them in language that the children can more easily understand. In addition, any task may be divided into a sequence of steps that the children can perform one at a time.

Precorrection and Specific Praise

Precorrective statements attend to both the demands of the setting and the desired behavior. The goal with precorrection is for the teacher to anticipate problems that may occur in the instructional environment, in this case the Skillstreaming setting. For example, if students typically have difficulty transitioning to a group activity, it is likely they will have similar difficulty moving to the area where Skillstreaming instruction occurs. Precorrective statements tell the students what is expected. In other words, the teacher tells the students, and perhaps models for them, the exact behavioral expectations. For transition, a precorrective statement might be something like "When it's time for Skillstreaming group, close your reading books and look at me so I know you're ready to come to the group. When I call your table, please walk slowly and sit on your carpet square. Now watch me and see what I do. What did I do first?" and so on. When the students follow the expectations, specific praise (e.g., "Thank you for walking quietly") will be necessary to reinforce the expectation. Both precorrective statements and behavior-specific praise have been shown to decrease problem behaviors in the classroom (Stormont & Reinke, 2009). Fullerton, Conroy, and Correa (2009), for example, trained early childhood teachers interacting with students with behavior problems to use specific praise during transitions. As the teachers increased their use of specific praise statements, children's engagement in the activity increased, as well as their compliance with expectations. Using these strategies also makes the environment more predictable for young students.

Offering Choices

Providing choices, initially selecting between two options, has been found to reduce behavior problems in young children with behavior challenges (Jolivette, McCormick, Jung, & Lingo, 2004). Furthermore, providing choices is also listed as a quality indicator in many early childhood programs. In the Skillstreaming session, young children should be offered choices as a matter of routine. For example, students may choose to role-play now or later, select a peer to participate in the role-play, and choose a situation in which to role-play. For some students with challenging behaviors or those who are reluctant to participate, it is appropriate to ask the student to make a choice. For example, the child may be asked to choose between sitting in the group or standing at the chart to note the skill steps as they are enacted or to role-play in the group or to role-play individually with the teacher at a later time. Jolivette, McCormick, Jung, and

Lingo (2004) offer several positive outcomes for providing choices:

- Promotes independence
- Teaches self-monitoring of appropriate behaviors
- Provides a sense of self-control
- Allows active participation
- Improves performance
- Fosters a positive, general sense of well-being
- Links behavior and values to responsibility

Simplifying

Simplifying, or asking less at one time, is another way to increase the likelihood that students will experience success in the Skillstreaming group. Children's abilities to handle particular group tasks will vary. Some may have difficulty following a series of instructions, understanding instructions, or knowing what to say during feedback time. Methods of simplifying include the following:

- Have the child role-play one behavioral step at a time. Reward minimal student accomplishment.
- Shorten the role-play.
- Coach the child through a prepared script that visually portrays the behavioral steps.
- Ask the student to take the role of coactor before that of main actor.

Prompting

The teacher needs to anticipate problems in the classroom or Skillstreaming session and then prompt desired behaviors. Prompting, or telling the child what to do in a given situation, can minimize behavior problems and also provides a positive, encouraging environment in which to foster learning. For example, if a group of five children are each given paper and scissors but are given only two bottles of glue, it is important for the teacher to anticipate the problem of sharing the glue. Once specific Skillstreaming skills are learned, the skills themselves can be used to prompt desired behaviors. In the preceding scenario, for example, the teacher might remind the group of the steps to Sharing (Skill 17) or Asking a Favor (Skill 7).

During Skillstreaming instruction, one of the teacher's main functions is to anticipate difficulties and be ready to prompt a desirable response during role-play activities. Children practicing a new skill in a session may easily forget a step or several steps, or they may not know how to behave to carry out a particular skill step. The teacher may then give instructional comments or hints to elicit the behavior (e.g., "We heard you think about your choices. Now you're going to make a choice") or coach the student from start to finish. Prompting may also prevent the child from acting in a disruptive or aggressive manner out of fear of failing. Such coaching will help the child practice performing the skill steps correctly rather than experience additional failure.

Surface Management Techniques

Redl and Wineman (1957) have suggested several techniques for unobtrusively managing mild and commonly occurring misbehaviors. These methods, termed *surface management techniques,* have been used successfully to deal with problem behaviors in Skillstreaming groups.

Planned ignoring

Mild misbehaviors can best be dealt with by simply ignoring them. Many times, drawing attention to such behaviors is more distracting to the learning process than the behaviors themselves. Positively reinforcing concurrent appropriate behavior helps eliminate the inappropriate action. This strategy is most effective when the group leader plans in advance which mild behaviors will be ignored.

> EXAMPLE. Susie often played with the laces on her new shoes during Skillstreaming sessions despite the fact that the teacher had taken her aside prior to the group to ask

that she sit cross-legged and keep her hands away from her shoes. Because Susie's behavior did not appear to distract others in the group, the teacher decided to ignore the behavior to see if, with lack of attention, the behavior would diminish.

Proximity control

In proximity control, the teacher moves closer to (stands near, sits next to) the student who is misbehaving. Often simply moving closer to the student who is engaging in problem or distracting behavior will draw the student's attention back to the learning situation. For students who do not mind being touched, a hand on the shoulder is an effective way of drawing the student back to task.

> EXAMPLE. While the group was providing feedback to role-players, Judy began singing. The leader quietly moved away from the front of the group, stood next to Judy, and touched her shoulder while continuing to elicit feedback about the role-play.

Signal interference

Signal interference includes nonverbal communicators that let the child know a behavior is unacceptable. This may include eye contact, hand gestures, or clearing one's throat. Some students who engage in mildly disruptive behavior may not even realize they are doing something distracting to others. In such cases, prearranging with the child a specific signal (e.g., a word or gesture) to cue the child that the behavior is occurring has been a useful strategy.

> EXAMPLE. While the teacher modeled the skill, Enrique began playing with Samantha's hair, distracting her from the modeling display. The teacher caught Enrique's eye, shook her head no, and continued with the modeling.

Interest boosting

When a student's attention appears to be drifting away from an activity, it is often helpful to boost the child's interest. This can be done by involving the child more directly in the activity, asking for his or her input, or directing a high-interest question to the group.

> EXAMPLE. While the teacher was generating situations in which the skill could be used, Cody became restless, turning around and trying to engage others in conversation. The teacher, changing her tone of voice to one of anticipation, asked the group if they had experienced similar situations. To increase the interest of all children, the teacher asked for a thumbs-up or thumbs-down as a response.

Humor

At times, a student in the Skillstreaming group may express something very clever or humorous. Such a humorous moment can quickly ease a tense situation. As long as the humor is not at the expense of a specific individual or group or the child is not being rewarded for being a class clown, it is fine to go ahead and laugh.

> EXAMPLE. While the group was getting ready to begin, one child told a silly knock-knock joke, and all the other group members laughed. Instead of reprimanding the child, the teacher laughed along with the others for a few moments and then began the instruction.

Restructuring the program/capturing teachable moments

At times, the planned lesson content must be abandoned in favor of dealing with a problem that has just occurred. If students appear tense and upset because of a playground problem, for example, requiring them to practice a less immediately relevant skill will not meet their needs. Instead, the teacher should abandon the preplanned lesson and restructure the lesson, changing the skill to be taught.

Capturing such teachable moments can take the form of employing Skillstreaming to better manage the instructional setting. Many problem behaviors—including withdrawal, disruptive-

ness, threats, and so forth—may be viewed as behavioral excess: too much talking, too much bullying, and so on. However, basic behaviors may equally well be construed as behavioral deficiencies: too little listening to others, too little concern for others, and so on. As Greene (2010) states, "In the past 30 years, research has told us that challenging kids are challenging because they lack the skills not to be challenging" (p. 29). Thus, an additional way to reduce problem behaviors is to replace them with desirable ones. The Skillstreaming curriculum consists of just such alternatives. Skills may be taught as previously scheduled (as part of regular sessions) or at spontaneous times that help students reduce behavior problems (i.e., teachable moments).

> EXAMPLE. Following recess, several children in the class were visibly agitated, and two children had been crying. After questioning the class, the teacher learned that some of the children had been bullied by an older child, and the playground supervisor hadn't seen the problem. Even though the teacher's plan for the day was to work on a different skill, he abandoned this plan and introduced the more timely skill of Knowing When to Tell (Skill 35) to encourage the children to tell the playground supervisor the next time.

Removing seductive objects

It is natural for children to be distracted by interesting objects and toys. Including the group guideline of leaving toys and other objects at one's desk may prevent such distractions from occurring during Skillstreaming sessions.

> EXAMPLE. Antonio brought a new toy to the group and began showing it to others. The teacher asked Antonio to finish showing the toy and then directed him to put it either in his desk or in her desk for safekeeping.

Taking a break

When a child's behavior is not easily controlled within the teaching setting, it may be best for the child to take a break. Redl and Wineman (1957) describe this approach as "antiseptic bouncing." This measure is not intended to be punitive but rather to remove the child from a situation before he or she loses control. With this technique, the child is asked to leave the room to get a drink of water, run an errand, and so forth.

> EXAMPLE. Joshua couldn't seem to settle down despite the teacher's attempts to involve him. The teacher quietly called Joshua away from the group, said she had neglected to take a folder to the director's office, and requested that he help her out by immediately delivering the folder.

Reality appraisal

This technique involves giving students an explanation of why a behavior is not acceptable, or "telling it like it is." This approach, which helps children understand the consequences of their behavior, is most effective if the teacher has established a positive relationship with the children in the group.

> EXAMPLE. During feedback, most of the children began talking all at once. The group leader responded, "If everyone talks at once, we won't be able to hear anyone's ideas."

Behavioral Redirection

One way to encourage a student's appropriate behavior while preventing the occurrence of negative actions is to employ behavioral redirection. This means calling the child's attention to a different task or activity, thus directing the child away from the inappropriate behavior or action. For example, a student who frequently disrupts the Skillstreaming sessions by standing up and wandering around the room may be asked to help the teacher by pointing to the skill steps as they are being role-played. Another example might be to request that a child who inappropriately brings toys to the group take other classroom materials and put them on the teacher's desk, replacing the toy on the way. Still another student who has

difficulty keeping her hands to herself might be asked to sit next to the teacher and hold the box of props needed for the role-play.

Relationship-Based Techniques

Psychologists and educators have long known that the better the relationship between helper and client (or teacher and student), the more positive and productive the outcome of their interaction. In fact, it has been demonstrated that a positive relationship affects academic achievement (Jones & Jones, 2008) in addition to long-term behavior change. Two such techniques, especially useful when working with young children, are empathic encouragement and threat reduction. Often, they can be combined with other management techniques for maximum effect.

Empathic encouragement

Empathic encouragement is a strategy in which the teacher first shows understanding of the difficulty the child is experiencing and then urges the child to participate as instructed. Often this additional one-to-one attention will motivate the child to participate and follow the teacher's guidance. In applying this technique, the teacher first listens to the child's explanation of the problem and expresses an understanding of the child's feelings and behavior (e.g., "I know it seems difficult to learn something new"). If appropriate, the teacher responds that the child's view is valid. The teacher then restates his or her own view with supporting reasons and outcomes and urges the child to try out the suggestion (e.g., "If you don't try it, you won't know that you can do it. Let's just try").

> EXAMPLE: While the children took turns role-playing Joining In (Skill 15), Ayul sits with her head resting in her hands and looks down. Despite the teacher's prompts and reminders of reinforcement to be earned by participating, Ayul continues to disengage. The teacher understands the skill of Joining In is likely a difficult one for her. The teacher

then walks to Ayul and sits beside her while the co-leader takes over facilitation of the group. The leader softly asks, "Ayul, you seem to be having some trouble participating today. Will you tell me the problem?" Ayul shrugs and remains quiet. The teacher responds, "I know this skill may seem difficult right now because we're just starting to learn how to join in. Is this the problem?" Ayul nods. "OK, then. I understand. But, I believe you can do it. Let's move closer to the group and start learning the skill by just watching the role-plays before you give it a try." Ayul takes the teacher's hand and follows to join the group.

Threat reduction

This technique is helpful in dealing with children's anxiety. Children who find role-playing or other types of participation threatening may react with inappropriate or disruptive behaviors or withdraw from the learning process. To deal with this problem, the teacher should provide reassurance or even physical contact (e.g., an arm around the child, a pat on the back). The teacher should also encourage group members to express support for the role-player and others who participate.

Other strategies for threat reduction include postponing the student's role-playing until last and clarifying and restructuring those aspects of the task that the student experiences as threatening. Simplifying and coaching may also help the child become more willing to engage in the learning activity.

TARGETED INTERVENTIONS

The universal interventions just described are designed to support students' desirable behaviors in an unobtrusive manner within the instructional setting while, in most cases, allowing instruction to continue. At times, however, more structured and directive interventions may be necessary. This section provides a brief review of behavior management techniques appropriate for this age group and describes a procedure for setting limits.

Before attempting to use these methods to manage problem behaviors, group leaders should ask themselves, Why at this moment is the student engaging in this particular behavior? All behavior serves a purpose or a function. To intervene in useful ways, teachers must be able to assess the problem behavior's function. Typical functions include obtaining something (attention or object), escape of a task or expectation, avoidance of a person, or self-regulation (e.g., reducing anxiety). Questions that may be asked include the following: Is the student's goal to seek attention or to avoid a task or a person? To avoid participation? To reduce anxiety? To confirm their hypothesis, leaders may directly ask children about their motivation: Could it be that you don't want to participate? Could it be that you want me to leave you alone? Or, could it be that this seems too difficult?

Perhaps the hypothesis is that the student is displaying resistive behavior to avoid a task he perceives as too complicated (e.g., one that has too many steps). In this case, the teacher may need to simplify the task. Another student may be experiencing anxiety as she realizes that her turn to role-play is approaching. In this situation, the teacher will likely need to offer reassurance. Still another student may not be receiving the desired amount of attention from others. Another may have been engaging in undesirable behaviors to belong and to be perceived as "cool." In these last two examples, the teacher may need to restructure the lesson to allow students to gain attention or belonging by being a helper or participant in the next role-play.

Behavior Management Techniques

Behavior management techniques (i.e., behavior modification) both promote skill learning and inhibit problematic behaviors. They are also central to effecting behavior change in individual interventions. The effectiveness of behavior modification technology rests upon a firm, well-validated foundation. Beyond the repeated demonstration of their effectiveness, behavior modification techniques are relatively easy to learn and use; may be administered by the teacher, parent, peers, or the child; and have a long history of successful use. For these reasons, the techniques can maximize time and opportunity for student learning. A major way to substitute appropriate for inappropriate behaviors is to present positive reinforcement to the student following and contingent upon the occurrence of appropriate behavior. Table 4 presents a variety of material and social reinforcers appropriate for the preschool and kindergarten child. A more detailed discussion of principles and techniques of behavior management is included as Appendix C in this book.

Setting Limits

As previously noted, in creating a safe learning environment, the teacher must correct any efforts to bully or treat others in an inappropriate or aggressive manner. The following plan has often been found useful in working with particularly difficult groups of young children.

Step 1: Reward Positive Behavior

Foremost among behavior management techniques for dealing with behavior problems is positive reinforcement, discussed previously. Many disruptions can be reduced or even eliminated by applying positive reinforcement to such desirable behaviors as listening, participating, and following group guidelines. Positive reinforcement also has a powerful effect on children who are behaving inappropriately if children who are engaging in desirable behavior are rewarded. As noted, if those who are listening are reinforced with behavior-specific verbal praise, a ripple effect is created, and the inattentive children will most likely begin to listen as well (Kounin, 1970). This strategy allows the teacher to control the group in a positive, helping way and decreases the impulse to nag children to pay attention.

Step 2: Offer Positive Consequences

Reminding students of the positive consequences of desirable behavior will often encourage them to stop an undesirable behavior and engage in the more desirable one. Offering positive consequences means telling students that a specific desirable behavior will earn a given reward. Examples include "When you listen, you may have a turn" and "When you put your materials away, you may join the group." Some behaviors may need a tangible positive consequence: "When you wait your turn, you'll earn your ticket (or sticker or star)." Reminding students to engage in a specific appropriate behavior to earn a privilege or reward lets them know that positive actions lead to good things—and it does so in an encouraging, helpful manner. It is important to present the positive consequences for stopping an undesirable action before informing children of any negative consequences.

Step 3: Inform the Child of Negative Consequences

The majority of minor behavioral difficulties (e.g., inattention, noisemaking) will likely be remedied by employing Steps 1 and 2 of this plan. However, if a child's inappropriate behavior does not cease, it may be necessary to inform him of the negative consequences of continuing the undesirable behavior. Examples of negative consequences include sitting away from the group for a minute, not earning stickers or other rewards that have been structured within the classroom plan, or not receiving a privilege such as extra recess time. Consequences should be as logically related to the misbehavior as possible. For example, if the child misuses classroom materials, she would then lose the privilege of using these materials for the rest of the day. Informing the child of negative consequences thus provides a warning of what will happen if the child continues to engage in that behavior. It is important for the teacher to have thought in advance of logically linked consequences that match the severity of the misbehavior. Thinking ahead in such a manner will prevent the application of consequences that are impossible to enforce or too severe.

Step 4: Allow the Child to Choose the Behavior

After being informed of both positive and negative consequences, the child is instructed to make a choice—either stop the behavior and earn the positive reinforcement or continue the behavior and accept the negative consequences.

Table 4: Material and Social Reinforcers

Material Reinforcers

Objects

Food (e.g., peanuts, raisins, apples, cereal, gum)

Stickers

Stars

Skill tickets

Happy faces

Awards

Good notes home

Ribbons

"Good Work" buttons

Rubber stamp on hand

Small toy or trinket

Photo of child

Activities

Feeding pets

Watering plants

Being first in line

One-on-one time with teacher

Extra free play

Sharpening pencils

Playing with a special toy

Listening to music or watching a DVD

Sitting at teacher's desk or chair

Extra outside play

Using teacher's equipment (e.g., stapler, hole punch)

Using colored chalk on chalkboard or sidewalk

Selecting a story to be read to the class

Earning a puzzle piece (completing the puzzle when all pieces are earned)

Listening to a story

Using the computer

Using the telephone

Social Reinforcers

Nonverbal

Smiling

Hugging

Looking interested

Physical closeness

A pat on the back

A wink

Nodding

Arm around the child

Holding hands

Verbal

Good listening, good thinking, and so forth

Thank you.

Wow!

I really like that.

That was nice.

You really waited.

Nice job!

Terrific!

Great work (or other behavior)!

When a child is given a choice, power struggles are eliminated. We cannot make a child behave in the way we would like him to behave; however, we can structure the consequences to encourage the child to make socially acceptable choices.

It is often helpful to allow the child time to make the choice. Informing the child that she will have two minutes to make the choice to put materials away or one minute to make the choice of whether or not to stop disrupting the group allows the teacher to leave the child alone, lessens the potential for a power struggle, reinforces the idea that the child can control both positive and negative consequences, and allows the child to maintain dignity.

Step 5: Enforce Positive or Negative Consequences

Either positive or negative consequences are next carried out. If the child chooses negative consequences by continuing the undesirable behavior, these are delivered in a calm and firm manner. For example, if the child continues to disrupt the Skillstreaming group by making noises, and the consequence for this behavior is to sit away from the group for two or three minutes, then the child is required to follow through. Once a negative consequence has been enforced, the teacher should reevaluate the structure of the learning environment, making supportive accommodations for the student—for example, seating the child closer to a group leader or implementing a structured management plan based on positive reinforcement (e.g., for meeting the goal of listening in the group, receiving stickers that can be traded for five minutes of free play following the group).

If the child makes the choice to stop the behavior as requested, then the child should receive the positive consequence (e.g., allowing the child to remain in the group or continue to use class materials). It is important to stress that once a child has earned a reward for a given positive behavior (e.g., stickers for listening), the reward should not be taken away as a negative consequence for another undesirable behavior. Loss of a reward previously earned may result in more severe maladaptive behavior, such as aggression or loss of motivation to earn the reward.

> EXAMPLE. When Serena began disrupting the group by making silly comments and laughing, the group leader rewarded those children who had been listening by giving verbal praise and participation tickets (Step 1). Serena continued the behavior, and the teacher responded, "Serena, when you show that you are listening, you may have your turn to role-play" (Step 2). Serena stopped the comments and laughing, and at the completion of the ongoing role-play, Serena received her turn. If she had continued, the teacher would have

calmly walked over to her, saying privately, "Serena, you need to stop the silly comments. It's distracting all of us. If you stop, you'll have the opportunity to role-play and earn your tickets for free time (Step 2). If you don't stop, you'll need to sit away from the group" (Step 3). If Serena persists, the teacher would say, "You need to choose. I'll set the timer for two minutes" (Step 4). Depending on the choice Serena makes, the teacher follows through with the positive or negative consequence (Step 5).

INDIVIDUAL INTERVENTIONS

Children who do not increase positive behaviors when provided with universal interventions (consistent structure and routines, along with supportive interventions) or with targeted procedures may require an individual behavior plan. A student for whom it is frequently necessary to use time-out, for example, will likely benefit from such a plan. Individual plans are more likely to be successful if they are based on consideration of the function of the student's problem behavior. Following is a brief summary of the processes of functional behavioral assessment and the corresponding development of a behavior intervention plan.

Functional Behavioral Assessment

Functional assessment is a method for identifying the variables that reliably predict and maintain problem behavior. The goal of the assessment is to better understand behavior and why the individual acts in this manner. Assessment includes evaluating the antecedents that prompt undesirable behavior to occur, the consequences that maintain the behavior, and the setting events or broad context in which it occurs.

It is important to distinguish between functional behavior analysis and functional behavioral assessment, or FBA, which is now widely used in schools and other application settings. Originally developed from the field of applied behavior analysis, functional behavior analysis has been used in highly controlled settings by manipulating variables to assess their impact on behavior (Gresham, Watson, & Skinner, 2001; Horner & Carr, 1997). Most frequently, it has been employed to assess the purpose of aberrant behavior, often self-abuse or severe aggression of individuals with developmental disabilities (Ingram, Lewis-Palmer, & Sugai, 2005).

The Individuals with Disabilities Education Act (IDEA, 1997, 2004) included the requirement that an FBA be conducted in schools when a change to a more restrictive placement due to disciplinary action is considered, when IEP behavioral goals are not sufficient, when a student has been suspended for more than 10 days, and when the student's behavior impedes school functioning or others' ability to learn (Cook et al., 2007). This requirement brought FBA technology into the daily lives of teachers, administrators, and support personnel as they worked to transfer the strategy to students in the schools in meaningful ways.

FBA is the process recommended most frequently to address severe maladaptive behaviors (Blood & Neel, 2007) and has been successful in early childhood and Head Start programs to reduce behavior problems and increase student engagement (Blair, Fox, & Lentini, 2010; Boyajian, DuPaul, Handler, Eckert, & McGoey, 2001; McLaren & Nelson, 2009).

The goal of completing an FBA is to design meaningful supports for individual students in need of intense interventions and support (Ingram, Lewis-Palmer, & Sugai, 2005). Outcomes of an FBA include operationally defining the problem behavior, identifying the antecedents that predict occurrence and nonoccurrence of the behavior, and identifying the consequences maintaining the behavior (McIntosh, Flannery, Sugai, Braun, & Cochrane, 2008). In other words, questions to be answered through the FBA process include the following (Horner & Carr, 1997):

1. What maintains the problem behavior?

2. What is our prediction of when the problem will occur and when it will not occur?

3. How can we prevent the problem behavior?

4. What do we do when the problem behavior does occur?

FBA is a team-based process involving obtaining information about the student from multiple sources (peers, parents, teachers) and from multiple environments and contexts (e.g., group versus independent; different school settings such as playground, various classrooms, cafeteria; Kulli, 2008). Information is gained through processes such as direct observations, rating scales, and record reviews (Gresham, Watson, & Skinner, 2001). Kern, Hilt, and Gresham (2004) found that, when assessing students with emotional-behavioral disorders and those at risk for these disorders, the most commonly applied methods for FBA in the schools were direct observation and teacher interviews. Once collected, the data are summarized in a way to make decisions regarding useful interventions (Gresham, Watson, & Skinner, 2001) and to describe the relationship among setting events, antecedents, behavior, and consequences (Ingram, Lewis-Palmer, & Sugai, 2005).

Behavior Intervention Plan

Typically, school behavior plans have been developed based on the disciplinary infraction rather than on individual student needs or the setting in which the challenging behavior occurs (Crone & Horner, 2003). Behavior intervention plans, or BIPs, include both instructional and environmental strategies. Based on the function of the student's problematic behavior (what gains accrue for the student or how the behavior serves to avoid a task, person, or situation), BIPs structure interventions to discourage the student's undesirable behavior, teach acceptable alternative or replacement behaviors, and provide the opportunity and motivation for the student to engage in positive behaviors (Cook et al., 2007). It is important to note here that the focus of both the FBA and the following BIP development is not solely to change the student's behavior through teaching skills and changing consequences but also to change the environment and what adults or peers do to prevent the occurrence of the undesirable behavior.

Replacement behaviors may be either academic or social and are those that (a) are considered appropriate; (b) serve the same function (e.g., attention, escape); (3) are incompatible with the behavior of concern (e.g., cannot be performed at the same time as the behavior of concern); and (d) are stated positively (Scott, Anderson, & Spaulding, 2008). Further, the replacement behavior should also be meaningful to the student and serve the student's real-life need.

BIPs must also include changing setting events and antecedents to reduce the occurrences of the behavior or concern. As Cook et al. (2007) state, "altering the environmental events that precede and follow the problem behavior allows educators to act in a proactive manner to deter student problem behavior" (p. 193). Reducing the problem behavior allows the student to learn an alternative replacement behavior (e.g., a prosocial skill). As Carr and his colleagues (2002) observe, "The best time to intervene on problem behavior is when the behavior is not occurring. Intervention takes place in the absence of problem behavior so that such behavior can be prevented from occurring again" (p. 9). In addition, consequences and crisis management procedures are included in the plan. Following the development of the BIP, decisions must be made regarding who must be trained, who will provide the training, and how outcomes for the student will be measured (Scott et al., 2008).

Matching interventions to the function of the problem behavior improves the effectiveness and efficiency of the selected interventions (LaRue, Weiss, & Ferraioli, 2008). Function-based behavior intervention plans have better reduced the number of problem behaviors (Ingram, Lewis-Palmer, & Sugai, 2005; Trussell, Lewis & Stichter, 2008) and increased academic engagement (Carter & Horner, 2007; Crone, Hawken, & Bergstrom, 2007).

Steps in the FBA/BIP Process

The FBA/BIP process follows these general steps:

1. Identify the behavior to be changed. To do this, list the student's problem behaviors in concrete, observable, and measurable terms. Then choose one behavior to decrease in frequency. This may be the behavior that bothers you the most or the one creating the greatest problem for the student.

2. Obtain baseline data to determine how frequently and under what conditions the undesirable behavior occurs. This process need not be complicated. For example, you may list the undesirable behavior and make a tally mark for each occurrence of the behavior on a given day, generally assessing whether the day has been "typical" for the child. Or you may find an A–B–C format useful (specifying antecedent conditions under which the behavior occurred, the specific behavior exhibited by the child, and the consequences that the child receives as a result of that behavior). The A–B–Cs can be written on a sheet of paper and quickly documented whenever the behavior of concern is observed.

3. On the basis of the preceding assessment and including other assessment data as appropriate, consider what setting events (characteristics of the environment) or antecedents (what happens right before the behavior occurs) seem to precipitate the behavior and what factors seem to maintain the problem behavior. Then hypothesize the function or purpose of the child's behavior (i.e., what that behavior achieves for the child). Instead of looking solely at the child's overt behavior (e.g., hitting, refusing, crying), ask what the child is accomplishing from this behavior. The answer to this question is a "best guess"

about the function of the child's behavior: to gain attention (e.g., from peers or adults), to escape or avoid (e.g., a task or person), or to gain access to something (e.g., a desired item or activity; Jolivette, Scott, & Nelson, 2000). Is the child's goal to seek attention or to belong? To avoid the group? To ruin the teaching opportunity? To avoid participation? Perhaps the student is displaying the particular resistive behavior to avoid a task he perceives as too complicated (e.g., one that has too many steps). Another student may be experiencing anxiety as she realizes that her turn to role-play is approaching. Still another child may not be receiving the desired amount of attention from others. Another may engage in undesirable behaviors to belong and gain friends.

4. When you have identified what is motivating the child's behavior (e.g., attention, escape, etc.), identify an alternative or replacement behavior. The replacement behavior serves the same function or purpose as the undesirable behavior. For example, if the undesirable behavior is aggression when the child wants a toy, the replacement behavior would be asking to play with the toy. Or, if a child screams to obtain attention from the teacher, the replacement behavior would be Interrupting (Skill 12). Then changes to the setting events, antecedents, and factors maintaining the problem behavior to decrease the efficiency of the problem behavior must also occur. Doing so is particularly important, as a reduction in the problem behavior will allow time for the child to learn and become proficient in performing the replacement behavior.

5. Teach the replacement behavior.

6. Determine an effective reinforcer and deliver it consistently when the replacement behavior occurs. If the reward is given immediately following the replacement behavior, it is more likely that the behavior will be repeated. Some small reinforcer (e.g., verbal encouragement, a sticker) should be given immediately following the behavior. A larger reward (e.g., a special privilege) may be given later—for example, when the child's sticker card is full.

7. Once the individual plan has been implemented, monitor behavior change. A chart or graph of the replacement behavior and the initial behavior of concern will show the degree of progress. It is important to evaluate the child's progress. If the replacement behavior is not increasing (or the problem behavior is not decreasing), the plan must be altered. It could be that the hypothesis about the problem behavior was incorrect, that the replacement behavior selected did not serve the same function for the child as the problem behavior, and so forth. Effective individual interventions are ones that work; as such, monitoring the effectiveness of the plan and making needed changes as indicated by the data are important aspects of behavior change.

Case Example

The following example illustrates use of these steps to address aggression, a significant behavioral concern that occurred in a Skillstreaming group.

While transitioning to the Skillstreaming group, Josef consistently hit and pushed peers out of his way. The group leaders were becoming frustrated, not only because Josef's actions disrupted the start of the group instruction, but also because other students whom he had hit needed consoling. In addition, while Josef was directed to sit in the quiet chair for three minutes, he missed out on the beginning of instruction. The group leaders had tried precorrection (informing the group what is expected during this transition), but this strategy had little positive impact on Josef's undesirable behavior. The group leaders thought about the function of Josef's behavior but didn't have any ready answers. So the leaders sought the advice of the school's intervention team.

A functional behavioral assessment was then conducted by the team, including Josef's parents. Through observation, checklists, and interviews with Josef, his parents, and other kindergarten teachers, it was discovered that he had similar issues when transitioning to lunch and outside play time. The antecedent to his aggression was being asked to transition, yet he did not display aggression when transitioning to gym or art class. The setting events seemed to be lining up with peers for what seems to be a preferred activity when his table wasn't called to line up first. The team hypothesized that, when Josef was to transition to a highly desired activity, he wanted to be one of the first to obtain the activity. The objective of Josef's behavior plan became to help him transition to a preferred activity without displaying aggression.

The team designed a BIP for Josef in which a replacement behavior was defined. Because the function of Josef's aggression seemed to be to obtain an activity, the team wanted to create a way for him to obtain the activity without having to use aggression. It was decided that Josef would be instructed to give an "activity ticket" to the teacher when transitioning to outside play, lunch, or Skillstreaming group. After handing the teacher the activity ticket, he could then get in line. The Skillstreaming leader even developed a new skill, "Using My Activity Ticket," and coached Josef in this skill.

Using My Activity Ticket

1. When it's time, give my ticket to the teacher.

2. Stop, turn around, and walk to the line.

3. Walk with my hands at my sides.

4. Say "Good for me! I did it!"

Because Josef's aggression was intense and occurred in more than one setting, additional interventions beyond Skillstreaming were indicated. In this case, Josef was instructed in relaxation techniques and was coached to use these strategies five minutes before a transition to one of his preferred activities. The teacher changed the antecedent to his aggression by setting the timer to provide increased warning when the transition was to occur. It was during this time Josef used his relaxation strategies. She also put tape on the floor midway to the classroom door so Josef would know this was his space to wait in line, no matter when he used his activity ticket. Consequences for not using his plan and hitting and shoving resulted in a time-out and transitioning to the activity after the other students had left.

Josef's plan and data related to aggressive incidents were periodically reviewed by the school's intervention team. Over time, data suggested Josef was learning to line up without physical aggression. While monitoring the data to be sure his aggression continued to decrease, the teacher removed the tape from the floor, allowing Josef to line up after the next child. Then a verbal reminder that a transition would soon occur replaced the timer. Instruction in Waiting Your Turn (Skill 16) was also provided to the Skillstreaming group, with additional coaching for Josef. He continued to use his activity tickets until, through a discussion with the teacher, he expressed his desire to try lining up with his table group.

CHAPTER 7

Building Positive Relationships with Parents

With very few exceptions, parents genuinely care about their children's academic and social progress as they enter the world of preschool and beyond. Often, cultural and socioeconomic differences impair the development of a common understanding between parents and teachers. Such misunderstandings are unfortunate and have the potential to put the social and emotional welfare of young children at risk. Although many teachers indicate that parent involvement is difficult to achieve, Skillstreaming is a productive and often nonemotional way to begin parent and school collaboration.

Traditionally, parent contact has taken the form of PTA/PTO meetings, parent-teacher conferences, or, as far too often has been the case with a child prone to behave aggressively or disruptively, the "bad news call." Teachers able to create positive relationships with parents often view and deal with parents quite differently. They demonstrate understanding of cultural and economic differences. They recognize and appreciate parents as the child's first (and continuing) teachers. They seek contact early and frequently, seeing this as an opportunity to collaborate in supportive, mutually reinforcing ways. Displaying such attitudes helps create the opportunity for the parent, teacher, and student to become a problem-solving team.

The role of parents and the family has gradually changed from being on the periphery to being a central focus in the child's education. It is more widely understood that establishing close working relationships with parents, especially in the early grades (i.e., kindergarten through third grade), can have a positive effect on the child's school adjustment (Adams, Womack, Shatzer, & Caldarella, 2010; Bruder, 2010; Strain & Timm, 2001; Walker, Colvin, & Ramsey, 1995). For young children with disabilities, as required by IDEA, goals for family outcomes include that families know their rights, effectively communicate their children's needs; and help their children develop and learn (Bruder, 2010). Thus, parents are not only expected to be involved with their child's education, but are expected to participate in their child's learning. Opportunities for the child to be successful in school, home, and peer group increase with a cooperative working relationship between parents and the school.

Although there is an increased emphasis on expanding the role of the family in the young child's school experience (e.g., involving parents to a greater degree in decision making, parent training), teachers and other professionals may not be sufficiently prepared for such collaboration (Friesen & Stephens, 1998). Fialka and Mikus (1999) have presented a model for the development of positive and productive relationships that may be helpful to the teacher or other Skillstreaming leader. This model calls for a partnership between home and school that can be developed through specific phases of parent-teacher interaction.

The first phase of relationship development, which Fialka and Mikus call *colliding and campaigning,* involves fostering understanding and beginning to build trust between parent and teacher. During this initial phase of relationship building, each party typically has difficulty listening to the other. Instead, it is often the goal to state their own perspectives about the child, the problem, or the intervention, with the hope of persuading the other to see the issue from their vantage point and to accept their solution. During initial parent contacts, then, it is important for each party to have the goal of listening for understanding, ask for more information, and be willing to explore different possibilities in resolving concerns. With successful work at the first phase, parents and teachers move to the middle phase, *coordinating, cooperating, and compromising,* in which their interactions are based on more effective listening and cooperation. Being able to suspend their personal agendas to explore a common ground and asking each other to explain ideas will give rise to respect for the other and increased capacity for problem solving. *Collaborating and creative partnering,* the third phase of relationship building, continues to be based on listening and inquiring. During this phase, there is more open sharing of each party's needs, hopes, and fears. Differences of opinion are more easily understood and accepted, and decision making becomes more balanced between the parties. Although these phases are described as discrete, relationships will often move back and forth among the phases as parents and teachers engage in problem solving.

Emotional and behavioral problems affect the child in all life situations—home, neighborhood, school, church, and so forth. In addition, families experience significant stress when their child has emotional and behavioral problems. Collaboration between teacher and parent best addresses the child's behavioral and social needs. Communication with the student's family should, therefore, be one of the most important components of any school program (Quinn et al., 2000).

PARENTING AND CHILDREN'S AGGRESSION

Overall, parents do the best they can with what they know. However, parenting styles and practices significantly affect the young child's later school and social adjustment. Considerable research evidence suggests that children exhibiting aggression during the preschool years, for example, often have been exposed to harsh, punitive, rigid, and authoritarian discipline and parents who model aggression (Jewett, 1992). Conversely, parenting practices related to prosocial behavior include appropriate and fair discipline, sufficient supervision, involvement in the child's life (e.g., school and peer contacts), an attitude of support, and the ability to resolve conflicts and handle crises in the family (Walker et al., 1995). Reid, Webster-Stratton, and Hammond (2007) have summarized effective parent training strategies, which include reducing harsh and inconsistent parenting, increasing positive and responsive parenting, promoting parent skills in cognitive stimulation, and increasing home-school bonding.

A seven-year follow-up study of parents of kindergarten children found that four types of parenting behavior promoted young children's later adjustment in school (Pettit, Bates, & Dodge, 2000). These positive parenting behaviors included warmth, supportive discipline (e.g., calm discussions), interest and involvement in the child's life (e.g., peer contacts), and the proactive teaching of social skills. In addition to promoting positive adaptation across the elementary school years, these parenting skills may also serve as a protective factor, buffering the risks associated with family stressors (e.g., financial stress, divorce).

PARENT INVOLVEMENT IN SKILLSTREAMING

Parents can and should be involved in Skillstreaming for a variety of important reasons. First, parenting practices may be at cross purposes with what is taught in the school (Cartledge & Milburn, 1995). A specific skill taught in the Skillstreaming group may not be supported at home, and its use may actually be discouraged. For example, a young child's attempt to use the skill Knowing When to Tell (Skill 35) may be met with the parent's response to "stop tattling." Such contradictions from important people in the child's life will be confusing and may discourage further use of the skill. When parents understand the goals of Skillstreaming, as well as the specific behaviors included, they are far more likely to be receptive to the child's skill initiations. Furthermore, because Skillstreaming provides a specific way of teaching children "what to do," the opportunity exists to alter how parents deal with the child's problems in the home and with peers and siblings. For example, when parents learn to reinforce and prompt prosocial skill use—and to change the consequences that maintain a child's aggression (Patterson, 1982)—more positive and supportive parenting will likely result. In this way, parent involvement and cooperation in Skillstreaming have the potential to improve parenting skills. In addition, parents' ratings of their child's self-control and social skills have been shown to improve when parents are trained as coaches and involved in the social skills training (Slim, Whiteside, Dittner, & Mellon, 2006).

Second, many social and behavioral problems originate in the home setting (Walker et al., 1995). Therefore, the more settings in which prosocial skill use is prompted and rewarded, the greater the likelihood that the skills taught will be maintained and will generalize. As discussed in chapter 5, on generalization, children may easily learn the Skillstreaming skills, but they are unlikely to continue to use skills over time or in a variety of situations and environments unless specific procedures are implemented to facilitate their use. Reinforcement and prompting of skill use in the home setting is a way to enhance continued use of skills.

A third rationale for including parents in Skillstreaming concerns the profound effect of modeling on the young child's behavior. When parents and siblings model behaviors for dealing with stress and anger, for example, the young child follows these models.

LEVELS OF PARENT INVOLVEMENT

In a survey of teachers, Brannon (2008) found the most successful ways of involving parents include: (a) involving the family in homework through discussion or activity; (b) informing parents what is occurring in class via newsletters or website; (c) informing parents of the class and school expectations so they understand and may be supportive; (d) asking parents to volunteer so they are exposed to behavioral expectations, and (e) holding events (such as breakfast or evening programs) to ease parents into the partnership and share what their children are learning.

In collaborating with parents on behalf of the young child, several goals are apparent. Cartledge and Milburn (1995) emphasize the value in conveying to parents the importance of social skills learning to the child's development, an awareness of the social skills needed to be successful outside the home, and actions parents may take to assist the child in skill learning. The level of involvement will vary according to the receptivity of both parents and professionals. The following levels should be prescriptively matched to the needs of the child targeted for skills training.

Orientation Level

The first level of parent involvement can best be described as an orientation to Skillstreaming skills and procedures. The purpose of this level is to promote parent awareness and understanding. An orientation meeting to describe Skillstreaming objectives and ways parents might help their child use the prosocial skills at home is very helpful. In such a meeting, leaders may present examples of skills, discuss the goals of Skillstreaming, and explain the learning process (modeling, role-playing, performance feedback, and generalization in the form of homework). Showing

The Skillstreaming Video (Goldstein & McGinnis, 1988) or conducting a mock group are specific activities that will increase parent understanding. Allowing time for questions and input about skills for instruction will also increase parents' understanding and involvement.

An alternative to an orientation meeting is to send a letter home explaining the goals of Skillstreaming instruction and the activities in which the child will be participating (i.e., watching leaders act out a skill, trying out the skill steps in the group, giving and receiving feedback about skill performance, and completing skill homework assignments). The Parent Orientation Note is helpful in this regard (see Figure 14). Orienting parents to the types of skills and procedures used is necessary because many of the skill-use situations occur in the family environment. If parents are uninformed about Skillstreaming goals, they may justifiably question the purpose of discussing home-related situations at school.

Other ways to promote parent involvement at the orientation level include the following:

1. Have parents assess their child's skill strengths and weaknesses by completing all or part of the Parent Checklist (in Appendix A) and talk with them about skills they value in the home. Conversations with parents about needed skills will help identify cultural aspects of the skills and permit better choices of where, when, and with whom individual skills will be most beneficial.

2. Frequently inform parents of the child's progress in the various skill areas, focusing on positive reports. (Parent Homework Notes, described in the following discussion, are a primary vehicle for communication.)

3. Videorecord the child in a role-play situation and share this videotape with the parents during a conference to encourage further understanding of Skillstreaming's goals and procedures.

4. Invite parents to participate in a mock Skillstreaming group in which parents learn a skill through modeling, role-playing, feedback, and generalization.

5. Encourage parents to support skill learning by giving the child positive feedback for practicing skills he or she has successfully role-played in the school or other learning environment.

Support Level

Following successful parent involvement at the orientation level, the teacher or other group leader should seek to involve parents at the support level. The goal at this level is to gain more active parental support. Parent activities at this level are as follows:

1. Support the child's demonstration of the social skill by helping the child complete assigned homework in the home environment. Feedback to the teacher will be given via Homework Report forms or Parent Homework Notes (see samples in Figures 15 and 16).

2. Notice and reward the child's specific skill use in the home and neighborhood environment and provide ongoing encouragement. Teachers may provide the child with Parent Awards to take home, then return to school (see Figure 12, chapter 5).

3. Observe a Skillstreaming group in progress and participate as coactors in the group.

4. Help assess the child's skill progress by judging skill performance at home and in neighborhood settings. The Early Childhood Rubric, included in Appendix A, may be used for this purpose.

Cooperative Level

At the cooperative level, parents are involved in selecting skills needed in the home and neighborhood setting and regularly give feedback to the teacher or other group leader about the

Figure 14: Sample Parent Orientation Note

Date 12/20

Dear Parent or Guardian:

Your child and his or her classmates are learning to handle a variety of day-to-day concerns in positive ways. Sharing, taking turns, handling teasing and anger, and following directions are some of the concerns we are working on. We are all learning specific steps to social skills in order to handle these problems in acceptable ways.

The process we are using to learn these skills is called Skillstreaming. First, your child is watching someone else use the skill. Then he or she will try out the skill and receive feedback about how well he or she performed the skill from both peers and adults. Finally, your child will be asked to practice the skill in real-life situations.

Each week we will be sending home a note describing the skill and its steps. We hope that you review this note with your child and help your child practice the skill at home. Please feel free to call me or e-mail me if you have any questions.

Sincerely,

Teacher/Leader

Phone 555-1234

E-mail teacherleader@anyschool.com

Figure 15: Sample Parent Homework Note I

Student _____Natalie_____ Date ___1/10_____

Dear Parent or Guardian:

This week we are working on the following skill:

_____Dealing with Mistakes (#33)_____

This is a very important skill for your child to learn. The steps of the skill are:

_____1.___Say, "It's OK to make mistakes. Everybody makes mistakes."_____

_____2.___Plan for next time._____

_____

_____

_____

_____

Your child has completed a homework assignment on this skill. Please review this assignment with your child.

Please feel free to call or e-mail me if you have any questions.

Sincerely,

_____Teacher/Leader_____

Phone ___555-1234_____

E-mail ___teacherleader@anyschool.com_____

Figure 16: Sample Parent Homework Note 2

Student   _Thomas_   Date   _1/15_

Dear Parent or Guardian:

This week we are working on the following skill:

Accepting No (#39)

This is a very important skill for your child to learn. The steps of the skill are:

    1.   _Stop and think._

    2.   _Choose._

          a. _Do something else._

          b. _Ask to talk._

    3.   _Do it._

Your child has learned this skill well but will need continued practice. Please watch for the skill at home! If you see a situation when the skill could be used, please encourage your child to use this skill. Enclosed is a Parent Award to complete and return to school when you see your child use this skill.

Please feel free to call or e-mail me if you have any questions.

Sincerely,

Teacher/Leader

Phone   _555-1234_

E-mail   _teacherleader@anyschool.com_

child's use of skills. Parent Homework Note 3 (Figure 17) is useful for structuring more direct parent involvement. Parents will also be involved in prompting the child's use of the skills at home and will provide encouragement and reinforcement for the child's performance (see the Skillstreaming Request to Parents, Figure 18). At the cooperative level, teachers and parents work together as a team to teach and support the child's skill development.

Family Skillstreaming Level

Program evaluations have suggested that children's prosocial responses are more likely to be rewarded, supported, and even reciprocated if significant others also participate in Skillstreaming training programs. Some of these joint efforts have involved teaching empathy skills to adolescents and their parents (Guzzetta, 1974), teaching delinquent youths and their families alternatives to aggression (Goldstein et al., 1989), and training adolescents and their peer groups in a variety of social skills (Gibbs, Potter, & Goldstein, 1995; Goldstein, Glick, Carthan, & Blancero, 1994). The success of these programs strongly suggests the effectiveness of instruction for both skill-deficient youth and the significant people in their lives.

For students and their families, schools are increasingly community resources, offering a range of health-related and social service programming. Expansion of the purposes of schools is likely to continue, and family Skillstreaming, in which children participate in Skillstreaming along with their siblings and parents, holds promise as a regular offering in this context, as well as in mental health, juvenile justice, and other settings.

Figure 17: Sample Parent Homework Note 3

Student _____Joleen_____ Date ___1/23_____

Dear Parent or Guardian:

This week we are working on the following skill:

_____Dealing with Feeling Mad (#28)_____

This is a very important skill for your child to learn. The steps of the skill are:

1. _Stop and think._____
2. _Choose._____
    a. _Turtle._____
    b. _Relax._____
    c. _Ask to talk._____
3. _Do it._____

Your child has been asked to complete this skill at home. Please help your child to follow these skill steps.

Please sign and return this form to ___Teacher/Leader____ with your comments (on the back) about quality of homework done and any questions/suggestions by ____1/27____.

Parent signature _____[signature]_____ Date ____1/27_____

Figure 18: Sample Request to Parents

Student _____Cory_____ Date ___1/23_____

Dear Parent or Guardian:

Your child is working on the following skill(s):

_____Waiting Your Turn (#16)_____

_____Sharing (#17)_____

_____Offering Help (#18)_____

_____

The steps to these skills are attached to this note. Please help your child practice at home by doing the following:

- ▶ Remind your child to use the skill when you see a time the skill could be helpful.
- ▶ Respond positively to your child's skill use (allow the skill use to be successful).
- ▶ Reward your child's use of the skill. (You may use a Parent Award and have your child return this to school.)
- ▶ Ask your child to teach you (or a brother or sister) the skill.
- ▶ Other ___Role-playing Skill 17 (Sharing) before his cousin's visit._____

Please write any comments on the back of this form about how your child is learning and practicing this skill at home.

Sincerely,

_____Teacher/Leader_____

CHAPTER 8

Skillstreaming in the School Context

Teachers and school administrators continue to report their greatest challenge is to reduce classroom and school disruption, often occurring in the form of student aggression and violence. In a 2004 Gallup poll (Rose & Gallup, 2004), educators cited discipline as the most serious issue in today's schools, second only to the lack of financial support. It is further estimated that between two and seven percent of students have significant emotional or behavioral problems, which often include anger and aggression (Kauffman, 2005). This chapter reviews issues surrounding school violence and aggression and suggests how Skillstreaming can play a role in reducing them.

VIOLENCE PREVENTION

Although it may be true that students today come to school with many more significant concerns than in the past, certain factors related to the school itself have been found to contribute to violence. Experts generally advocate a multifaceted or combined program of school safety, including the development of school policies addressing weapons and crisis response, environmental factors such as school facilities and family and community resources, and prevention through education. Educational strategies, school climate, and disciplinary policy and methods play a central role.

Educational Strategies

Educational approaches to preventing violence and aggression include conflict management, social skills instruction, mentoring programs, behavioral programs, intensive academic instruction, drug prevention, student advocacy programs, peer helper programs, student assistance (counseling) programs, prejudice reduction/cultural sensitivity curricula, and community service. An important goal of such schoolwide approaches is "to give everyone involved in the school the same skills, language and terminology for handling stress and conflict—to create an environment that is consistently nonviolent and nurturing" (Ascher, 1994, p. 4).

To be effective in reducing discipline problems, improving school climate, and increasing students' self-esteem and ability to assume responsibility (Walker, Colvin, & Ramsey, 1995), such programs need to be instituted at an early age and should include many individuals in the child's environment (teachers, peers, and other school staff, such as custodians and paraprofessionals). Furthermore, teachers and other school personnel will need professional staff development in the areas of conflict resolution, how to respond to violence, and team building.

School Climate

The culture or climate of a school is reflected in the prevailing values and beliefs held by school staff, parents, and students. These values and beliefs define acceptable behavior and determine the manner in which the school should function. As Modro (1995) has stated:

> The most important factor that needs to be addressed even before policies that will support school safety is the atmosphere, or "feeling tone," in which education takes place. Does our educational system reflect a genuine belief in the essential dignity of each child? Do educators believe in the inherent value of the people they serve? The fear is that many mirror for our children what some of them already see reflected in society. (p. 11)

Johnson (2009) reviewed 25 studies published in 2007–2008 that addressed the relationship between the school environment and school violence and considered both the social and physical environments. Lower rates of school violence were associated with positive relationships with teachers, students' clear understanding of the rules and their perceptions that the rules were fair, students' feelings of ownership in their school, positive classrooms and other school environments that focused on student understanding, and safety interventions that increased the perception of physical order.

A positive school climate not only provides an environment for students to learn prosocial skills but also enhances academic achievement and teacher retention (Cohen, Pickeral, & McCloskey, 2009; MacNeil, Prater, & Busch, 2009). To learn, students must believe their school is a safe environment, free from harassment and aggression (Goldstein, Young, & Boyd, 2008). Indeed, half of all students who take a weapon to school say they do so for their own protection (Sprague & Walker, 2000).

Learning environments need to create opportunities for children to participate in rule setting and to accept responsibility, and children must be taught the skills necessary for prosocial participation in these activities. Creating a better balance of positive to negative consequences is also necessary to foster a positive school climate. Some children, in particular those who have well-established patterns of undesirable behavior, are more likely to receive an overabundance of negative consequences. For these individuals, positive feelings about school and learning itself are unlikely. Such children need more instruction, not less.

Disciplinary Policy and Methods

Exclusionary practices remain the primary way the schools deal with student disruption, aggression, and violence. This fact also applies to students at the preschool level, with those in this age group being three times as likely to be expelled than students in grades K through 12 (Gilliam, 2005). The problem is that such practices fail to work in the long run. Suspension and other forms of traditional punishment do not prevent or deter future misconduct for students with chronic or intense behavior problems (Goldstein, Glick, & Gibbs, 1998). Neither do such policies make schools safer; in fact, the opposite appears to be true (Brownstein, 2010). For example, Nickerson and Martens (2008) explored different approaches to school violence prevention through a survey of over 2,000 school principals. These authors found that a focus on security/enforcement and suspending students actually related to a higher incidence of disruption and crime.

In addition, suspension and other exclusionary practices often exacerbate the very behaviors they are designed to extinguish (Mendler & Curwin, 1999). Because we know that time spent in learning is the best predictor of increased academic achievement (Skiba & Sprague, 2008), suspensions often contribute to a student's academic failure. Such long-term negative outcomes include poor academic achievement, grade retention, negative feelings about school, truancy, and dropping out (Bock, Tapscott, & Savner, 1998; Dupper & Bosch, 1996; Hickman, Batholomew, Mathwig, & Heinrichs, 2008). For example, Hickman et al. (2008) examined the histories of school dropouts and graduates. Students who dropped out showed higher rates of behavior problems in early grades, a history of absenteeism as early as first grade, more often repeated a grade, and showed lower grades and test scores than did graduates. Students themselves have reported that suspensions were "not at all" helpful (Costenbader & Markson, 1998). In addition, issues of equity exist: Minority students are more likely to be suspended more than nonminority students and are disciplined more severely for minor disciplinary infractions (Advancement Project/Civil Rights Project, 2000; Applied Research Center, 1999; Brownstein, 2010; Cartledge, 2003; Costenbader & Markson, 1998; Skiba, Peterson, & Williams, 1997).

Furthermore, the positive relationship between school attendance and academic success has been well documented, encouraging the examination of the relationship of school suspension to academic achievement (Andrews, Taylor, Martin, & Slate, 1998; Zins, Bloodworth, Weissberg, & Walberg, 2004). The more students are excluded from school, the more likely they are to fall behind academically. And because it is more acceptable to act bad than it is to act stupid (Brendtro et al., 2002), students are more likely to act disruptively and aggressively to avoid work that is not understood. It makes sense that students who are not in school will fail to learn what they need to learn.

Mayer (2001) summarizes what schools can do to create an environment that will facilitate the reduction of behavior problems:

1. Reduce punitive methods of control

2. Provide clear rules (expectations) for student conduct

3. Assure support to educators

4. Minimize academic failure experiences

5. Teach critical social skills

6. Use function-based behavior management

7. Respect, value, and understand ethnic and cultural differences

8. Support student involvement and participation

Johns, Carr, and Hoots (1995, p. 2-2) recommend that school discipline be evaluated by asking the following questions:

1. Does the disciplinary process allow students to accept responsibility for their actions?

2. Does the disciplinary process continually place importance on the value of academic participation and achievement?

3. Does the disciplinary action build positive self-image?

4. Does the disciplinary action teach students alternative methods of dealing with problems?

In other words, disciplinary programs in schools today and in the future need to be instructional in nature. Instructional alternatives may include assigning the student to a social skills class (dealing with specific alternatives to the conflict that resulted in suspension and where more desirable behaviors may be learned), requiring the student to complete community service (where he or she will be more likely to be exposed to appropriate models and receive the attention needed to foster a more positive self-image), and having the student complete an in-school intervention focusing on conflict resolution.

Bullying

One form of aggression that deserves closer scrutiny is bullying. Bullying is common in preschool and elementary school classrooms (Beane, 1999; Manning, Heron, & Marshall, 1978; Smith & Levan, 1995). Bullying often begins in preschool and presents significant behavioral issues not only for the young child who is the target but for the bully and observers as well.

It is important to distinguish between bullying and other types of aggression that may occur in the preschool and kindergarten setting. The most common form of bullying is teasing;

however, occasional teasing does not constitute bullying. Neither is bullying considered rough play or accidentally hurtful events. Instead, in bullying, there is a physical or psychological imbalance of power (Newman, Horne, & Bartolomucci, 2000). The most accepted definition of bullying is presented by Olweus (1991), who states, "A person is being bullied or victimized when he or she is exposed, repeatedly and over time, to negative actions on the part of one or more persons" (p. 413).

This type of aggression can be either direct or indirect (Olweus, 1993). Direct, or overt, bullying typically is observable verbal or physical aggression. Direct bullying includes hitting, pushing, kicking, and tripping, as well as the verbal behaviors of yelling, threatening, and cursing (Ahmad & Smith, 1994). Indirect bullying includes behaviors such as spreading rumors, backbiting or scapegoating, and convincing others to ignore or isolate the victim. Both types can be very harmful.

Bullying also may be a precursor to more severe and dangerous violence (Greenbaum, Turner, & Stephens, 1989; Hoover & Oliver, 1996; Olweus, 1991). Kauffman, Mostert, Trent, and Hallahan (1998) note that "engaging in aggressive antisocial acts is not good for children; it does not help them develop appropriate behavior, but increases the likelihood of further aggression, maladjustment, and academic and social failure" (p. 14). When ignored, bullying often escalates in intensity and continues in frequency (Goldstein, 1999a).

Young children often engage in bullying or other aggressive acts to exert their power over others or to control a situation—for example, to get what they want, whether it is a toy, candy, a peer's lunch, or attention from peers. Bullying often is unreported because it typically occurs in places without sufficient adult supervision (e.g., playground, lunchroom, hallways, neighborhood park, to and from school). Many children do not report bullying for fear that they will receive even more aggression from the bully. Based on what

adults often teach children, children are likely to question whether anything will be done about the provocation. After all, haven't adults reinforced the belief that children shouldn't tattle? Sometimes the target is even reprimanded by the adult, further rewarding the bully for the aggression.

The goal of Skillstreaming is to teach prosocial alternatives. By experiencing direct teaching of behavioral skill steps, children who are targets or observers of bullying can learn assertiveness skills to deal effectively with being teased and with other peer provocation (Using Brave Talk, Skill 3; Dealing with Teasing, Skill 27), to tell an adult about a problem (Knowing When to Tell, Skill 35), to problem solve (Solving a Problem, Skill 30), and to say no (Saying No, Skill 38). Other skills from the Skillstreaming curriculum also may be effectively used in bullying contexts.

The bully also deserves our attention and instructional efforts. The bully, although often maintaining a level of social status with peers (Hoover & Oliver, 1996), often feels isolated from others. It is important to expand this child's repertoire of choices by teaching friendship-making skills (Group III), as well as ways to deal with anger (Dealing with Feeling Mad, Skill 28) and skills for dealing with feelings (Group IV). In addition, because the bully seeks power or control, he or she can be given influence in a prosocial, positive way by helping to teach the skills to peers or younger children or in other ways assuming a leadership role in Skillstreaming.

SCHOOLWIDE APPLICATIONS OF SKILLSTREAMING

Although preschool and elementary students are now taught prosocial skills primarily in individual classrooms, Skillstreaming is increasingly a part of the school curriculum on a schoolwide basis. One example of schoolwide use is Edmunds Elementary School in Des Moines, Iowa, where instruction occurs in all preschool through fifth-grade classrooms on a regular basis. Therefore, all teachers and students are aware of the skills and behaviors expected. In addition, because all teachers provide the Skillstreaming instruction, they prompt prosocial skill use throughout the school day.

Polaris K–12 School in Anchorage, Alaska, also uses Skillstreaming in the form of whole-class and group instruction for all students in kindergarten through third grade, as well as providing targeted instruction for students who need to learn positive social behaviors in particular skill areas. This program provides for the prevention of behavior problems by clearly defining behavioral expectations, teaching the skills in a relevant way, and structuring reinforcement of these behaviors by other adults in the school.

The potential for student participation, including generalization and maintenance of learned skills, is greatly enhanced the more the environment is involved in the program. Including entire schools in the skills training process has the potential to increase both student motivation and skill awareness. Large-scale program involvement means that many more teachers and other school staff are involved as instructors, thus providing greater opportunity for students to be rewarded for correct skill use and to receive prompting or coaching following incorrect use. In addition, when entire schools are involved, especially at the lower grade levels, added potential exists for Skillstreaming to operate at a preventive level—before youth get into difficulty in school, at home, or with the law. At the preschool level, implementing such prevention strategies holds special promise to alter the patterns of future aggression.

INTEGRATION IN THE CURRICULUM

As we move into the 21st century, schools are paying more attention to students' emotional health and are more likely to integrate Skillstreaming within the general education curricula. Marx (2006), for example, recommends that schools "expand programs in thinking and reasoning skills as well as civic and character education" (p. 45). As the Partnership for 21st Century Skills (2008) states, "All Americans must be skilled at

interacting competently and respectfully with others" (p. 10). In *Connecting Teachers, Students, and Standards: Strategies for Success in Diverse and Inclusive Classrooms* and citing the work of Mercer and Pullen (2005), Voltz, Sims, and Nelson (2010) call for including social skills strategy instruction into the curriculum. They state:

> [Social skill strategy instruction] . . . is designed to teach students how to interact appropriately with others across a variety of situations and settings. Skills such as resisting pressure, accepting criticism, negotiating, following directions, and asking for help are included. (p. 78)

In addition, it is continuing to become more well-accepted that social skills are essential in achieving needed academic outcomes (Schoenfeld, Rutherford, Gable, & Rock, 2008). Indeed, the relationship between problem behavior and low academic skills has been widely investigated (Lassen, Steele, & Sailor, 2006; McIntosh & Mackay, 2008; Rock, Fessler, & Church, 1997; Trzesniewski, Moffit, Caspi, Taylor, & Maughan, 2006). Further, Marzano and Haystead (2008) provide examples for including standards in life skills, such as the following:

► Expectations for participation (asking questions, staying focused, raising hand, waiting for appropriate time to ask a question)

► Work completion (following directions, bringing necessary materials to class)

► Behavior (following routines, helping others, treating others with respect, such as keeping hands to oneself)

Schoenfeld et al. (2008) describe a way to include social skills instruction into daily academic instruction. Their ENGAGE blueprint includes the following steps:

1. Examine the demands of curriculum and instruction.

2. Note essential social skills (e.g., raising hands, sharing materials). Consider skills for

the entire class, small groups, and individual students.

3. Go forward and teach. Implement the teaching plan.

4. Actively monitor (e.g., scan, move about the room, prompt students in skill use, provide positive reinforcement).

5. Gauge progress. Monitor the use of the skills.

6. Exchange reflections. Debrief with students on social skill use and expectations.

It is clear from this brief review that social skills instruction lends itself to being imbedded within the academic curricula as a central goal for all students and that it can be considered as a prevention as well as intervention strategy.

INCLUSION

Another current initiative in schools today provides for increasing inclusion of youth with special needs in regular education classrooms. The Individuals with Disabilities Education Act (IDEA, 2004) calls for educating students with disabilities within the least restrictive environment. In other words, as much as possible, students with disabilities should be educated with nondisabled peers within the general education setting. It has been accepted in recent years that if academic or social benefit can be attained in the regular classroom setting, then a student with disabilities should receive his or her instruction there. Yet many experts in the field of special education believe social benefits are unlikely to occur unless planned and systematic instruction in social skills also takes place. Outcomes for preschool students with disabilities required by IDEA include that they have positive social-emotional skills, demonstrate acquisition of use of knowledge and skills, and use appropriate behavior to meet their needs (Bruder, 2010). Students without disabilities may also need instruction in accepting students with differences. Skillstreaming is often used to teach the proso-

cial behaviors that will enhance successful inclusion. For example, in Placer County, California schools, students with emotional and behavioral disorders receive direct Skillstreaming instruction. In addition, all staff members are involved in the instruction and prompt skill use throughout the school day. In Fayette County Schools, Georgia, Skillstreaming instruction includes students with a variety of disabilities participating in modeling and role-plays with nondisabled peers. Skillstreaming is also used with students with Asperger's syndrome. This project, Connections Research and Treatment Program, provides services for six hours per day, five days per week, for a period of six weeks. Students receive Skillstreaming for four 20-minute cycles each day. An additional 50 minutes in each cycle is devoted to activities in which children practice the social skills they learned and emotion recognition and expand on their interests.

In the effort to increase prospective teachers' awareness and understanding of students with disabilities, the preservice teaching program at St. Mary's College in Notre Dame, Indiana, implements a field experience called Campus Friends (Turner, 2003). Once per week, students with disabilities come to the campus to interact with college students. Using Skillstreaming, students are taught a variety of prosocial skills. Students also visit areas of the campus community and are prompted to use the prosocial skills they have been taught. In brief, the trend toward inclusion makes it even more important to teach all students (both with and without disabilities) the social skills they need.

MULTI-TIERED SYSTEMS OF SUPPORT

Many schools and districts are developing systems to address both academic and behavioral interventions to meet the learning needs of all students. Tiered systems of support have been evidenced to address student academic concerns through Response to Intervention (RTI) and behavioral concerns through Positive Behavioral Interventions and Supports (PBIS).

Recently, social and behavioral concerns have begun to be addressed through RTI in addition to academics. These tiered supports are often composed of three or four levels and offer schools a systematic way to look at the intensity of intervention needed. School teams then develop interventions to address the needs of all and implement academic, behavioral, and social interventions along this continuum. Recognizing that academic needs impact behavior and vice versa, schools and districts are now designing multi-tiered systems of support (MTSS) considering both academic and social-behavioral interventions in such tiered models.

For example, Farmer, Farmer, Estell and Hutchins (2007) offer a three-level system to address both academic and behavioral need. Such systems often include (a) universal strategies to meet the needs of all students, (b) selective or targeted interventions for students who continue to struggle even after high-quality universal instruction is provided, and (c) individual or intense interventions for students not responding to the first two levels. The goal of such systems is to match the intensity of student need with the intensity of interventions.

Positive Behavior Intervention and Supports

PBIS is rapidly gaining acceptance across the country largely because of its strong research base and procedures for training schools in implementation. Funded by a federal grant, The Center on Positive Behavioral Interventions and Supports (www.pbis.org) provides ongoing training assistance to state departments of education and school districts and is a clearinghouse for updated information and new evidence.

The universal (primary) level of prevention includes the development and instruction of school and classroom routines and behavioral expectations through schoolwide social skills training. Skillstreaming is used at this level to instruct all students in skills such as Asking for Help (Skill 6), Listening (Skill 1), and Follow-ing Directions (Skill 10). How these skills look in each area of the school (e.g., cafeteria, hallway, commons, classroom) is demonstrated, and all students in the school have the opportunity to see the skills modeled and to follow through with group role-plays and feedback. New skills are also created depending upon the expectations of each school. For example, skills may be developed to teach school routines, such as Passing from Class to Class, Bringing Needed Materials to Class, or Appropriate Talk in the Lunchroom. A new social skill is developed for whatever problem behaviors are experienced by most students. The goal here is to reduce predictable problems so that more time and effort can be directed toward students needing more interventions at the other levels.

Targeted (secondary) prevention provides a system of behavioral supports for those students, fewer in number, who continue to have behavioral difficulties that may result in a school suspension. While still participating in universal interventions, these students experience additional targeted instruction in Skillstreaming in small groups. At this level, the selection of skills becomes more prescriptive—that is, the specific skills selected for group instruction are those related to the students' problematic behavior. Skills for targeted instruction often include Concentrating on a Task (Skill 50), Using Self-Control (Skill 26), Making a Complaint (Skill 32), and Keeping Out of Fights (Skill 30). Other types of targeted interventions may include a staff member's checking in with a group of students to better prepare them for the school day or providing group mentoring activities.

For the few students who remain unresponsive to targeted interventions, individual interventions are designed. Students at this level may experience multiple problems and will therefore need multiple interventions. For example, wrap-around supports or a behavior intervention plan (BIP) may be necessary to assist students needing this level of support. At this level,

Skillstreaming is a part of the student's overall support program, often implemented to teach the student replacement behaviors (acceptable behaviors that serve the same function and are incompatible with problem behavior), as determined through the functional behavioral assessment (FBA) process. This process is described in more depth in chapter 6, on managing behavioral problems.

Response to Intervention

In part because of dissatisfaction with the discrepancy model for identifying students with learning disabilities, the RTI process is advocated as an alternative method for identifying students who have a learning disability. Used primarily to address academic deficits, it is becoming more common to include behavioral and social deficits within this framework (Sugai, Guardino, & Lathrop, 2007). Most RTI models include these components (Bender, 2009):

▶ Universal screening to identify students who are not making adequate progress

▶ Increasingly intensive interventions presented in levels or tiers

▶ Use of evidence-based strategies at all tiers

▶ Progress monitoring of student progress

▶ Making data-based decisions when considering moving a student to another tier

What does RTI look like related to social behaviors, and how is Skillstreaming used within this framework? Universal screening for behavior problems and social skills deficits is conducted. This process is often quite easy; most teachers can readily identify at least the students who are acting out. Reviewing the data from office discipline and counseling referrals is another method of such screening. Once students have been identified, Tier I (or universal social skills instruction) is provided to all students in a manner similar to the PBIS process. The teacher provides whole-class instruction in the skills needed by most students. While con-

tinuing to monitor behavioral data, the teacher checks in with a small group of students 10 minutes before school begins and again at the end of the school day (Tier II). This brief check-in time allows the teacher to review the students' behavioral self-monitoring systems and provide encouragement and reinforcement for use of the Tier I skills. Students not making adequate behavioral progress (e.g., continued office referrals) are also assigned to a skills group (Tier II). This group is co-instructed by the teacher and a school counselor or other support staff member, and in this group, skills for which those in the group have had been sent to the office are addressed. Based on progress monitoring data, students still not making adequate behavioral progress receive more intense Skillstreaming instruction in a Tier III after-school alternative to suspension skills group, along with other strategies, as determined on an individual student basis (e.g., counseling support, wrap-around supports). A student needing Tier III intervention continues to benefit from interventions at Tiers I and II. As this example shows, Skillstreaming can be a valuable part of a student's program at all three tiers.

NEW INTERVENTION COMBINATIONS

Although Skillstreaming is effective in teaching prosocial skills and interpersonal competencies, quite often students do not perform the skills learned where and when needed. Chapter 5 examined the bases for generalization failures, as well as means for their remediation. As discussed earlier, some students fail to display newly learned skill behaviors because earlier learned behaviors, such as aggression, have been well practiced and therefore are more readily available and frequently used.

For this purpose, Goldstein and colleagues (Goldstein, Glick, Reiner, Zimmerman, & Coultry, 1986; Goldstein, Glick & Gibbs, 1998) developed Aggression Replacement Training (ART). Used primarily for aggressive adolescents, ART incorporates both anger control training (Feindler,

1979, 1995) and moral reasoning (Kohlberg, 1969, 1973). Students learn what to do from Skillstreaming and what not to do from anger control training. The final component, moral reasoning, is designed to engage students in discussion of values to increase motivation to choose prosocial skill alternatives. A third edition of this widely used program is available (Glick & Gibbs, 2010). The Prepare Curriculum (Goldstein, 1999b) expands the three components of ART to include such areas as empathy training, situational perception training, and problem solving.

Based on ART, The Peace4Kids and Families Program (centerforsafeschools.org) was developed for use in schools to provide youth in grades prekindergarten through 12. Based in Broomfield, Colorado, the program includes the four components of social skills training, empathy, anger control, and character education. Peace4Kids provides strategies for all students (universal interventions); targeted strategies for students who are at risk; and intensive, individualized interventions for students who do not show improved behavior through the first two levels of intervention. The goal of the program is to implement an effective prevention program and to create a culture of learning and behaving in schools, community-based programs, day treatment, and residential services. An effective parent empowerment component is also included.

PART 2

Skill Outlines and Homework Reports

Group 1

Beginning Social Skills

Skills 1–8

Skill 1: Listening

SKILL STEPS

1. **Look.**

   Discuss the importance of looking at the person who is talking. Point out that sometimes you may think someone isn't listening, even though he or she really is. These steps are to show someone that you really are listening.

2. **Stay still.**

   Remind the children that staying still means keeping hands and feet still and not talking with friends.

3. **Think.**

   Encourage the children to think about what the person is saying, and be sure they understand if the person is asking them to do something.

SUGGESTED MODELING SITUATIONS

School: Your teacher tells you that you are to go to the art center; your teacher gives you instructions on how to do an activity.

Home: A parent is telling you plans for the weekend.

Peer group: A friend is telling you a story.

COMMENTS

This is a good skill with which to begin your Skillstreaming group. Adults often tell young children to listen without explaining the specific behaviors or steps necessary to do so. Once the skill of listening is learned, it can be incorporated into classroom rules. Giving the children a special cue to listen (e.g., "Do you have your listening ears on?") may help them apply the skill when needed.

RELATED SKILL-SUPPORTING ACTIVITIES

Play the listening game of Simon Says.

Have students listen to follow the directions to complete a drawing.

In small groups, have students listen to complete a cooperative drawing or group project.

Skill 1: Listening

Name_____Date_____

SKILL STEPS

1. Look.

2. Stay still.

3. Think.

Who?   When?

How I did

Skillstreaming

From *Skillstreaming in Early Childhood: Teaching Prosocial Skills* (3rd ed.), © 2012 by E. McGinnis, Champaign, IL: Research Press (www.researchpress.com, 800-519-2707).

Skill 1: Listening

Name_____Date_____

SKILL STEPS

1. Look.

2. Stay still.

3. Think.

I did it!

From *Skillstreaming in Early Childhood: Teaching Prosocial Skills* (3rd ed.), © 2012 by E. McGinnis, Champaign, IL: Research Press (www.researchpress.com, 800-519-2707).

Skill 2: Using Nice Talk

SKILL STEPS

1. **Use a friendly look.**

   Discuss how your body and facial expressions can give a friendly or unfriendly look. You may want to act out different facial expressions and body postures to help the children identify what is friendly.

2. **Use a friendly voice.**

   Tell the children that a friendly voice is an "inside" voice—not loud like they might use outside, angry, or whining. Again, you may wish to act out different voice tones and volumes and have the children identify which ones are friendly.

SUGGESTED MODELING SITUATIONS

School: A teacher asks you to do a favor.

Home: A parent has just reminded you to pick up your toys.

Peer group: A friend is playing with the toy you wanted.

COMMENTS

This skill is intended to be used with other skills that require a verbal response. The children can be helped to understand that often it's not so much what is said as the way it is said that may elicit an angry response. Once children have learned this skill, reminding them to use nice talk can reduce the frequency of loud talking and/or whining.

RELATED SKILL-SUPPORTING ACTIVITY

Make a chart titled "Using Nice Talk." During free play, circulate around the classroom. When a student talks in an unfriendly or angry way, quietly take the child aside and prompt him or her to use "nice talk." When the student uses the skill, put a smiley-face sticker on the chart. Provide a total class special activity when the chart is filled with stickers.

Skillstreaming

From *Skillstreaming in Early Childhood: Teaching Prosocial Skills* (3rd ed.), © 2012 by E. McGinnis, Champaign, IL: Research Press (www.researchpress.com, 800-519-2707).

Skill 2: Using Nice Talk

Name_____Date_____

SKILL STEPS

1. Use a friendly look.

2. Use a friendly voice.

Who?   When?

How I did

Skill 2: Using Nice Talk

Name_____Date_____

SKILL STEPS

1. Use a friendly look.

2. Use a friendly voice.

I did it!

Skillstreaming

From *Skillstreaming in Early Childhood: Teaching Prosocial Skills* (3rd ed.), © 2012 by E. McGinnis, Champaign, IL: Research Press (www.researchpress.com, 800-519-2707).

Skill 3: Using Brave Talk

SKILL STEPS

1. **When?**

   Discuss situations in which children should use a brave (i.e., assertive) response.

2. **Use a brave look.**

   Discuss body posture and facial expressions that convey a brave look. Distinguish this look from an angry look (e.g., clenching teeth) and a friendly look (e.g., smiling).

3. **Use a brave voice.**

   Discuss that a brave voice is one slightly louder than a friendly one and in which the words are spoken more clearly. Show examples of this voice versus friendly and angry voices.

SUGGESTED MODELING SITUATIONS

School: A friend keeps pressuring you to take one of the school computer games home with you.

Home: A brother or sister encourages you to draw a picture on the outside of the house with markers.

Peer group: A friend wants you both to play in your parents' car.

COMMENTS

Another situation in which children could use this skill is when an older peer urges them to behave in ways that make them feel uncomfortable (e.g., crossing the street when they aren't supposed to). The use of puppets may help to lessen the anxiety when children are role-playing such situations.

RELATED SKILL-SUPPORTING ACTIVITY

Show different expressions and tones of voice to the children by using pictures, videotapes, and/or performing the actions live. Have the children hold up cards to indicate whether the actions are friendly, brave, or angry.

From *Skillstreaming in Early Childhood: Teaching Prosocial Skills* (3rd ed.), © 2012 by E. McGinnis, Champaign, IL: Research Press (www.researchpress.com, 800-519-2707).

Skill 3: Using Brave Talk

Name_____Date_____

SKILL STEPS

1. When?

2. Use a brave look.

3. Use a brave voice.

Who?   When?

How I did

Skillstreaming
From *Skillstreaming in Early Childhood: Teaching Prosocial Skills* (3rd ed.), © 2012
by E. McGinnis, Champaign, IL: Research Press (www.researchpress.com, 800-519-2707).

Skill 3: Using Brave Talk

Name_____Date_____

SKILL STEPS

1. When?

2. Use a brave look.

3. Use a brave voice.

I did it!

 From *Skillstreaming in Early Childhood: Teaching Prosocial Skills* (3rd ed.), © 2012 by E. McGinnis, Champaign, IL: Research Press (www.researchpress.com, 800-519-2707).

Skill 4: Saying Thank You

SKILL STEPS

1. **Was it nice to do?**

   Talk about nice things that parents, teachers, and friends do for others. Tell the children that saying thank you is a way to let someone know you are happy about what that person did for you.

2. **When?**

   Discuss appropriate times to say thank you (i.e., when the person isn't busy).

3. **Say, "Thank you."**

   Let the children know that they may want to tell the person why they are saying thank you (e.g., that they really wanted that toy or that something the person did made them feel good), especially if they must thank the person later.

SUGGESTED MODELING SITUATIONS

School: Someone gives you a school toy that you wanted.

Home: A parent fixes your favorite dinner.

Peer group: A friend invites you to a birthday party; a friend lets you play with a special toy.

COMMENTS

If children have already learned Using Nice Talk (Skill 2), they can be reminded to use it when they are saying thanks.

RELATED SKILL-SUPPORTING ACTIVITIES

Generate with the children other ways to say thank you, such as smiling, giving a hug, or doing something nice for the person.

Practice different ways of saying thank you, such as "That was nice of you to do for me" or "I felt good when you said that to me."

Develop a "thank you" list of people within the school who have helped students. Each week, plan a way to thank one of the people on that list (e.g., make a card or banner; write a note and tuck it inside a balloon, then blow up the balloon and give it to the person).

Skillstreaming

From *Skillstreaming in Early Childhood: Teaching Prosocial Skills* (3rd ed.), © 2012 by E. McGinnis, Champaign, IL: Research Press (www.researchpress.com, 800-519-2707).

Skill 4: Saying Thank You

Name_____Date_____

SKILL STEPS

1. Was it nice to do?

2. When?

3. Say, "Thank you."

Who?   When?

How I did

Skillstreaming   From *Skillstreaming in Early Childhood: Teaching Prosocial Skills* (3rd ed.), © 2012
by E. McGinnis, Champaign, IL: Research Press (www.researchpress.com, 800-519-2707).

127

Skill 4: Saying Thank You

Name_____Date_____

SKILL STEPS

1. Was it nice to do?

2. When?

3. Say, "Thank you."

I did it!

Skillstreaming

From *Skillstreaming in Early Childhood: Teaching Prosocial Skills* (3rd ed.), © 2012 by E. McGinnis, Champaign, IL: Research Press (www.researchpress.com, 800-519-2707).

Skill 5: Rewarding Yourself

SKILL STEPS

1. **How did you do?**

   Discuss ways of evaluating one's own performance. These might include feeling as though something was hard but that you tried, hearing someone else praise your efforts, or having a good feeling inside about how you did.

2. **Say, "Good for me!"**

   Discuss the feeling of being proud of yourself. Have the children talk about times when they have felt this way. Give examples of other things they might say to reward themselves (e.g., "Way to go," "I really did a good job").

SUGGESTED MODELING SITUATIONS

School: You helped the teacher or another child; you did a good job on an activity.

Home: You cleaned up your room; you helped clear the table.

Peer group: You helped a friend learn how to play a game on the computer.

COMMENTS

Emphasize that a person doesn't always have to depend on others to reward his or her actions.

RELATED SKILL-SUPPORTING ACTIVITY

If the group is large, divide into smaller groups of four to six students each. Have the children take turns telling one thing they did well that day. Have the children reward themselves (e.g., say, "Good for me," or give themselves a pat on the back). Each day, write a note to several parents about their children's achievement. Be sure at the end of the week that all children have had an "I did it" note to take home.

From *Skillstreaming in Early Childhood: Teaching Prosocial Skills* (3rd ed.), © 2012 by E. McGinnis, Champaign, IL: Research Press (www.researchpress.com, 800-519-2707).

Skill 5: Rewarding Yourself

Name_____Date_____

SKILL STEPS

1. How did you do?

2. Say, "Good for me!"

Who?   When?

How I did

Skill 5: Rewarding Yourself

Name_____Date_____

SKILL STEPS

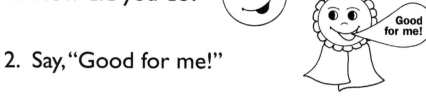

1. How did you do?

2. Say, "Good for me!"

I did it!

Skillstreaming

From *Skillstreaming in Early Childhood: Teaching Prosocial Skills* (3rd ed.), © 2012
by E. McGinnis, Champaign, IL: Research Press (www.researchpress.com, 800-519-2707).

Skill 6: Asking for Help

SKILL STEPS

1. **Try it.**

   Talk about the importance of trying on your own first. Sometimes people ask for help instead of trying something difficult by themselves, but doing something difficult on your own can give you a feeling of pride.

2. **Say, "I need help."**

   Acknowledge that sometimes it's frustrating when something is difficult to do, but stress the importance of Using Nice Talk (Skill 2).

SUGGESTED MODELING SITUATIONS

School: You need help putting the paints back up on the shelf.

Home: You need help from a parent in getting dressed for school or finding your swimming suit.

Peer group: You want to ask a friend to help you learn to ride your bike.

COMMENTS

Remind the children that they may want to use the skill of Saying Thank You (Skill 4) after the help is given. This will help the child understand how to use a sequence of prosocial skills.

RELATED SKILL-SUPPORTING ACTIVITIES

Have children list and/or illustrate the activities or skills each is particularly good at. Discuss individual differences; stress that it is OK to ask for help if it's needed. These lists may also stimulate the children to ask for help from peers who have listed certain areas as strengths.

Create a classroom "yellow pages," which lists strengths or services (e.g., math skills, playing a certain board game, tying shoes). (Be sure each child has his or her name in the pages at least once!) Encourage students to look in the yellow pages if they need help with something.

Skillstreaming

From *Skillstreaming in Early Childhood: Teaching Prosocial Skills* (3rd ed.), © 2012 by E. McGinnis, Champaign, IL: Research Press (www.researchpress.com, 800-519-2707).

Skill 6: Asking for Help

Name_____ Date_____

SKILL STEPS

1. Try it.

2. Say, "I need help."

Who?   When?

How I did

Skillstreaming   From *Skillstreaming in Early Childhood: Teaching Prosocial Skills* (3rd ed.), © 2012
by E. McGinnis, Champaign, IL: Research Press (www.researchpress.com, 800-519-2707).   133

Skill 6: Asking for Help

Name_____Date_____

SKILL STEPS

1. Try it.

2. Say, "I need help."

I did it!

Skillstreaming

From *Skillstreaming in Early Childhood: Teaching Prosocial Skills* (3rd ed.), © 2012 by E. McGinnis, Champaign, IL: Research Press (www.researchpress.com, 800-519-2707).

Skill 7: Asking a Favor

SKILL STEPS

1. **What do you want?**

   Explain that this skill may be used to express children's wants or needs but that the favor should be a fair one. Deciding If It's Fair (Skill 29) will help them determine this.

2. **Plan what to say.**

   Talk about the importance of planning what to say and suggest several possible ways to ask. The children may also want to give a reason for asking the favor (e.g., "Could you please move a little? I can't see when you sit there").

3. **Ask.**

4. **Say, "Thank you."**

   Refer to Saying Thank You (Skill 4).

SUGGESTED MODELING SITUATIONS

School: You want to use the markers another child is using.

Home: You ask your parent to make popcorn.

Peer group: You want to ride a friend's bicycle.

COMMENTS

Once the children have been successful in using this skill in role-play situations, it is particularly important that they practice what to do when the favor isn't granted. Adding the statement "Thanks anyway" or having the child get involved in something else may be helpful.

RELATED SKILL-SUPPORTING ACTIVITY

Make a list of favors that would be fair and those that would not. For example, if a person has a pack of gum, would it be fair to ask for a stick? If a person has one stick of gum, would it be fair to ask for it?

From *Skillstreaming in Early Childhood: Teaching Prosocial Skills* (3rd ed.), © 2012 by E. McGinnis, Champaign, IL: Research Press (www.researchpress.com, 800-519-2707).

Skill 7: Asking a Favor

Name_____Date_____

SKILL STEPS

1. What do you want?

2. Plan what to say.

3. Ask.

4. Say, "Thank you."

Who?   When?

How I did

Skillstreaming

From *Skillstreaming in Early Childhood: Teaching Prosocial Skills* (3rd ed.), © 2012 by E. McGinnis, Champaign, IL: Research Press (www.researchpress.com, 800-519-2707).

Skill 7: Asking a Favor

Name_____Date_____

SKILL STEPS

1. What do you want?

2. Plan what to say.

3. Ask.

4. Say, "Thank you."

I did it!

Skill 8: Ignoring

SKILL STEPS

1. **Look away.**

   Tell the children not to look at the person they want to avoid. They can turn their heads away, look at a friend, or pick up a book or toy to look at.

2. **Close your ears.**

   Tell children not to listen to what the annoying person is saying. If they are supposed to be listening to someone else (such as a teacher), they can listen to that person.

3. **Be quiet.**

   Remind children not to say anything back to the person who is annoying.

SUGGESTED MODELING SITUATIONS

School: Another child is talking when you are supposed to be listening to the teacher.

Home: A brother or sister is trying to keep you from listening to your CD.

Peer group: Another child is trying to interfere with a game you are playing.

COMMENTS

Discuss that sometimes someone who is acting silly is trying to get attention. A good way to teach that person not to act silly is to avoid giving him any attention at all. Also discuss the idea that sometimes friends will bother others because they really want to play, too. In this case, the children may want to ask the child to join in. Finally, talk about other ways of ignoring, such as leaving the room (at home) or getting involved in another activity (at school).

RELATED SKILL-SUPPORTING ACTIVITIES

Tell the class that during this class activity, one that they are to do independently at their work stations, you will walk around the room and try to distract them. They are to practice Ignoring. Be sure each child has a copy of the steps of the skill to serve as a reminder.

In pairs, have one child tell what he or she did last night. First, have the other child listen to what is being said. (It may be necessary to review Skill 1, Listening.) Next have the child tell again what he or she did, directing the other child to use the skill of Ignoring. As a group, discuss how it felt to be listened to and how it felt to be ignored.

From *Skillstreaming in Early Childhood: Teaching Prosocial Skills* (3rd ed.), © 2012 by E. McGinnis, Champaign, IL: Research Press (www.researchpress.com, 800-519-2707).

Skill 8: Ignoring

Name_____Date_____

SKILL STEPS

1. Look away.

2. Close your ears.

3. Be quiet.

Who?   When?

How I did

139

Skill 8: Ignoring

Name_____Date_____

SKILL STEPS

1. Look away.

2. Close your ears.

3. Be quiet.

I did it!

Skillstreaming

From *Skillstreaming in Early Childhood: Teaching Prosocial Skills* (3rd ed.), © 2012 by E. McGinnis, Champaign, IL: Research Press (www.researchpress.com, 800-519-2707).

Group II

School-Related Skills

Skills 9–12

Skill 9: Asking a Question

SKILL STEPS

1. **What to ask?**

   Discuss what children need to ask and how to decide whether the question is really necessary. Help them plan out what they need to ask.

2. **Whom to ask?**

   Discuss how to decide if they should ask the teacher, a parent, or someone else.

3. **When to ask?**

   Talk about how to choose a good time to ask (i.e., when the other person isn't busy).

4. **Ask.**

   Stress the importance of Using Nice Talk (Skill 2).

SUGGESTED MODELING SITUATIONS

School: You want to ask your teacher about when the field trip is; you want to ask to use the markers and glue.

Home: You want to ask a parent if you can visit a friend.

Peer group: You want to ask a friend if she would like to play at your house; you want to ask how a friend made something.

COMMENTS

Young children often phrase questions as statements. Modeling the question form when such situations arise will help them learn an alternate way of expressing themselves.

RELATED SKILL-SUPPORTING ACTIVITIES

Practice asking questions via a game format. For example, make a statement such as "I want a glass of milk," and ask the children to change the statement to a question ("May I have a glass of milk?").

State a topic (e.g., swimming) and, as a group, generate several questions that could be asked about that topic. Discourage questions unrelated to the topic.

Skill 9: Asking a Question

Name_____Date_____

SKILL STEPS

1. What to ask?

2. Whom to ask?

3. When to ask?

4. Ask.

Who?   When?

How I did

Skillstreaming

From *Skillstreaming in Early Childhood: Teaching Prosocial Skills* (3rd ed.), © 2012
by E. McGinnis, Champaign, IL: Research Press (www.researchpress.com, 800-519-2707).

Skill 9: Asking a Question

Name_____Date_____

SKILL STEPS

1. What to ask?

2. Whom to ask?

3. When to ask?

4. Ask.

I did it!

Skill 10: Following Directions

SKILL STEPS

1. **Listen.**

   Review Listening (Skill 1). Discuss the importance of having children show that they are listening.

2. **Think about it.**

   Remind the children to think about what is being said.

3. **Ask if needed.**

   Encourage children to ask questions about anything they don't understand. (Review or teach Skill 9, Asking a Question).

4. **Do it.**

SUGGESTED MODELING SITUATIONS

School: Your teacher gives you the directions to do some work at a learning center.

Home: A parent gives you directions to make a snack.

Peer group: A friend tells you how to play a game at recess.

COMMENTS

Sometimes directions given to young children are too complex for them to complete successfully. Give directions consisting of only one or two steps until the children are familiar with following directions. It's helpful to preface a direction with a consistent cue, such as "Here's the direction."

RELATED SKILL-SUPPORTING ACTIVITIES

Play the Treasure Hunt game, giving the children verbal directions to find a special treat or activity (e.g., "Walk to the bookshelf and look on the bottom shelf under the big book").

Read the book *Strega Nona,* by Tomie de Paola (Simon and Schuster, 1979). Discuss the consequences in this story when Big Anthony didn't follow directions. Discuss the consequences of not following directions in the children's own lives.

Skillstreaming

From *Skillstreaming in Early Childhood: Teaching Prosocial Skills* (3rd ed.), © 2012 by E. McGinnis, Champaign, IL: Research Press (www.researchpress.com, 800-519-2707).

Skill 10: Following Directions

Name_____Date_____

SKILL STEPS

1. Listen.

2. Think about it.

3. Ask if needed.

4. Do it.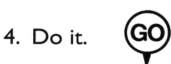

Who?   When?

How I did

From *Skillstreaming in Early Childhood: Teaching Prosocial Skills* (3rd ed.), © 2012 by E. McGinnis, Champaign, IL: Research Press (www.researchpress.com, 800-519-2707).

Skill 10: Following Directions

Name_____Date_____

SKILL STEPS

1. Listen.

2. Think about it.

3. Ask if needed.

4. Do it.

I did it!

Skillstreaming From *Skillstreaming in Early Childhood: Teaching Prosocial Skills* (3rd ed.), © 2012 by E. McGinnis, Champaign, IL: Research Press (www.researchpress.com, 800-519-2707).

Skill 11: Trying When It's Hard

SKILL STEPS

1. **Stop and think.**

   Discuss the feeling of frustration, and point out that lots of people get frustrated when something is difficult.

2. **Say, "It's hard, but I'll try."**

   Talk about feeling proud when something is hard but you try it anyway. Also stress that it's OK to try and fail.

3. **Try it.**

   Point out that a person might need to try more than once.

SUGGESTED MODELING SITUATIONS

School: Your teacher gives you an assignment that you don't think you can do.

Home: A parent wants you to do a chore that you don't think you can do (e.g., make the beds).

Peer group: A friend wants you to roller blade with him, but you think it's too hard.

COMMENTS

For the child who is afraid of failure, this will be a particularly valuable skill. Reinforce the idea that the only way to learn new things is to try those that are difficult. When assigning preacademic or academic skills, be sure that tasks asked of the children are ones they are capable of completing with effort.

RELATED SKILL-SUPPORTING ACTIVITY

Read *The Little Engine That Could,* by Watty Piper (Platt and Munk, 1976), and discuss the feelings of each of the characters in the story. Also discuss what might have happened if the little engine didn't try. Substitute stories with similar themes, such as *The Little Red Ant and the Great Big Crumb: A Mexican Fable,* by Shirley Climo (Clarion, 1999).

Skill 11: Trying When It's Hard

Name_____Date_____

SKILL STEPS

1. Stop and think.

2. Say, "It's hard, but I'll try."

3. Try it.

Who?   When?

How I did

Skillstreaming

From *Skillstreaming in Early Childhood: Teaching Prosocial Skills* (3rd ed.), © 2012 by E. McGinnis, Champaign, IL: Research Press (www.researchpress.com, 800-519-2707).

Skill 11: Trying When It's Hard

Name_____Date_____

SKILL STEPS

1. Stop and think.

2. Say, "It's hard, but I'll try."

3. Try it.

I did it!

Skillstreaming From *Skillstreaming in Early Childhood: Teaching Prosocial Skills* (3rd ed.), © 2012
by E. McGinnis, Champaign, IL: Research Press (www.researchpress.com, 800-519-2707). **151**

Skill 12: Interrupting

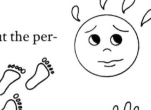

SKILL STEPS

1. **Decide if you need to.**

   Discuss when it is appropriate to interrupt (i.e., when you need help but the person you want to talk to isn't looking at you).

2. **Walk to the person.**

3. **Wait.**

   Emphasize the importance of waiting without talking. Tell children to wait until the person stops talking and looks at you.

4. **Say, "Excuse me."**

   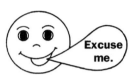

   Discuss how to know the person is ready to hear you (e.g., the person looks at you). The children can then ask what they need to.

SUGGESTED MODELING SITUATIONS

School: Your teacher is talking with another adult, and you need help with your activity.

Home: A parent is talking on the telephone, and you want to ask whether you can go outside.

Peer group: Your friend is talking with another person, and you want to ask whether you can play with your friend's video game.

COMMENTS

It will be important to discuss situations in which children should not interrupt (i.e., to ask a question that could wait) and situations in which they should interrupt immediately (i.e., in an emergency). It may be helpful to have the children actually say to the adult, "This is an emergency" when such cases arise.

RELATED SKILL-SUPPORTING ACTIVITY

Provide pictures of a variety of situations and, as a group, have the children put the pictures under one of the following headings: "Do Not Interrupt," "OK to Interrupt," or "Emergency."

Skillstreaming

From *Skillstreaming in Early Childhood: Teaching Prosocial Skills* (3rd ed.), © 2012 by E. McGinnis, Champaign, IL: Research Press (www.researchpress.com, 800-519-2707).

Skill 12: Interrupting

Name_____Date_____

SKILL STEPS

1. Decide if you need to.

2. Walk to the person.

3. Wait.

4. Say, "Excuse me."

Who?   When?

How I did

Skill 12: Interrupting

Name_____Date_____

SKILL STEPS

1. Decide if you need to.

2. Walk to the person.

3. Wait.

4. Say, "Excuse me."

I did it!

Skillstreaming

Group III

Friendship-Making Skills

Skills 13–20

Skill 13: Greeting Others

SKILL STEPS

1. **Smile.**

2. **Say, "Hi, _____."**

   Encourage children to use the person's name if
   they know it.

3. **Walk on.**

   This step should be used if the children are supposed to be following along
   with the group or if they don't know the person well. The children may wish
   to begin a conversation if the person is a friend and if it is an OK time to have
   a conversation.

SUGGESTED MODELING SITUATIONS

School: You pass by the school secretary in the hallway.

Home: A friend of your parents is visiting.

Peer group: Another child is walking past your house with her parents.

COMMENTS

This skill is intended for use with people the child knows only casually or in situations in which starting
a conversation would likely be inappropriate.

RELATED SKILL-SUPPORTING ACTIVITY

With the children, take a walk around the school and practice greeting others.

From *Skillstreaming in Early Childhood: Teaching Prosocial Skills* (3rd ed.), © 2012
by E. McGinnis, Champaign, IL: Research Press (www.researchpress.com, 800-519-2707).

Skill 13: Greeting Others

Name_____Date_____

SKILL STEPS

1. Smile.

2. Say, "Hi, _____."

3. Walk on.

Who? When?

How I did

Skillstreaming

From *Skillstreaming in Early Childhood: Teaching Prosocial Skills* (3rd ed.), © 2012 by E. McGinnis, Champaign, IL: Research Press (www.researchpress.com, 800-519-2707).

Skill 13: Greeting Others

Name_____Date_____

SKILL STEPS

1. Smile.

2. Say, "Hi, _____."

3. Walk on.

I did it!

Skillstreaming From *Skillstreaming in Early Childhood: Teaching Prosocial Skills* (3rd ed.), © 2012
by E. McGinnis, Champaign, IL: Research Press (www.researchpress.com, 800-519-2707).

Skill 14: Reading Others

SKILL STEPS

1. **Look at the face.**

   Discuss the importance of watching for different facial expressions, such as smiling, frowning, clenching teeth together, and so forth.

2. **Look at the body.**

   Talk about the feelings shown in a person's body position, such as putting head down, making fists with hands, placing hands on hips, and so on.

SUGGESTED MODELING SITUATIONS

School: The teacher walks into the class and smiles, or she has her hands on her hips and frowns.

Home: A parent is sitting with his head resting on his hands and not saying anything.

Peer group: A friend keeps turning away from you and doesn't answer you when you try to talk.

COMMENTS

For some children, paying attention to nonverbal communication (facial expressions and body posture) will be quite difficult, and considerable practice with this skill will be necessary.

RELATED SKILL-SUPPORTING ACTIVITIES

Show a variety of pictures of people engaged in everyday activities. (These pictures can be cut from magazines.) Have children describe the facial expressions and body postures shown in the pictures.

When reading picture books to the class, draw attention to the characters' facial expressions and body postures as clues to how the characters might feel.

From *Skillstreaming in Early Childhood: Teaching Prosocial Skills* (3rd ed.), © 2012 by E. McGinnis, Champaign, IL: Research Press (www.researchpress.com, 800-519-2707).

Skill 14: Reading Others

Name_____Date_____

SKILL STEPS

1. Look at the face.

2. Look at the body.

Who?   When?

How I did

From *Skillstreaming in Early Childhood: Teaching Prosocial Skills* (3rd ed.), © 2012 by E. McGinnis, Champaign, IL: Research Press (www.researchpress.com, 800-519-2707).

Skill 14: Reading Others

Name_____Date_____

SKILL STEPS

1. Look at the face.

2. Look at the body.

I did it!

Skillstreaming
From *Skillstreaming in Early Childhood: Teaching Prosocial Skills* (3rd ed.), © 2012 by E. McGinnis, Champaign, IL: Research Press (www.researchpress.com, 800-519-2707).

Skill 15: Joining In

SKILL STEPS

1. **Move closer.**

   Point out that the children should be fairly close to where the activity is taking place.

2. **Watch.**

   Tell the children to watch the ongoing activity and wait for a pause. Discuss the importance of choosing a time to follow through with the next step (i.e., before the activity has begun or when there is a break in the activity).

3. **Ask.**

   Suggest possible things to say, such as "That looks fun! Could I play, too?" Stress the importance of Using Brave Talk (Skill 3).

SUGGESTED MODELING SITUATIONS

School: You want to join in a game at recess or during free play.

Home: You want to play a game with a brother, sister, or parent.

Peer group: You want to join a group of children at the park.

COMMENTS

Attempts to join in are more successful if the child hovers near the ongoing activity before asking to join. Children may need to use alternative skills if they are repeatedly rejected by a certain peer group. Practice in Reading Others (Skill 14) may help them assess other children's receptivity to such overtures.

RELATED SKILL-SUPPORTING ACTIVITY

During free play in the classroom or on the playground, tell the children that they will be practicing this skill. For each activity, review the steps with three or four children, then have them try out the skill. Discuss the outcomes with the class.

Skill 15: Joining In

Name_____Date_____

SKILL STEPS

1. Move closer.

2. Watch.

3. Ask.

Who?   When?

How I did

.Skillstreaming

From *Skillstreaming in Early Childhood: Teaching Prosocial Skills* (3rd ed.), © 2012
by E. McGinnis, Champaign, IL: Research Press (www.researchpress.com, 800-519-2707).

Skill 15: Joining In

Name_____Date_____

SKILL STEPS

1. Move closer.

2. Watch.

3. Ask.

I did it!

From *Skillstreaming in Early Childhood: Teaching Prosocial Skills* (3rd ed.), © 2012 by E. McGinnis, Champaign, IL: Research Press (www.researchpress.com, 800-519-2707).

Skill 16: Waiting Your Turn

SKILL STEPS

1. **Say, "It's hard to wait, but I can do it."**

   Discuss how the children feel when they have to wait.

2. **Choose.**

   a. **Wait quietly.**

      Discuss that this choice means not talking or bothering anyone else and remembering not to get angry or frustrated.

   b. **Do something else.**

      Talk about what things the children could do while they are waiting.

3. **Do it.**

   Children should make one of these choices.

SUGGESTED MODELING SITUATIONS

School: You are waiting your turn to play a game or to use the playground equipment.

Home: You are waiting until it's time for you to go to a movie or to the park.

Peer group: You are waiting your turn to have a toy.

COMMENTS

Remember to use a coping model during the modeling displays because this skill can be a difficult one for the young child, who may be impulsive.

RELATED SKILL-SUPPORTING ACTIVITY

To practice this skill, as well as to show the group a product resulting from working together and taking turns, structure round-robin activities in the classroom, such as cooperatively making a collage, putting together a puzzle, or making a card or banner as a thank-you for someone. If the group is large, three or four groups could be completing the activity simultaneously. Remind the children to use the skill (post the steps or give each child a skill card).

Skillstreaming

From *Skillstreaming in Early Childhood: Teaching Prosocial Skills* (3rd ed.), © 2012 by E. McGinnis, Champaign, IL: Research Press (www.researchpress.com, 800-519-2707).

Skill 16: Waiting Your Turn

Name_____Date_____

SKILL STEPS

1. Say, "It's hard to wait, but I can do it."

2. Choose.

    a. Wait quietly.

    b. Do something else.

3. Do it. GO

Who?   When?

How I did

Skill 16: Waiting Your Turn

Name_____Date_____

SKILL STEPS

1. Say, "It's hard to wait, but I can do it."

2. Choose.

    a. Wait quietly.

    b. Do something else.

3. Do it.

I did it!

Skillstreaming

From *Skillstreaming in Early Childhood: Teaching Prosocial Skills* (3rd ed.), © 2012 by E. McGinnis, Champaign, IL: Research Press (www.researchpress.com, 800-519-2707).

Skill 17: Sharing

SKILL STEPS

1. **Make a sharing plan.**

   Discuss the different plans children could make, such as playing with a toy together or having each child take a turn with the toy for a set period of time.

2. **Ask.**

   Remind the children of the importance of Using Nice Talk (Skill 2) when asking friends if they agree to the plan.

3. **Do it.**

   Talk about the importance of following through with the plan until a different plan is decided on.

SUGGESTED MODELING SITUATIONS

School: You have to share the glue and other art materials with two other children.

Home: You must share the last cookie with a brother or sister.

Peer group: You have to share your toys with a friend who has come to your house to play.

COMMENTS

It is appropriate to discuss how the children feel when someone doesn't share with them and to encourage them to think about their feelings when someone asks them to share.

RELATED SKILL-SUPPORTING ACTIVITIES

Plan activities to encourage this skill, such as sharing art materials, taking turns when cooking, or engaging in other cooperative activities.

Divide children into groups of four or five at each table. Instruct each child to complete his or her own art activity. However, provide only one or two pairs of scissors and glue containers for each table. Remind the students to use the skill of Sharing.

Skill 17: Sharing

Name_____Date_____

SKILL STEPS

1. Make a sharing plan.

2. Ask.

3. Do it.

Who? When?

How I did

Skillstreaming

From *Skillstreaming in Early Childhood: Teaching Prosocial Skills* (3rd ed.), © 2012
by E. McGinnis, Champaign, IL: Research Press (www.researchpress.com, 800-519-2707).

Skill 17: Sharing

Name_____Date_____

SKILL STEPS

1. Make a sharing plan.

2. Ask.

3. Do it.

I did it!

From *Skillstreaming in Early Childhood: Teaching Prosocial Skills* (3rd ed.), © 2012
by E. McGinnis, Champaign, IL: Research Press (www.researchpress.com, 800-519-2707).

Skillstreaming

Skill 18: Offering Help

SKILL STEPS

1. **Decide if someone needs help.**

   Discuss how to tell when someone might want or need help (e.g., someone has lots to carry or is showing frustration).

2. **Ask.**

   Discuss appropriate ways of asking, such as saying, "May I help you?" or "How can I help you?"

3. **Do it.**

   Discuss what to do if the person does not want your help.

SUGGESTED MODELING SITUATIONS

School: Your teacher looks frustrated while trying to pass out snacks and help a child who is upset at the same time.

Home: A parent is hurrying to get dinner ready.

Peer group: A friend is having trouble getting her coat on.

COMMENTS

Discuss what to do if the person doesn't want the help (e.g., walk away, get involved in another activity, say to yourself, "I did a good job asking" or "It was nice of me to ask").

RELATED SKILL-SUPPORTING ACTIVITIES

Include this skill when teaching units on community helpers by asking the people who come in to talk to the class to discuss ways they offer help to others.

Generate a class list of ways the children could help someone at home. Ask students to follow through with one of these suggestions. (Having the children draw a picture of what they plan to do, then take the picture home, will serve as a reminder.)

Skillstreaming

From *Skillstreaming in Early Childhood: Teaching Prosocial Skills* (3rd ed.), © 2012 by E. McGinnis, Champaign, IL: Research Press (www.researchpress.com, 800-519-2707).

Skill 18: Offering Help

Name_____Date_____

SKILL STEPS

1. Decide if someone needs help.

2. Ask.

3. Do it.

Who?   When?

How I did

Skillstreaming   From *Skillstreaming in Early Childhood: Teaching Prosocial Skills* (3rd ed.), © 2012 by E. McGinnis, Champaign, IL: Research Press (www.researchpress.com, 800-519-2707).

Skill 18: Offering Help

Name_____Date_____

SKILL STEPS

1. Decide if someone needs help.

2. Ask.

3. Do it.

I did it!

Skillstreaming

From *Skillstreaming in Early Childhood: Teaching Prosocial Skills* (3rd ed.), © 2012 by E. McGinnis, Champaign, IL: Research Press (www.researchpress.com, 800-519-2707).

Skill 19: Asking Someone to Play

SKILL STEPS

1. **Decide if you want to.**

   Discuss how to decide whether you want someone to play with or you would rather play alone. Point out that there might be times when you would rather be alone.

2. **Decide who.**

   Talk about whom the child might choose (e.g., someone who is playing alone, someone new in the class the child would like to get to know, someone who isn't busy).

3. **Ask.**

   Discuss and practice ways to ask (e.g., "Do you want to play?" or "Will you play this with me?")

SUGGESTED MODELING SITUATIONS

School: You want to play with someone when it's free play time.

Home: You want to ask a brother, sister, or parent to play.

Peer group: You want to play with a friend in the neighborhood.

COMMENTS

It is important to point out that it is best to ask someone to play after the person has finished his or her work at school or at home.

RELATED SKILL-SUPPORTING ACTIVITY

Write each child's name on a small index card or sheet of paper. During free play, have children draw a name. This is the child they will ask to play. (You may have to guide the children in an activity that they both would enjoy.)

Skill 19: Asking Someone to Play

Name_____Date_____

SKILL STEPS

1. Decide if you want to.

2. Decide who.

3. Ask.

Who?   When?

How I did

From *Skillstreaming in Early Childhood: Teaching Prosocial Skills* (3rd ed.), © 2012 by E. McGinnis, Champaign, IL: Research Press (www.researchpress.com, 800-519-2707).

Skill 19: Asking Someone to Play

Name_____Date_____

SKILL STEPS

1. Decide if you want to.

2. Decide who.

3. Ask.

I did it!

From *Skillstreaming in Early Childhood: Teaching Prosocial Skills* (3rd ed.), © 2012 by E. McGinnis, Champaign, IL: Research Press (www.researchpress.com, 800-519-2707).

Skill 20: Playing a Game

SKILL STEPS

1. **Know the rules.**

   Discuss that everyone playing should agree on the rules before the game begins.

2. **Who goes first?**

   Talk about ways to decide, such as rolling a die or offering to let the other person go first.

3. **Wait for a turn.**

   Emphasize the importance of paying attention to the game and watching and waiting for your own turn.

SUGGESTED MODELING SITUATIONS

School: You are practicing shooting baskets at recess with two other friends.

Home: You are playing a board game with your mom.

Peer group: You are playing a video game with a friend.

COMMENTS

Two good skills to teach along with this one are Dealing with Losing (Skill 36) and Wanting to Be First (Skill 37).

RELATED SKILL-SUPPORTING ACTIVITY

Provide opportunities for the children to play board or computer games in pairs or small groups, emphasizing use of this skill. Teach a variety of games children may play at recess or during free play in the classroom.

From *Skillstreaming in Early Childhood: Teaching Prosocial Skills* (3rd ed.), © 2012 by E. McGinnis, Champaign, IL: Research Press (www.researchpress.com, 800-519-2707).

Skill 20: Playing a Game

Name_____ Date_____

SKILL STEPS

1. Know the rules.

2. Who goes first?

3. Wait for a turn.

Who?   When?

How I did

Skill 20: Playing a Game

Name_____Date_____

SKILL STEPS

1. Know the rules.

2. Who goes first?

3. Wait for a turn.

I did it!

Skillstreaming

From *Skillstreaming in Early Childhood: Teaching Prosocial Skills* (3rd ed.), © 2012 by E. McGinnis, Champaign, IL: Research Press (www.researchpress.com, 800-519-2707).

Group IV

Dealing with Feelings

Skills 21–26

Skill 21: Knowing Your Feelings

SKILL STEPS

1. **Think about what happened.**

   Discuss what happened that may have caused the feeling. Also talk about the signals the children's bodies give that indicate they are having a strong feeling.

2. **Decide on the feeling.**

   Discuss a variety of feelings, such as anger, happiness, frustration, fear, and so on.

3. **Say, "I feel _____."**

SUGGESTED MODELING SITUATIONS

School: You have to go to a new school where you don't know any of the kids.

Home: Your parent announces that the whole family is going to a movie that you had been wanting to see.

Peer group: You didn't get invited to a friend's birthday party.

COMMENTS

Explore as many different feeling words as the children can handle, trying to expand their vocabulary beyond the typical feelings of happy, sad, and mad.

RELATED SKILL-SUPPORTING ACTIVITIES

Read the story *I Was So Mad,* by Mercer Mayer (Western, 1983). Discuss how the main character's body might feel during different parts of the story.

Read the book *Feelings,* by Aliki (William Morrow, 1986). Discuss times when the children have had similar feelings. Ask how they knew (how their bodies felt) when they were having those feelings.

Present pictures of people and animals, and help children identify what feelings may be expressed. Generate ideas as to what may have caused these feelings.

From *Skillstreaming in Early Childhood: Teaching Prosocial Skills* (3rd ed.), © 2012 by E. McGinnis, Champaign, IL: Research Press (www.researchpress.com, 800-519-2707).

Skill 21: Knowing Your Feelings

Name_____Date_____

SKILL STEPS

1. Think about what happened.

2. Decide on the feeling.

3. Say, "I feel _____."

Who?   When?

How I did

Skillstreaming
From *Skillstreaming in Early Childhood: Teaching Prosocial Skills* (3rd ed.), © 2012 by E. McGinnis, Champaign, IL: Research Press (www.researchpress.com, 800-519-2707).

Skill 21: Knowing Your Feelings

Name_____ Date_____

SKILL STEPS

1. Think about what happened.

2. Decide on the feeling.

3. Say, "I feel _____."

I did it!

Skillstreaming From *Skillstreaming in Early Childhood: Teaching Prosocial Skills* (3rd ed.), © 2012
by E. McGinnis, Champaign, IL: Research Press (www.researchpress.com, 800-519-2707).

Skill 22: Feeling Left Out

SKILL STEPS

1. **Decide what happened.**

   Discuss situations in which the children may feel left out and help them decide what caused them to feel this way. Talk about reasons why someone may not be included (e.g., a friend could invite only three people to her birthday party).

2. **Choose.**

   a. **Join in.**

   Children may need prior instruction in Joining In (Skill 15).

   b. **Do something else.**

   Generate ideas for other things children could do. Suggest that they may want to invite a friend to do one of these activities.

3. **Do it.**

   Children should make one of these choices.

SUGGESTED MODELING SITUATIONS

School: You are left out of a game during free play.

Home: Your sister won't let you come into her room.

Peer group: A friend has invited someone else to go skating.

COMMENTS

The children may need practice in Reading Others (Skill 14) or Deciding How Someone Feels (Skill 25) to assess whether or not the other child or group of children is approachable.

RELATED SKILL-SUPPORTING ACTIVITIES

Discuss the types of feelings that result from being left out, such as anger, hurt, loneliness, or frustration.

Read the story *Alejandro's Gift,* by Richard Albert (Chronicle Publishing, 1996). Discuss how Alejandro felt and what he did about it.

From *Skillstreaming in Early Childhood: Teaching Prosocial Skills* (3rd ed.), © 2012 by E. McGinnis, Champaign, IL: Research Press (www.researchpress.com, 800-519-2707).

Skill 22: Feeling Left Out

Name_____Date_____

SKILL STEPS

1. Decide what happened.

2. Choose.

   a. Join in.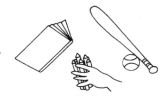

   b. Do something else.

3. Do it. GO

Who?   When?

How I did

Skill 22: Feeling Left Out

Name_____Date_____

SKILL STEPS

1. Decide what happened.

2. Choose.

   a. Join in.

   b. Do something else.

3. Do it.

I did it!

Skillstreaming

From *Skillstreaming in Early Childhood: Teaching Prosocial Skills* (3rd ed.), © 2012 by E. McGinnis, Champaign, IL: Research Press (www.researchpress.com, 800-519-2707).

Skill 23: Asking to Talk

SKILL STEPS

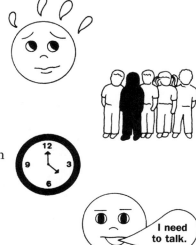

1. **Decide if you need to talk.**

   Discuss times when something might bother children and they might want to talk to someone about it.

2. **Who?**

   Decide whom to talk with (i.e., a parent, teacher, or friend).

3. **When?**

   Decide when would be a good time to ask (i.e., when the person isn't busy with something or someone else).

4. **Say, "I need to talk."**

   Stress the importance of Using Nice Talk (Skill 2) to say this.

SUGGESTED MODELING SITUATIONS

School: You are feeling sad because you didn't have a turn at the painting center.

Home: Your parent bought your brother something that you had wanted.

Peer group: You feel that a friend would rather play with someone other than you.

COMMENTS

Stress that everyone experiences problems at some time and, although talking with someone may not actually solve the problem, it will likely help make you feel better.

RELATED SKILL-SUPPORTING ACTIVITY

Write descriptions of times when talking with someone would be helpful (include the situations the students generated during initial instruction in this skill). Have the children, in turn, draw a card on which one of these situations has been listed. (Depending upon the reading skills of the class, it may be necessary to select a reader from the class or to read the situations yourself.) Ask each child whom he or she would ask to talk with, and follow through by role-playing the skill.

Skill 23: Asking to Talk

Name_____ Date_____

SKILL STEPS

1. Decide if you need to talk.

2. Who?

3. When?

4. Say, "I need to talk."

Who?   When?

How I did

Skillstreaming

From *Skillstreaming in Early Childhood: Teaching Prosocial Skills* (3rd ed.), © 2012 by E. McGinnis, Champaign, IL: Research Press (www.researchpress.com, 800-519-2707).

Skill 23: Asking to Talk

Name_____ Date_____

SKILL STEPS

1. Decide if you need to talk.

2. Who?

3. When?

4. Say, "I need to talk."

I did it!

Skillstreaming From *Skillstreaming in Early Childhood: Teaching Prosocial Skills* (3rd ed.), © 2012
by E. McGinnis, Champaign, IL: Research Press (www.researchpress.com, 800-519-2707).

Skill 24: Dealing with Fear

SKILL STEPS

1. **What?**

   Discuss situations that cause children to be afraid.

2. **Choose.**

   a. **Ask to talk.**

      Refer to Asking to Talk (Skill 23).

   b. **Relax.**

      Refer to Relaxing (Skill 32).

3. **Do it.**

   Children should make one of these choices.

SUGGESTED MODELING SITUATIONS

School: A parent is late, and you're afraid he or she isn't coming.

Home: A brother or sister is watching a scary movie.

Peer group: You are afraid to go out of the house because an older child said he would get you.

COMMENTS

Discuss that there are events in which a real danger is present and fear is appropriate. Many other situations, such as being afraid of the dark, are quite normal for this age group and likely present no serious problems for most children. However, explain that sometimes we may be afraid to try new things; in this case, the children should be encouraged to use Trying When It's Hard (Skill 11) after first using one of the choices listed in this skill.

RELATED SKILL-SUPPORTING ACTIVITIES

Read the story *Bootsie Barker Bites,* by Barbara Bottner (Putnam, 1997). Discuss what the girl in the story did to overcome her fear of being bullied.

Read the story *Mirette on the High Wire,* by Emily Arnold McCully (Putnam, 1997). Discuss how each character in the story felt and how Mirette helped Bellini to overcome his fear.

Skillstreaming

From *Skillstreaming in Early Childhood: Teaching Prosocial Skills* (3rd ed.), © 2012 by E. McGinnis, Champaign, IL: Research Press (www.researchpress.com, 800-519-2707).

Skill 24: Dealing with Fear

Name_____Date_____

SKILL STEPS

1. What?

2. Choose.

   a. Ask to talk.

   b. Relax.

3. Do it.

Who?   When?

How I did

Skillstreaming From *Skillstreaming in Early Childhood: Teaching Prosocial Skills* (3rd ed.), © 2012 by E. McGinnis, Champaign, IL: Research Press (www.researchpress.com, 800-519-2707).

Skill 24: Dealing with Fear

Name_____Date_____

SKILL STEPS

1. What?

2. Choose.

    a. Ask to talk.

    b. Relax.

3. Do it.

I did it!

Skillstreaming

From *Skillstreaming in Early Childhood: Teaching Prosocial Skills* (3rd ed.), © 2012 by E. McGinnis, Champaign, IL: Research Press (www.researchpress.com, 800-519-2707).

Skill 25: Deciding How Someone Feels

SKILL STEPS

1. **Watch the person.**

   Discuss a variety of feelings, such as frustration, anger, happiness, fear, and so on. Help children describe the kinds of body language and words that correspond to these feelings.

2. **Name the feeling.**

3. **Ask.**

   Decide whether to ask the person if he or she is feeling this way or whether to do something to help that person. If the person seems very angry or upset, point out that it may be best to wait until the person is calm.

SUGGESTED MODELING SITUATIONS

School: A large jar of paint was spilled on a child, and he has started to cry.

Home: A parent has dropped a sack of groceries, and he is shaking his head and sighing.

Peer group: A friend of yours asked someone to play, but the person said no.

COMMENTS

This skill extends Reading Others (Skill 14) to include the verbal expression of feelings. Children might also be encouraged to use Offering Help (Skill 18) following this skill if the circumstances warrant.

RELATED SKILL-SUPPORTING ACTIVITY

When reading stories to the children, ask how they think the characters in the story feel and why.

Skill 25: Deciding How Someone Feels

Name_____ Date_____

SKILL STEPS

1. Watch the person.

2. Name the feeling.

3. Ask.

Who?   When?

How I did

Skillstreaming From *Skillstreaming in Early Childhood: Teaching Prosocial Skills* (3rd ed.), © 2012 by E. McGinnis, Champaign, IL: Research Press (www.researchpress.com, 800-519-2707).

Skill 25: Deciding How Someone Feels

Name_____Date_____

SKILL STEPS

1. Watch the person.

2. Name the feeling.

3. Ask.

I did it!

Skillstreaming From *Skillstreaming in Early Childhood: Teaching Prosocial Skills* (3rd ed.), © 2012 by E. McGinnis, Champaign, IL: Research Press (www.researchpress.com, 800-519-2707).

Skill 26: Showing Affection

SKILL STEPS

1. **Decide if you have nice feelings.**

   Discuss how to decide if you have positive feelings about someone. Talk about the people children might want to show affection to (friends, parents, and teachers versus strangers).

2. **Choose.**

   a. **Say it.**

      Talk about things the children might say to friends, parents, or teachers. Guide the children in appropriate things to say.

   b. **Hug.**

      Discuss that in many situations it would be appropriate to ask if it's OK to give the person a hug (e.g., a new friend, a teacher).

   c. **Do something.**

      Discuss nice things that could be done for someone to show caring.

3. **When?**

   Talk about appropriate times to show affection.

4. **Do it.**

   Children should make one of these choices.

SUGGESTED MODELING SITUATIONS

School: You want to show your teacher that you like her.

Home: You want to show affection to your grandparents.

Peer group: You want to let a friend know that you like him.

COMMENTS

Because several choices are included in this skill, it may be a difficult one for some younger preschoolers. If so, limit the choices. Some children will need additional help to distinguish between people they know well and comparative strangers. Greeting Others (Skill 13) can be suggested for use with people they know less well.

RELATED SKILL-SUPPORTING ACTIVITY

Display the following headings on the chalkboard or easel pad: "Strangers," "New Friends," "Good Friends." Ask the children for examples of each type (e.g., a store clerk, a sister's friend, your best friend). Write the examples under their respective categories. Ask students whether or not they would show affection to this person and, if so, how.

From *Skillstreaming in Early Childhood: Teaching Prosocial Skills* (3rd ed.), © 2012 by E. McGinnis, Champaign, IL: Research Press (www.researchpress.com, 800-519-2707).

Skill 26: Showing Affection

Name_____Date_____

SKILL STEPS

1. Decide if you have nice feelings.

2. Choose.

   a. Say it.

   b. Hug.

   c. Do something.

3. When?

4. Do it.

Who?   When?

How I did

Skill 26: Showing Affection

Name_____Date_____

SKILL STEPS

1. Decide if you have nice feelings.

2. Choose.

    a. Say it.

    b. Hug.

    c. Do something.

3. When?

4. Do it.

I did it!

Skillstreaming

From *Skillstreaming in Early Childhood: Teaching Prosocial Skills* (3rd ed.), © 2012 by E. McGinnis, Champaign, IL: Research Press (www.researchpress.com, 800-519-2707).

Group V

Alternatives to Aggression

Skills 27–31

Skill 27: Dealing with Teasing

SKILL STEPS

1. **Stop and think.**

   Discuss the importance of giving yourself time before reacting and the likely consequences of saying something back or acting aggressively. Talk about the reasons people tease (to get others mad or to get their attention).

2. **Say, "Please stop."**

   Stress the importance of Using Brave Talk (Skill 3), and practice this skill.

3. **Walk away.**

   This step is important to help end the teasing situation. After walking away, the child may need to use other skills, such as Asking to Talk (Skill 23) or Relaxing (Skill 32).

SUGGESTED MODELING SITUATIONS

School: On the playground, someone is calling you a name.

Home: A brother or sister tells you something that you know isn't true—for example, that your face is blue or that you're going out to dinner when you know you're not.

Peer group: A friend is teasing you that she can ride a bike better than you can.

COMMENTS

It may be important for the young child to talk with another friend or adult about the teasing. If the manner in which the child is talking appears to be "tattling," it is valuable for the child to be guided in Knowing When to Tell (Skill 35). To ensure safe school environments, it is critical that the student's concern be addressed. Teachers should assess the severity and frequency of the teasing; if the child's responses do not stop the teasing, teacher intervention with the teaser is indicated.

RELATED SKILL-SUPPORTING ACTIVITIES

Read and discuss the story *The Cow That Went Oink,* by Bernard Most (Harcourt Brace, 1990).

Make a paper chain with the names of students who have used the skill. Add a link whenever a student reports that he or she has used the skill.

Skill 27: Dealing with Teasing

Name_____ Date_____

SKILL STEPS

1. Stop and think.

2. Say, "Please stop."

3. Walk away.

Who?   When?

How I did

Skillstreaming

From *Skillstreaming in Early Childhood: Teaching Prosocial Skills* (3rd ed.), © 2012 by E. McGinnis, Champaign, IL: Research Press (www.researchpress.com, 800-519-2707).

Skill 27: Dealing with Teasing

Name_____Date_____

SKILL STEPS

1. Stop and think.

2. Say, "Please stop."

3. Walk away.

I did it!

Skill 28: Dealing with Feeling Mad

SKILL STEPS

1. **Stop and think.**

   Discuss the importance of stopping and not doing anything. Talk about the negative consequences of acting out this feeling in an aggressive way (e.g., hitting the person). Also discuss that stopping and thinking gives a person time to make choices.

2. **Choose.**

   a. **Turtle.**

   Instruct children to act like turtles, curling up in their shells where they can't see the person with whom they are angry.

   b. **Relax.**

   Refer to Relaxing (Skill 32).

   c. **Ask to talk.**

   Discuss people children can talk to. Refer to Asking to Talk (Skill 23) as needed.

3. **Do it.**

   Children should make one of these choices.

SUGGESTED MODELING SITUATIONS

School: The teacher won't let you have free play.

Home: It's raining, and a parent won't let you ride your bike.

Peer group: A friend has taken your basketball and won't give it back.

COMMENTS

It is important to offer children a choice involving a physical response, such as relaxing or doing the turtle. The turtle technique is taken from Schneider and Robin's (1974) *Turtle Manual.*

RELATED SKILL-SUPPORTING ACTIVITY

Read the story and do the activities included in the *Turtle Manual.*

Skillstreaming

From *Skillstreaming in Early Childhood: Teaching Prosocial Skills* (3rd ed.), © 2012 by E. McGinnis, Champaign, IL: Research Press (www.researchpress.com, 800-519-2707).

Skill 28: Dealing with Feeling Mad

Name_____Date_____

SKILL STEPS

1. Stop and think.

2. Choose.

   a. Turtle.

   b. Relax.

   c. Ask to talk.

3. Do it.

Who?   When?

How I did

From *Skillstreaming in Early Childhood: Teaching Prosocial Skills* (3rd ed.), © 2012 by E. McGinnis, Champaign, IL: Research Press (www.researchpress.com, 800-519-2707).

Skill 28: Dealing with Feeling Mad

Name_____Date_____

SKILL STEPS

1. Stop and think.

2. Choose.

    a. Turtle.

    b. Relax.

    c. Ask to talk.

3. Do it.

I did it!

Skillstreaming

Skill 29: Deciding If It's Fair

SKILL STEPS

1. **Think about how the other person feels.**

   Discuss thinking about how the other person might feel in a situation that isn't fair (e.g., if the teacher always seems to choose one child to help). Talk about how children feel when they perceive things that aren't fair.

2. **What can you do?**

   Decide if there is anything that could be done to make the situation more fair (e.g., sharing).

3. **Do it.**

SUGGESTED MODELING SITUATIONS

School: You or another child has asked the teacher to use the computer that someone else is using.

Home: Both you and your brother or sister want to watch different programs on TV, and your parent says you can watch your program.

Peer group: You want to let another friend play, but the child you're playing with doesn't want the other friend to play, too.

COMMENTS

It is very important that the children begin to understand that things can't always be fair. For example, it might rain when you'd planned to go swimming, or you might get the flu and have to stay home from the school skating party.

RELATED SKILL-SUPPORTING ACTIVITY

Present children with several situations (use situations you have observed in the classroom). Give each child a "Fair" and "Not Fair" card. Ask the children to indicate, by holding up the appropriate card, if the situation is fair or not fair.

From *Skillstreaming in Early Childhood: Teaching Prosocial Skills* (3rd ed.), © 2012 by E. McGinnis, Champaign, IL: Research Press (www.researchpress.com, 800-519-2707).

Skill 29: Deciding If It's Fair

Name_____Date_____

SKILL STEPS

1. Think about how the other person feels.

2. What can you do?

3. Do it. (GO)

Who?   When?

How I did

Skillstreaming

From *Skillstreaming in Early Childhood: Teaching Prosocial Skills* (3rd ed.), © 2012 by E. McGinnis, Champaign, IL: Research Press (www.researchpress.com, 800-519-2707).

Skill 29: Deciding If It's Fair

Name_____Date_____

SKILL STEPS

1. Think about how the other person feels.

2. What can you do?

3. Do it.

I did it!

From *Skillstreaming in Early Childhood: Teaching Prosocial Skills* (3rd ed.), © 2012 by E. McGinnis, Champaign, IL: Research Press (www.researchpress.com, 800-519-2707).

Skill 30: Solving a Problem

SKILL STEPS

1. **Decide on the problem.**

   Children may need help in defining the problem.

2. **Think of choices.**

   Generate different alternatives children could choose, and discuss the likely consequences of each choice.

3. **Make a plan.**

   Decide on one choice to try and plan how to do this.

4. **Do it.**

SUGGESTED MODELING SITUATIONS

School: You have trouble following the teacher's directions.

Home: You have a problem going to bed on time.

Peer group: You like playing with one friend but get upset when another friend comes over to play, too.

COMMENTS

Generating alternatives and anticipating consequences are necessary skills for students to learn. Alternative and consequential thinking, along with goal setting and communication skills, enhance children's social competence.

RELATED SKILL-SUPPORTING ACTIVITY

Have children generate a plan for solving a real-life problem and draw a picture of the plan to share with parents and serve as a reminder to themselves.

Skillstreaming

From *Skillstreaming in Early Childhood: Teaching Prosocial Skills* (3rd ed.), © 2012 by E. McGinnis, Champaign, IL: Research Press (www.researchpress.com, 800-519-2707).

Skill 30: Solving a Problem

Name_____ Date_____

SKILL STEPS

1. Decide on the problem.

2. Think of choices.

3. Make a plan.

4. Do it.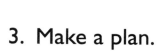

Who?   When?

How I did

From *Skillstreaming in Early Childhood: Teaching Prosocial Skills* (3rd ed.), © 2012 by E. McGinnis, Champaign, IL: Research Press (www.researchpress.com, 800-519-2707).

Skill 30: Solving a Problem

Name_____Date_____

SKILL STEPS

1. Decide on the problem.

2. Think of choices.

3. Make a plan.

4. Do it.

I did it!

Skillstreaming

From *Skillstreaming in Early Childhood: Teaching Prosocial Skills* (3rd ed.), © 2012 by E. McGinnis, Champaign, IL: Research Press (www.researchpress.com, 800-519-2707).

Skill 31: Accepting Consequences

SKILL STEPS

1. **Stop and think.**

   Stress that this step will give children time to calm down and follow the rest of the steps.

2. **Decide if you're wrong.**

   Discuss that it's OK for people to be wrong. Everyone makes mistakes sometimes.

3. **Say, "Yes, I did it. I'm sorry."**

   Emphasize the importance of Using Nice Talk (Skill 2) when apologizing and being honest when admitting to doing something wrong.

4. **Follow the direction.**

   Explain that children may need to do something to resolve the problem (e.g., clean up a mess or help pay for something they broke).

SUGGESTED MODELING SITUATIONS

School: You spilled another child's glass of juice.

Home: You broke something of your parents.

Peer group: You took a friend's toy without permission.

COMMENTS

Some children may have difficulty verbally admitting their behavior or saying they are sorry. If so, this step could be deleted or another step (perhaps nodding your head yes) could be substituted.

RELATED SKILL-SUPPORTING ACTIVITIES

Read *The Tale of Peter Rabbit,* by Beatrix Potter (Warner, 1976). Discuss the mistakes Peter made and how he accepted the consequences.

List common mistakes that children of this age make. Use a puppet or present a picture of an unknown child. As a group, discuss the probable consequences and decide how the puppet or child might respond.

From *Skillstreaming in Early Childhood: Teaching Prosocial Skills* (3rd ed.), © 2012 by E. McGinnis, Champaign, IL: Research Press (www.researchpress.com, 800-519-2707).

Skill 31: Accepting Consequences

Name_____ Date_____

SKILL STEPS

1. Stop and think.

2. Decide if you're wrong.

3. Say, "Yes, I did it. I'm sorry."

4. Follow the direction.

Who?   When?

How I did

Skillstreaming

From *Skillstreaming in Early Childhood: Teaching Prosocial Skills* (3rd ed.), © 2012 by E. McGinnis, Champaign, IL: Research Press (www.researchpress.com, 800-519-2707).

Skill 31: Accepting Consequences

Name_____Date_____

SKILL STEPS

1. Stop and think.

2. Decide if you're wrong.

3. Say, "Yes, I did it. I'm sorry."

4. Follow the direction.

I did it!

From *Skillstreaming in Early Childhood: Teaching Prosocial Skills* (3rd ed.), © 2012
by E. McGinnis, Champaign, IL: Research Press (www.researchpress.com, 800-519-2707).

Group VI

Dealing with Stress

Skills 32–40

Skill 32: Relaxing

SKILL STEPS

1. **Think about how you feel.**

   Talk about how children feel when they are tense (jittery inside, getting a stomachache, tight or warm all over, etc.).

2. **Take three deep breaths.**

   Teach the children how to take relaxing breaths: Take a big breath in slowly, then let the air out through an open mouth. Have everyone practice this step.

3. **Squeeze the oranges.**

   Pretend to give each child an orange in each hand. Have children tighten their fists to squeeze all the juice out of each orange in turn, then both oranges together. Finally, have them drop the oranges and shake the rest of the juice off their hands.

SUGGESTED MODELING SITUATIONS

School: You are putting on an important puppet show for another class.

Home: You are going on vacation, and you're excited; a parent seems angry with you, and you don't know why.

Peer group: You are waiting to go to a friend's birthday party.

COMMENTS

Children may need a great deal of training in relaxation before they will be able to use this skill effectively. Having them practice this skill each day before rest time may help them to fall asleep more easily.

RELATED SKILL-SUPPORTING ACTIVITY

Practice this skill as a group before a change in routine (e.g., field trips, assemblies) and before classroom activities that are typically difficult for the children.

Skill 32: Relaxing

Name_____ Date_____

SKILL STEPS

1. Think about how you feel.

2. Take three deep breaths.

3. Squeeze the oranges.

Who?   When?

How I did

Skillstreaming

From *Skillstreaming in Early Childhood: Teaching Prosocial Skills* (3rd ed.), © 2012
by E. McGinnis, Champaign, IL: Research Press (www.researchpress.com, 800-519-2707).

Skill 32: Relaxing

Name_____Date_____

SKILL STEPS

1. Think about how you feel.

2. Take three deep breaths.

3. Squeeze the oranges.

I did it!

Skillstreaming   From *Skillstreaming in Early Childhood: Teaching Prosocial Skills* (3rd ed.), © 2012 by E. McGinnis, Champaign, IL: Research Press (www.researchpress.com, 800-519-2707).

Skill 33: Dealing with Mistakes

SKILL STEPS

1. **Say, "It's OK to make mistakes. Everybody makes mistakes."**

   Discuss mistakes that you have made. Encourage the children to talk about mistakes they have made. Use humor if appropriate.

2. **Plan for next time.**

   Have children plan how they could avoid making the same mistakes again. Ideas might include taking more time, asking for help, asking a question, and so on.

SUGGESTED MODELING SITUATIONS

School: You make a mistake on an art project.

Home: You make a mistake while helping your parent with cooking.

Peer group: You invited a friend over but forgot to ask your parent's permission.

COMMENTS

Discuss how making a plan before engaging in a difficult task may help prevent mistakes, and encourage each child to make such a plan. Because the skill does not require the child to take immediate action, it will be helpful to post the plan in the classroom or at home so the child will have easy reference to it when needed. (Use pictures to illustrate plans for nonreaders.)

RELATED SKILL-SUPPORTING ACTIVITY

Have everyone who wants to (including yourself) share "most embarrassing moments."

Skillstreaming

From *Skillstreaming in Early Childhood: Teaching Prosocial Skills* (3rd ed.), © 2012 by E. McGinnis, Champaign, IL: Research Press (www.researchpress.com, 800-519-2707).

Skill 33: Dealing with Mistakes

Name_____Date_____

SKILL STEPS

1. Say, "It's OK to make mistakes. Everybody makes mistakes."

2. Plan for next time.

Who?   When?

How I did

From *Skillstreaming in Early Childhood: Teaching Prosocial Skills* (3rd ed.), © 2012 by E. McGinnis, Champaign, IL: Research Press (www.researchpress.com, 800-519-2707).   **225**

Skill 33: Dealing with Mistakes

Name_____Date_____

SKILL STEPS

1. Say, "It's OK to make mistakes. Everybody makes mistakes."

2. Plan for next time.

I did it!

Skillstreaming

From *Skillstreaming in Early Childhood: Teaching Prosocial Skills* (3rd ed.), © 2012 by E. McGinnis, Champaign, IL: Research Press (www.researchpress.com, 800-519-2707).

Skill 34: Being Honest

SKILL STEPS

1. **Think of what can happen.**

   Help children construct lists of likely consequences of telling and not telling the truth. Also discuss how being honest can sometimes be hurtful (e.g., saying you don't like a person's haircut).

2. **Decide to tell the truth.**

   Discuss how punishing consequences are usually less severe if a person is honest at the start.

3. **Say it.**

   Discuss and practice examples of telling the truth, such as "I'm sorry I did it" or "Yes, but I didn't mean to." Emphasize Using Nice Talk (Skill 2).

SUGGESTED MODELING SITUATIONS

School: You accidentally broke one of the school's toys.

Home: You hit your brother or sister when you were angry; you went across the street without permission.

Peer group: You said something about a friend that was true but not very nice.

COMMENTS

Children should be rewarded for telling the truth, even though there may be other negative consequences for their actions. Encourage children to use Rewarding Yourself (Skill 5) for being honest.

RELATED SKILL-SUPPORTING ACTIVITY

Spend time discussing the difference between telling "tall tales" and being dishonest. Read the story of Paul Bunyan, and explain that this is a tall tale. Have the children make up their own tall tales. Later, if a child's honesty is questionable, it's OK to ask if he or she is telling a tall tale.

Skill 34: Being Honest

Name_____Date_____

SKILL STEPS

1. Think of what can happen.

2. Decide to tell the truth.

3. Say it.  I did it.

Who?   When?

How I did

Skillstreaming

Skill 34: Being Honest

Name_____Date_____

SKILL STEPS

1. Think of what can happen.

2. Decide to tell the truth.

3. Say it.

I did it!

From *Skillstreaming in Early Childhood: Teaching Prosocial Skills* (3rd ed.), © 2012 by E. McGinnis, Champaign, IL: Research Press (www.researchpress.com, 800-519-2707).

Skill 35: Knowing When to Tell

SKILL STEPS

1. **Decide if someone will get hurt.**

   Explain that children need to decide if the action is likely to hurt the person involved, themselves, or someone else.

2. **Whom should you tell?**

   If the action will not result in someone's getting hurt (e.g., one child's taking a toy from another), the child should first talk to the person with whom he or she has the problem, perhaps using Asking a Favor (Skill 7) or Dealing with Teasing (Skill 27) as needed. If the action will cause harm, the child should tell a teacher, parent, or other responsible adult immediately.

3. **Do it.**

   This should be done in a helpful, friendly way.

SUGGESTED MODELING SITUATIONS

School: Someone threatens to hit you; someone takes your crayons without asking.

Home: A brother or sister is playing with matches.

Peer group: A friend won't share her candy with you.

COMMENTS

This skill is designed to help children know when to involve an adult in a problem and when to attempt to deal with the problem themselves. Toward this end, discuss different types of things that cause hurt to others, such as hitting, pinching, inappropriate touching, or excessive tickling.

Even when no actual harm will be done, children should feel free to approach adults to discuss ways of dealing with a problem or to talk about the feelings associated with a situation. These are positive behaviors, as opposed to tattling, which has a negative purpose. If a child does approach you about minor peer conflicts, a helpful response is "How can I help you deal with that?"

RELATED SKILL-SUPPORTING ACTIVITY

Develop a list of common situations, and write these (or display pictures of them) on a chart. As a class, decide if children should tell or try to solve the problem themselves. Relative to each situation, discuss or role-play following through with the decision.

From *Skillstreaming in Early Childhood: Teaching Prosocial Skills* (3rd ed.), © 2012 by E. McGinnis, Champaign, IL: Research Press (www.researchpress.com, 800-519-2707).

Skill 35: Knowing When to Tell

Name_____Date_____

SKILL STEPS

1. Decide if someone will get hurt.

2. Whom should you tell?

3. Do it.

Who?   When?

How I did

From *Skillstreaming in Early Childhood: Teaching Prosocial Skills* (3rd ed.), © 2012 by E. McGinnis, Champaign, IL: Research Press (www.researchpress.com, 800-519-2707).

Skill 35: Knowing When to Tell

Name_____ Date_____

SKILL STEPS

1. Decide if someone will get hurt.

2. Whom should you tell?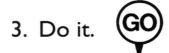

3. Do it.

I did it!

Skillstreaming

From *Skillstreaming in Early Childhood: Teaching Prosocial Skills* (3rd ed.), © 2012 by E. McGinnis, Champaign, IL: Research Press (www.researchpress.com, 800-519-2707).

Skill 36: Dealing with Losing

SKILL STEPS

1. **Say, "Everybody can't win."**

   Point out the absurdity of having everyone win a game. Affirm that it is normal to feel disappointed at not winning; discuss the feelings that children have when they don't win.

2. **Say, "Maybe I'll win next time."**

   Children should be encouraged to say this in a hopeful, coping manner.

3. **Do something else.**

   Point out that, although it's OK to feel disappointed, continuing to think about the disappointment may only cause children to have a bad time.

SUGGESTED MODELING SITUATIONS

School: Your group loses at Duck-Duck-Goose (or another game).

Home: You didn't win when playing a game with a brother, sister, or parent.

Peer group: You came in second in a running race with friends.

COMMENTS

Cooperative games and activities have been found to teach more positive skills than do competitive activities. When possible, cooperative activities, versus competitive ones, should be included in the school curriculum.

RELATED SKILL-SUPPORTING ACTIVITY

Create times in the classroom when the children can play board games. Prior to beginning the games, set out Dealing with Losing Skill Cards (one fewer than the number of students playing). Tell students that each student who uses the skill after the game should take a card and bring it to you. Congratulate the students for using the skill.

Skill 36: Dealing with Losing

Name_____ Date_____

SKILL STEPS

1. Say, "Everybody can't win."

2. Say, "Maybe I'll win next time."

3. Do something else.

Who?   When?

How I did

Skillstreaming

From *Skillstreaming in Early Childhood: Teaching Prosocial Skills* (3rd ed.), © 2012 by E. McGinnis, Champaign, IL: Research Press (www.researchpress.com, 800-519-2707).

Skill 36: Dealing with Losing

Name_____Date_____

SKILL STEPS

1. Say, "Everybody can't win."

2. Say, "Maybe I'll win next time."

3. Do something else.

I did it!

From *Skillstreaming in Early Childhood: Teaching Prosocial Skills* (3rd ed.), © 2012 by E. McGinnis, Champaign, IL: Research Press (www.researchpress.com, 800-519-2707).

Skill 37: Wanting to Be First

SKILL STEPS

1. **Say, "Everybody can't be first."**

   Discuss how the children feel when they are first and when they aren't first. Talk about how it would be impossible for everyone to be first.

2. **Say, "It's OK not to be first."**

3. **Stay with it.**

   Talk about what children would miss if they quit the activity because they weren't first (e.g., the pleasure of playing a game or being part of an activity).

SUGGESTED MODELING SITUATIONS

School: You're not first in line for recess or lunch.

Home: A brother or sister gets to sit in the front seat on the way to the park, but you have to wait until the ride home.

Peer group: A friend gets to be first when playing a game.

COMMENTS

Many teachers of preschool or kindergarten children find it helpful to initiate a "Child of the Week" program, in which one child is chosen to share personal things, such as pictures and special toys, and gets to be the line leader and first at special activities. Other teachers choose children to perform specific classroom duties and to be line leaders on a daily basis. Such activities tend to diminish the frequency of children's distress at not being first.

RELATED SKILL-SUPPORTING ACTIVITY

With the children, make a class plan to help them handle the disappointment of not being first (e.g., one child's telling another child to go first). Have the children practice the plan while putting together a jigsaw puzzle. For example, one child is to say, "You can go first." The other can say, "Thank you." Periodically, direct children to use the class plan.

From *Skillstreaming in Early Childhood: Teaching Prosocial Skills* (3rd ed.), © 2012 by E. McGinnis, Champaign, IL: Research Press (www.researchpress.com, 800-519-2707).

Skill 37: Wanting to Be First

Name_____Date_____

SKILL STEPS

1. Say, "Everybody can't be first."

2. Say, "It's OK not to be first."

3. Stay with it.

Who?   When?

How I did

Skill 37: Wanting to Be First

Name_____Date_____

SKILL STEPS

1. Say, "Everybody can't be first."

2. Say, "It's OK not to be first."

3. Stay with it.

I did it!

Skillstreaming From *Skillstreaming in Early Childhood: Teaching Prosocial Skills* (3rd ed.), © 2012 by E. McGinnis, Champaign, IL: Research Press (www.researchpress.com, 800-519-2707).

Skill 38: Saying No

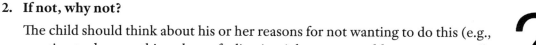

SKILL STEPS

1. **Decide if you want to do it.**

   The child needs to decide whether or not he or she wants to do what is being asked. Discuss situations when saying no is appropriate and when it is not.

2. **If not, why not?**

   The child should think about his or her reasons for not wanting to do this (e.g., wanting to do something else or feeling it might cause trouble or unnecessarily hurt someone else's feelings).

3. **Say, "No."**

   Stress the importance of Using Nice Talk (Skill 2) when saying no. Point out that the child might also want to give the reason for saying no.

SUGGESTED MODELING SITUATIONS

School: A friend wants you to leave the classroom.

Home: A younger brother or sister wants you to stay home and play, but you want to play at a friend's house.

Peer group: A friend wants you to go to the park, but you want to go swimming with another friend.

COMMENTS

Most situations will require Using Nice Talk (Skill 2). However, if a child is being pressured to do something he or she knows is wrong, Using Brave Talk (Skill 3) would be more appropriate.

RELATED SKILL-SUPPORTING ACTIVITY

Read the story *The Toll-Bridge Troll,* by Patricia Rae Wolff (Browndeer, 1995). Discuss how Trigg said no to the troll and whether this was a good way of saying this.

Skill 38: Saying No

Name_____Date_____

SKILL STEPS

1. Decide if you want to do it.

2. If not, why not?

3. Say, "No."

Who?   When?

How I did

Skillstreaming
From *Skillstreaming in Early Childhood: Teaching Prosocial Skills* (3rd ed.), © 2012
by E. McGinnis, Champaign, IL: Research Press (www.researchpress.com, 800-519-2707).

Skill 38: Saying No

Name_____Date_____

SKILL STEPS

1. Decide if you want to do it.

2. If not, why not?

3. Say, "No."

_____

I did it!

Skillstreaming From *Skillstreaming in Early Childhood: Teaching Prosocial Skills* (3rd ed.), © 2012 by E. McGinnis, Champaign, IL: Research Press (www.researchpress.com, 800-519-2707).

Skill 39: Accepting No

SKILL STEPS

1. **Stop and think.**

   Discuss the possible reasons children might be told no in various situations.

2. **Choose.**

   a. **Do something else.**

      Discuss the fact that, even though you are told you can't do or have something, you can still have fun by doing something else.

   b. **Ask to talk.**

      Stress that children can use Asking to Talk (Skill 23) if they do not understand the reason for being told no. However, point out that Using Nice Talk (Skill 2) is very important, or the parent or teacher may interpret their questions as arguing. Discuss that the goal of asking is to better understand the adult's decision, not to have the adult change the decision.

3. **Do it.**

   Children should make one of these choices.

SUGGESTED MODELING SITUATIONS

School: A teacher tells you that it's time to do art and that you can't have free play.

Home: A parent tells you that it's too late to go to a friend's house to play or that you can't get a toy at the grocery store.

Peer group: A friend tells you that he can't play today or won't let you play with one of his toys.

COMMENTS

This skill may be difficult for many young children to accomplish; many practice sessions should be planned.

RELATED SKILL-SUPPORTING ACTIVITY

Accepting being told no is often very difficult for young children. Develop "Accepting No" cards that depict a special privilege on the back (e.g., computer, book, rocking chair). Throughout the day, when a child uses the skill, let that child choose a card to show which privilege he or she has earned.

Skillstreaming

From *Skillstreaming in Early Childhood: Teaching Prosocial Skills* (3rd ed.), © 2012 by E. McGinnis, Champaign, IL: Research Press (www.researchpress.com, 800-519-2707).

Skill 39: Accepting No

Name_____Date_____

SKILL STEPS

1. Stop and think.

2. Choose.

    a. Do something else.

    b. Ask to talk.

3. Do it.

Who?   When?

How I did

Skillstreaming From *Skillstreaming in Early Childhood: Teaching Prosocial Skills* (3rd ed.), © 2012 by E. McGinnis, Champaign, IL: Research Press (www.researchpress.com, 800-519-2707).

Skill 39: Accepting No

Name_____Date_____

SKILL STEPS

1. Stop and think.

2. Choose.

   a. Do something else.

   b. Ask to talk.

3. Do it.

I did it!

Skillstreaming

From *Skillstreaming in Early Childhood: Teaching Prosocial Skills* (3rd ed.), © 2012 by E. McGinnis, Champaign, IL: Research Press (www.researchpress.com, 800-519-2707).

Skill 40: Deciding What to Do

SKILL STEPS

1. **Think about what you like to do.**

   Help the children generate lists of things they like to do that would be acceptable in different situations.

2. **Decide on one thing.**

3. **Do it.**

SUGGESTED MODELING SITUATIONS

School: It's free-play time.

Home: It's a rainy afternoon, and everyone in the house is busy.

Peer group: You and a friend can't think of anything to do.

COMMENTS

After children successfully complete this skill, you may want to encourage them to use Rewarding Yourself (Skill 5).

RELATED SKILL-SUPPORTING ACTIVITY

Have children draw pictures on index cards of activities they enjoy. Have each child place his or her cards in a file box under the headings "Home," "School," and "Outdoors." When a child complains of not having anything to do, the child can consult his or her own personal card file.

Skill 40: Deciding What to Do

Name_____Date_____

SKILL STEPS

1. Think about what you like to do.

2. Decide on one thing.

3. Do it.

Who?   When?

How I did

From *Skillstreaming in Early Childhood: Teaching Prosocial Skills* (3rd ed.), © 2012 by E. McGinnis, Champaign, IL: Research Press (www.researchpress.com, 800-519-2707).

Skill 40: Deciding What to Do

Name_____Date_____

SKILL STEPS

1. Think about what you like to do.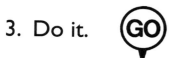

2. Decide on one thing.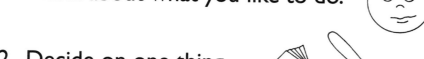

3. Do it. GO

I did it!

APPENDIX A

Program Forms

TEACHER/STAFF CHECKLIST

Student _____ Class/age _____

Teacher/staff _____ Date _____

INSTRUCTIONS: Listed below are a number of skills that children are more or less proficient in using. This checklist will help you evaluate how well each child uses the various skills. For each child, rate his/her use of each skill, based on your observations of his/her behavior in various situations.

Circle 1 if the child is *almost never* good at using the skill.

Circle 2 if the child is *seldom* good at using the skill.

Circle 3 if the child is *sometimes* good at using the skill.

Circle 4 if the child is *often* good at using the skill.

Circle 5 if the child is *almost always* good at using the skill.

Please rate the child on all skills listed. If you know of a situation in which the child has particular difficulty using the skill well, please note it briefly in the space marked "Problem situation."

	almost never	seldom	sometimes	often	almost always

1. **Listening:** Does the child appear to listen when someone is speaking and make an effort to understand what is said?

   Problem situation: 1 2 3 4 5

2. **Using Nice Talk:** Does the child speak to others in a friendly manner?

   Problem situation: 1 2 3 4 5

3. **Using Brave Talk:** Does the child use a brave or assertive tone of voice in a conflict with another child?

   Problem situation: 1 2 3 4 5

4. **Saying Thank You:** Does the child say thank you or in another way let others know he/she appreciates help given, favors, and so forth?

   Problem situation: 1 2 3 4 5

5. **Rewarding Yourself:** Does the child say when he/she has done a good job?

   Problem situation: 1 2 3 4 5

From *Skillstreaming in Early Childhood: Teaching Prosocial Skills* (3rd ed.), © 2012 by E. McGinnis, Champaign, IL: Research Press (www.researchpress.com, 800-519-2707).

251

6. **Asking for Help:** Does the child request help when needed in an acceptable manner?

    Problem situation:

1   2   3   4   5

7. **Asking a Favor:** Does the child ask favors of others in an acceptable way?

    Problem situation:

1   2   3   4   5

8. **Ignoring:** Does the child ignore other children or situations when it is desirable to do so?

    Problem situation:

1   2   3   4   5

9. **Asking a Question:** Does the child ask questions about something he/she doesn't understand?

    Problem situation:

1   2   3   4   5

10. **Following Directions:** Does the child seem to understand directions and follow them?

    Problem situation:

1   2   3   4   5

11. **Trying When It's Hard:** Does the child continue to try when something is difficult instead of giving up?

    Problem situation:

1   2   3   4   5

12. **Interrupting:** Does the child interrupt when necessary in an appropriate manner?

    Problem situation:

1   2   3   4   5

13. **Greeting Others:** Does the child acknowledge acquaintances when it is appropriate to do so?

    Problem situation:

1   2   3   4   5

14. **Reading Others:** Does the child pay attention to a person's nonverbal language and seem to understand what is being communicated?

    Problem situation:

1   2   3   4   5

	almost never	seldom	sometimes	often	almost always

15. **Joining In:** Does the child use acceptable ways of joining in an ongoing activity or group?

Problem situation:

      1   2   3   4   5

16. **Waiting Your Turn:** Does the child wait his/her turn when playing a game with others?

Problem situation:

      1   2   3   4   5

17. **Sharing:** Does the child share most materials and toys with peers?

Problem situation:

      1   2   3   4   5

18. **Offering Help:** Does the child recognize when someone needs or wants help and offer assistance?

Problem situation:

      1   2   3   4   5

19. **Asking Someone to Play:** Does the child ask other children to play or extend an invitation to others to join in his/her activity?

Problem situation:

      1   2   3   4   5

20. **Playing a Game:** Does the child play games with peers in a fair manner?

Problem situation:

      1   2   3   4   5

21. **Knowing Your Feelings:** Does the child identify his/her feelings?

Problem situation:

      1   2   3   4   5

22. **Feeling Left Out:** Does the child deal with being left out of an activity without losing control or becoming upset?

Problem situation:

      1   2   3   4   5

23. **Asking to Talk:** Does the child verbally express when he/she seems upset?

Problem situation:

      1   2   3   4   5

	almost never	seldom	sometimes	often	almost always
24. **Dealing with Fear:** When afraid, does the child know why he/she is afraid and deal with this fear in an acceptable way (e.g., by talking about it)? Problem situation:	1	2	3	4	5
25. **Deciding How Someone Feels:** Does the child identify how another person appears to be feeling by what the person says? Problem situation:	1	2	3	4	5
26. **Showing Affection:** Does the child show that he/she likes someone in an acceptable way? Problem situation:	1	2	3	4	5
27. **Dealing with Teasing:** Does the child deal with being teased in acceptable ways? Problem situation:	1	2	3	4	5
28. **Dealing with Feeling Mad:** Does the child use acceptable ways to express his/her anger? Problem situation:	1	2	3	4	5
29. **Deciding If It's Fair:** Does the child accurately assess what is fair and unfair? Problem situation:	1	2	3	4	5
30. **Solving a Problem:** When a problem occurs, does the child state alternative, prosocial ways to solve the problem? Problem situation:	1	2	3	4	5
31. **Accepting Consequences:** Does the child accept the consequences for his/her behavior without becoming angry or upset? Problem situation:	1	2	3	4	5
32. **Relaxing:** Is the child able to relax when tense or upset? Problem situation:	1	2	3	4	5

33. **Dealing with Mistakes:** Does the child accept making mistakes without becoming upset?

     Problem situation:

almost never 1 seldom 2 sometimes 3 often 4 almost always 5

34. **Being Honest:** Is the child honest when confronted with a negative behavior?

     Problem situation:

1 2 3 4 5

35. **Knowing When to Tell:** Does the child refrain from telling on others about small problems?

     Problem situation:

1 2 3 4 5

36. **Dealing with Losing:** Does the child accept losing at a game or activity without becoming upset or angry?

     Problem situation:

1 2 3 4 5

37. **Wanting to Be First:** Does the child accept not being first at a game or activity?

     Problem situation:

1 2 3 4 5

38. **Saying No:** Does the child say no in an acceptable manner to things he/she doesn't want to do or to things that may get him/her into trouble?

     Problem situation:

1 2 3 4 5

39. **Accepting No:** Does the child accept being told no without becoming upset?

     Problem situation:

1 2 3 4 5

40. **Deciding What to Do:** Does the child choose acceptable activities on his/her own when feeling bored?

     Problem situation:

1 2 3 4 5

PARENT CHECKLIST

Name_____ Date_____

Child's name _____ Birth date _____

INSTRUCTIONS: Based on your observations in various situations, rate your child's use of the following skills.

Circle 1 if the child is *almost never* good at using the skill.

Circle 2 if the child is *seldom* good at using the skill.

Circle 3 if the child is *sometimes* good at using the skill.

Circle 4 if the child is *often* good at using the skill.

Circle 5 if the child is *almost always* good at using the skill.

	almost never	seldom	sometimes	often	almost always
1. **Listening:** Does your child listen and understand when you or others talk to him/her? Comments:	1	2	3	4	5
2. **Using Nice Talk:** Does your child speak to others in a friendly manner? Comments:	1	2	3	4	5
3. **Using Brave Talk:** Does your child use a brave or assertive tone of voice in a conflict with another child? Comments:	1	2	3	4	5
4. **Saying Thank You:** Does your child say thank you or in another way show thanks when someone does something nice for him/her? Comments:	1	2	3	4	5
5. **Rewarding Yourself:** Does your child tell you when he/she has done a good job? Comments:	1	2	3	4	5
6. **Asking for Help:** Does your child ask in a friendly way when he/she needs help? Comments:	1	2	3	4	5

From *Skillstreaming in Early Childhood: Teaching Prosocial Skills* (3rd ed.), © 2012 by E. McGinnis, Champaign, IL: Research Press (www.researchpress.com, 800-519-2707).

almost never	seldom	sometimes	often	almost always

7. **Asking a Favor:** Does your child ask favors of others in an acceptable way?

    1   2   3   4   5

Comments:

8. **Ignoring:** Does your child ignore other children or situations when it is desirable to ignore them?

    1   2   3   4   5

Comments:

9. **Asking a Question:** Does your child ask questions about something he/she doesn't understand?

    1   2   3   4   5

Comments:

10. **Following Directions:** Does your child seem to understand and follow directions that you give?

    1   2   3   4   5

Comments:

11. **Trying When It's Hard:** Does your child continue to try when something is difficult instead of giving up?

    1   2   3   4   5

Comments:

12. **Interrupting:** Does your child know when and how to interrupt when he/she needs something?

    1   2   3   4   5

Comments:

13. **Greeting Others:** Does your child acknowledge acquaintances when it is appropriate to do so?

    1   2   3   4   5

Comments:

14. **Reading Others:** Does your child pay attention to a person's nonverbal language and seem to understand what is being communicated?

    1   2   3   4   5

Comments:

15. **Joining In:** Does your child use acceptable ways of joining in an activity with friends or family?

    1   2   3   4   5

Comments:

	almost never	seldom	sometimes	often	almost always

16. **Waiting Your Turn:** Does your child wait his/her turn when playing a game with others?

    Comments:

                      1 2 3 4 5

17. **Sharing:** Does your child share most materials and toys with his/her friends?

    Comments:

                      1 2 3 4 5

18. **Offering Help:** Does your child recognize when someone needs or wants help and offer this help?

    Comments:

                      1 2 3 4 5

19. **Asking Someone to Play:** Does your child ask other children to play or join in his/her activity?

    Comments:

                      1 2 3 4 5

20. **Playing a Game:** Does your child play games with friends in a fair manner?

    Comments:

                      1 2 3 4 5

21. **Knowing Your Feelings:** Does your child identify his/her feelings?

    Comments:

                      1 2 3 4 5

22. **Feeling Left Out:** Does your child deal with being left out of an activity without losing control or becoming upset?

    Comments:

                      1 2 3 4 5

23. **Asking to Talk:** Does your child talk about his/her problems when upset?

    Comments:

                      1 2 3 4 5

24. **Dealing with Fear:** Does your child know why he/she is afraid and deal with this fear in an acceptable way (e.g., by talking about it)?

    Comments:

                      1 2 3 4 5

25. **Deciding How Someone Feels:** Does your child identify how another person appears to be feeling by what the person says?

          1   2   3   4   5

Comments:

26. **Showing Affection:** Does your child show that he/she likes someone in an acceptable way?

          1   2   3   4   5

Comments:

27. **Dealing with Teasing:** Does your child deal with being teased in acceptable ways?

          1   2   3   4   5

Comments:

28. **Dealing with Feeling Mad:** Does your child use acceptable ways to express his/her anger?

          1   2   3   4   5

Comments:

29. **Deciding If It's Fair:** Does your child accurately assess what is fair and unfair?

          1   2   3   4   5

Comments:

30. **Solving a Problem:** When a problem occurs, does your child state alternative, acceptable ways to solve the problem?

          1   2   3   4   5

Comments:

31. **Accepting Consequences:** Does your child accept the consequences for his/her behavior without becoming angry or upset?

          1   2   3   4   5

Comments:

32. **Relaxing:** Is your child able to relax when tense or upset?

          1   2   3   4   5

Comments:

33. **Dealing with Mistakes:** Does your child accept making mistakes without becoming upset?

          1   2   3   4   5

Comments:

34. **Being Honest:** Does your child admit that he/she has done something wrong when confronted?

       1   2   3   4   5

Comments:

35. **Knowing When to Tell:** Does your child refrain from telling on others about small problems?

       1   2   3   4   5

Comments:

36. **Dealing with Losing:** Does your child accept losing at a game or activity without becoming upset or angry?

       1   2   3   4   5

Comments:

37. **Wanting to Be First:** Does your child accept not being first at a game or activity?

       1   2   3   4   5

Comments:

38. **Saying No:** Does your child say no in an acceptable way to things he/she doesn't want to do or to things that may get him/her into trouble?

       1   2   3   4   5

Comments:

39. **Accepting No:** Does your child accept being told no without becoming upset?

       1   2   3   4   5

Comments:

40. **Deciding What to Do:** Does your child choose acceptable activities on his/her own when feeling bored?

       1   2   3   4   5

Comments:

CHILD CHECKLIST

INSTRUCTIONS: Ask the child to point to the picture on the Child Response Record corresponding to each question (rabbit, teddy bear, cat, etc.), listen carefully as you read the question, then color the face that shows how he/she feels. Repeat each question at least once.

SESSION 1

1. **Skill 1/rabbit:** Is it easy for you to listen and understand when someone is talking to you?

2. **Skill 2/teddy bear:** Is it easy for you to talk to others in a friendly way?

3. **Skill 3/cat:** Do you tell a person to stop when that person is bothering you without getting upset or mad?

4. **Skill 4/owl:** Do you say thank you or show thanks when someone has said or done something nice for you?

5. **Skill 5/elephant:** Do you tell about things that you do a good job with?

6. **Skill 6/flower:** Is it easy for you to ask in a friendly way when you need help?

7. **Skill 7/pig:** Is it easy for you to ask a favor of someone else?

8. **Skill 8/mouse:** Do you ignore others when they are acting silly?

9. **Skill 9/dog:** Do you ask questions about things you don't understand?

10. **Skill 10/bird:** Do you know what to do when directions are given?

SESSION 2

1. **Skill 11/rabbit:** Do you keep trying when something is hard to do?

2. **Skill 12/teddy bear:** When you want or need something from a teacher or parent who is busy, do you interrupt in a nice way?

3. **Skill 13/cat:** When you walk by somebody you know a little bit, do you smile and say hi?

4. **Skill 14/owl:** Can you tell when someone is sad or mad by how the person looks?

5. **Skill 15/elephant:** Is it easy for you to join in a game if you want to play?

6. **Skill 16/flower:** Is it easy for you to wait your turn when playing a game?

7. **Skill 17/pig:** Is it easy for you to share toys with friends?

8. **Skill 18/mouse:** Do you notice when someone needs or wants help and try to help the person?

9. **Skill 19/dog:** Is it easy for you to ask a friend to play?

10. **Skill 20/bird:** When playing a game, do you play fair?

From *Skillstreaming in Early Childhood: Teaching Prosocial Skills* (3rd ed.), © 2012 by E. McGinnis, Champaign, IL: Research Press (www.researchpress.com, 800-519-2707).

SESSION 3

1. **Skill 21/rabbit:** Is it easy for you to say how you feel (mad, happy, frustrated)?

2. **Skill 22/teddy bear:** Do you still feel OK if you are left out of a game or activity?

3. **Skill 23/cat:** When you feel upset, is it easy for you to talk about why you're upset?

4. **Skill 24/owl:** When you feel afraid, do you talk to somebody about it?

5. **Skill 25/elephant:** Can you tell if somebody else is feeling mad, sad, or afraid by what the person says?

6. **Skill 26/flower:** Is it easy for you to show the people you like that you like them?

7. **Skill 27/pig:** When somebody teases you, can you keep from being upset?

8. **Skill 28/mouse:** Is it easy for you to stay in control when you are mad?

9. **Skill 29/dog:** Can you tell what is fair or not fair?

10. **Skill 30/bird:** If a problem happens, can you think of different ways to handle it—ways that won't get you into trouble?

SESSION 4

1. **Skill 31/rabbit:** Do you accept your punishment when you've done something wrong without getting mad or upset?

2. **Skill 32/teddy bear:** When you feel tense or upset, is it easy for you to calm down?

3. **Skill 33/cat:** When you make a mistake on an activity or in a game, do you still feel OK?

4. **Skill 34/owl:** Do you tell the truth if you have done something wrong?

5. **Skill 35/elephant:** Can you keep from telling on someone else who does something wrong?

6. **Skill 36/flower:** If you lose at a game, can you keep from becoming upset or angry?

7. **Skill 37/pig:** Do you still feel OK if you are not first at a game or activity?

8. **Skill 38/mouse:** Is it easy to say no to something a friend wants you to do that you don't want to do or that might get you into trouble?

9. **Skill 39/dog:** When you are told no to something you want to do, can you keep from becoming upset?

10. **Skill 40/bird:** When you feel bored, can you choose something to do?

Child Checklist (page 2 of 2)

CHILD RESPONSE RECORD

Name _____ Birth date _____

School/program _____

Teacher/evaluator _____ Assessment date _____

1.

2.

3.

4.

Child Response Record (page 2 of 2)

GROUPING CHART

	student names															
GROUP I: Beginning Social Skills																
1. Listening																
2. Using Nice Talk																
3. Using Brave Talk																
4. Saying Thank You																
5. Rewarding Yourself																
6. Asking for Help																
7. Asking a Favor																
8. Ignoring																
GROUP II: School-Related Skills																
9. Asking a Question																
10. Following Directions																
11. Trying When It's Hard																
12. Interrupting																
GROUP III: Friendship-Making Skills																
13. Greeting Others																
14. Reading Others																
15. Joining In																
16. Waiting Your Turn																
17. Sharing																
18. Offering Help																
19. Asking Someone to Play																
20. Playing a Game																
GROUP IV: Dealing with Feelings																
21. Knowing Your Feelings																
22. Feeling Left Out																
23. Asking to Talk																
24. Dealing with Fear																
25. Deciding How Someone Feels																
26. Showing Affection																

	student names																		
GROUP V: Alternatives to Aggression																			
27. Dealing with Teasing																			
28. Dealing with Feeling Mad																			
29. Deciding If It's Fair																			
30. Solving a Problem																			
31. Accepting Consequences																			
GROUP VI: Dealing with Stress																			
32. Relaxing																			
33. Dealing with Mistakes																			
34. Being Honest																			
35. Knowing When to Tell																			
36. Dealing with Losing																			
37. Wanting to Be First																			
38. Saying No																			
39. Accepting No																			
40. Deciding What to Do																			

EARLY CHILDHOOD RUBRIC

Student name _____ Date _____

Evaluator name _____ Position _____

INSTRUCTIONS: Circle the number corresponding to your best assessment of the child's skills. Pre- and postassessment may be completed by circling the number corresponding to skill proficiency in different colors. The specific area of concern (i.e., Academic, Peer Relations, Self-Control, Assertion, or Cooperation) may be circled or highlighted to indicate problematic situations and areas for instruction.

A. Listens (Academic; Cooperation; Peer Relations).

4. Consistently and actively listens to others in almost all academic and behavioral group situations and seems to understand what is said.

3. Consistently listens to others in most academic and behavioral situations and most of the time seems to understand what is being said.

2. Sporadically demonstrates listening and understanding in some group and individual academic and behavioral situations.

1. Rarely, if ever, demonstrates listening behaviors in any situation or setting.

Skills for instruction: Skill 1 (Listening)

Skill 8 (Ignoring)

B. Speaks to others in friendly or assertive ways (Academic; Peer Relations).

4. Consistently speaks to others in friendly or assertive ways appropriate to the social or academic situation.

3. Most of the time speaks to others in friendly or assertive ways appropriate to the social or academic situation.

2. Sporadically is able to speak to others in friendly or assertive ways in some social or academic situations.

1. Rarely, if ever, is able to speak to others appropriately in social or academic situations.

Skills for instruction: Skill 2 (Using Nice Talk)

Skill 3 (Using Brave Talk)

Skill 14 (Reading Others)

C. Asks for help or favors when needed (Academic; Assertion; Peer Relations).

4. Consistently asks for help or favors in appropriate ways whenever needed in academic and social situations.

3. Most of the time asks for help or favors in appropriate ways when needed in most academic and social situations.

2. Sporadically asks for help or favors in appropriate ways when needed in some academic and social situations.

1. Rarely, if ever, asks for help or favors appropriately when needed.

Skills for instruction: Skill 6 (Asking for Help)
Skill 7 (Asking a Favor)
Skill 23 (Asking to Talk)

D. Expresses appreciation (Academic; Peer Relations).

4. Consistently thanks others for help or favors given in appropriate ways in almost all academic and social situations.

3. Most of the time thanks others for help or favors given in appropriate ways in most academic and social situations.

2. Occasionally thanks others for help or favors given in appropriate ways in some academic and social situations.

1. Rarely, if ever, thanks others appropriately for help or favors given in either academic or social situations.

Skill for instruction: Skill 4 (Saying Thank You)

E. Evaluates own performance (Academic; Self-Control; Assertion).

4. Consistently and accurately identifies and rewards self for a job well done.

3. Most of the time identifies when a job is well done and rewards self appropriately.

2. Occasionally identifies when a job is well done and rewards self appropriately.

1. Rarely, if ever, identifies when a job is well done and rewards self appropriately.

Skill for instruction: Skill 5 (Rewarding Yourself)

F. Avoids problematic or conflict situations by ignoring (Peer Relations; Academic; Self-Control; Cooperation).

4. Consistently ignores distracting or problematic peer behavior in academic and social situations when it is appropriate to do so.

3. Most of the time ignores distracting or problematic peer behavior in most academic and social situations when it is appropriate to do so.

2. Occasionally ignores distracting or problematic peer behavior in some academic and social situations when it is appropriate to do so.

1. Rarely, if ever, ignores distracting or problematic peer behavior in any situation.

Skills for instruction: Skill 8 (Ignoring)
Skill 35 (Knowing When to Tell)

G. Follows directions and completes tasks (Academic; Self-Control; Cooperation).

4. Consistently follows directions in almost all academic and cooperative situations, asking questions to clarify and following through to the completion of the task or direction.

3. Most of the time follows directions in most academic and cooperative situations, asking questions to clarify and following through to the completion of the task or direction.

2. Occasionally follows directions in some academic and cooperative situations, at times asking questions to clarify and occasionally following through to the completion of the task or direction.

1. Rarely, if ever, follows directions, asks clarifying questions, or completes tasks.

Skill 9 (Asking a Question)
Skills for instruction: Skill 10 (Following Directions)
Skill 11 (Trying When It's Hard)

H. Interrupts appropriately and under appropriate circumstances (Self-Control; Academic; Assertion).

   4. Consistently interrupts others appropriately when necessary in social and academic situations.

   3. Most of the time interrupts others appropriately when necessary in social and academic situations.

   2. Occasionally interrupts others appropriately when necessary in social and academic situations.

   1. Rarely, if ever, interrupts in an appropriate manner.

     Skills for instruction: Skill 12 (Interrupting)
     Skill 35 (Knowing When to Tell)

I. Initiates contacts with others (Peer Relations; Assertion).

   4. Consistently and actively acknowledges others and joins in activities in the classroom or with peers in an appropriate and natural manner.

   3. Most of the time acknowledges others and joins in activities in the classroom or with peers in an appropriate and natural manner.

   2. Occasionally acknowledges others and sometimes joins in activities in the classroom or with peers in a somewhat appropriate manner.

   1. Rarely, if ever, initiates interaction with others in an appropriate manner.

     Skills for instruction: Skill 13 (Greeting Others)
     Skill 15 (Joining In)
     Skill 19 (Asking Someone to Play)

J. Is sensitive to nonverbal communication (Peer Relations; Self-Control).

   4. Consistently demonstrates understanding of and insight about the nonverbal communication of others in almost all situations.

   3. Most of the time demonstrates understanding of and insight about the nonverbal communication of others in most situations.

   2. Occasionally demonstrates understanding of and insight about the nonverbal communication of others in some situations.

   1. Rarely, if ever, demonstrates understanding and insight, misreading others' nonverbal communication.

     Skills for instruction: Skill 14 (Reading Others)
     Skill 25 (Deciding How Someone Feels)
     Skill 28 (Dealing with Feeling Mad)

K. Plays appropriately with others (Academic; Peer Relations; Self-Control; Assertion; Cooperation).

   4. Consistently and actively cooperates with others during almost all academic or social games.

3. Most of the time cooperates with others during academic or social games.

2. Occasionally cooperates with others during academic or social games.

1. Rarely, if ever, cooperates with others during academic or social games.

   Skills for instruction: Skill 16 (Waiting Your Turn)
       Skill 17 (Sharing)
       Skill 20 (Playing a Game)
       Skill 36 (Dealing with Losing)
       Skill 37 (Wanting to Be First)

L. Understands the feelings of others (Peer Relations; Cooperation; Self-Control).

4. Consistently and actively seeks to understand the feelings of another in almost all appropriate situations when that person is experiencing a problem.

3. Most of the time actively seeks to understand the feelings of another in most appropriate situations when that person is experiencing a problem.

2. Occasionally seeks to understand the feelings of another in most appropriate situations when that person is experiencing a problem.

1. Rarely, if ever, notices or seeks to understand the feelings of another.

   Skill for instruction: Skill 25 (Deciding How Someone Feels)

M. Demonstrates empathy (Peer Relations; Cooperation).

4. Consistently and actively demonstrates empathy toward another when that person is upset or sad.

3. Most of the time demonstrates empathy toward another when that person is upset or sad.

2. Occasionally demonstrates empathy toward another when that person is upset or sad.

1. Rarely, if ever, demonstrates empathy toward another.

   Skills for instruction: Skill 18 (Offering Help)
       Skill 26 (Showing Affection)

N. Identifies own feelings (Self-Control).

4. Consistently identifies own feelings in appropriate situations.

3. Most of the time identifies own feelings in appropriate situations.

2. Occasionally identifies own feelings in appropriate situations.

1. Rarely, if ever, identifies own feelings.

   Skill for instruction: Skill 21 (Knowing Your Feelings)

O. Identifies feelings appropriate to a situation (Assertion; Peer Relations; Academic; Self-Control).

4. Consistently interprets situations accurately and identifies appropriate feelings.

3. Most of the time interprets situations accurately and identifies appropriate feelings.

2. Occasionally interprets situations accurately and identifies appropriate feelings.

1. Rarely, if ever, interprets situations accurately and identifies appropriate feelings.

   Skills for instruction: Skill 11 (Trying When It's Hard)
       Skill 14 (Reading Others)

Skill 21 (Knowing Your Feelings)
Skill 22 (Feeling Left Out)
Skill 24 (Dealing with Fear)
Skill 28 (Dealing with Feeling Mad)
Skill 33 (Dealing with Mistakes)
Skill 36 (Dealing with Losing)

P. Shows affection (Peer Relations; Cooperation).

4. Consistently displays affection appropriate to the person and in appropriate ways when it is relevant to do so.

3. Most of the time displays affection appropriate to the person and in appropriate ways when it is relevant to do so.

2. Occasionally displays affection appropriate to the person and in appropriate ways when it is relevant to do so.

1. Rarely, if ever, displays affection appropriately when it is relevant to do so.

   Skill for instruction: Skill 26 (Showing Affection)

Q. Deals with anger and conflict (Self-Control; Peer Relations; Cooperation).

4. Consistently deals with anger and conflict appropriately in almost all situations.

3. Most of the time deals with anger and conflict appropriately in most situations.

2. Occasionally deals with anger and conflict appropriately in some situations.

1. Rarely, if ever, deals with anger and conflict appropriately in any situation.

   Skills for instruction: Skill 23 (Asking to Talk)
   Skill 28 (Dealing with Feeling Mad)
   Skill 30 (Solving a Problem)
   Skill 31 (Accepting Consequences)
   Skill 32 (Relaxing)
   Skill 33 (Dealing with Mistakes)
   Skill 39 (Accepting No)

R. Deals with peer provocation (Self-Control; Peer Relations).

4. Consistently deals with peer provocation in productive ways.

3. Most of the time deals with peer provocation in productive ways.

2. Occasionally deals with peer provocation in productive ways.

1. Rarely, if ever, deals with peer provocation in productive ways.

   Skills for instruction: Skill 23 (Asking to Talk)
   Skill 27 (Dealing with Teasing)
   Skill 35 (Knowing When to Tell)

S. Decides what is fair (Self-Control; Peer Relations).

4. Consistently and accurately assesses what is fair and unfair in almost all situations when appropriate.

3. Most of the time accurately assesses what is fair and unfair in most situations when appropriate.

2. Occasionally accurately assesses what is fair and unfair in some situations when appropriate.

1. Rarely, if ever, accurately assesses what is fair and unfair.

   Skill for instruction: Skill 29 (Deciding If It's Fair)

T. Accepts consequences (Self-Control; Cooperation; Academic).

4. Consistently accepts consequences of own actions appropriately in almost all situations.

3. Most of the time accepts consequences of own actions appropriately in most situations.

2. Occasionally accepts consequences of own actions appropriately in some situations.

1. Rarely, if ever, accepts consequences of own actions appropriately.

   Skills for instruction: Skill 31 (Accepting Consequences)
   Skill 32 (Relaxing)
   Skill 33 (Dealing with Mistakes)
   Skill 34 (Being Honest)

U. Resists peer pressure (Cooperation; Peer Relations; Self-Control).

4. Consistently says no in an acceptable manner to things he/she doesn't want to do or to things that may be trouble.

3. Most of the time says no in an acceptable manner to things he/she doesn't want to do or to things that may be trouble.

2. Occasionally says no in an acceptable manner to things he/she doesn't want to do or to things that may be trouble.

1. Rarely, if ever, says no in an acceptable manner to things he/she doesn't want to do or to things that may be trouble.

   Skills for instruction: Skill 29 (Deciding If It's Fair)
   Skill 30 (Solving a Problem)
   Skill 38 (Saying No)

V. Accepts being told no (Cooperation; Peer Relations; Self-Control).

4. Consistently accepts being told no in an acceptable way.

3. Most of the time accepts being told no in an acceptable way.

2. Occasionally accepts being told no in an acceptable way.

1. Rarely, if ever, accepts being told no in an acceptable way.

   Skill for instruction: Skill 39 (Accepting No)

W. Uses free time appropriately (Cooperation; Assertion).

4. Consistently selects acceptable activities when feeling bored.

3. Most of the time selects acceptable activities when feeling bored.

2. Occasionally selects acceptable activities when feeling bored.

1. Rarely, if ever, selects acceptable activities when feeling bored.

   Skill for instruction: Skill 40 (Deciding What to Do)

Name_____Date_____

Skill _____

SKILL STEPS

_____

Who?   ## When?

_____

How I did

Name_____Date_____

Skill _____

SKILL STEPS

_____

I did it!

Skillstreaming From *Skillstreaming in Early Childhood: Teaching Prosocial Skills* (3rd ed.), © 2012 by E. McGinnis, Champaign, IL: Research Press (www.researchpress.com, 800-519-2707).

I reached
my goal!

Name _____

Date _____

Skill _____

Great job!

Name _____

Date _____

Skill _____

Good for me!

Name _____

Date _____

Skill _____

Together we can!

Skill _____

Skillstreaming

From *Skillstreaming in Early Childhood: Teaching Prosocial Skills* (3rd ed.), © 2012 by E. McGinnis, Champaign, IL: Research Press (www.researchpress.com, 800-519-2707).

We can do it!

Skill _____

From *Skillstreaming in Early Childhood: Teaching Prosocial Skills* (3rd ed.), © 2012 by E. McGinnis, Champaign, IL: Research Press (www.researchpress.com, 800-519-2707).

Skill Ticket

_____
Name

Skill Ticket

_____
Name

Skill Ticket

_____
Name

Skill Ticket

_____
Name

Skill Ticket

_____
Name

Skill Ticket

_____
Name

Skill Ticket

_____
Name

Skill Ticket

_____
Name

Skillstreaming

From *Skillstreaming in Early Childhood: Teaching Prosocial Skills* (3rd ed.), © 2012 by E. McGinnis, Champaign, IL: Research Press (www.researchpress.com, 800-519-2707).

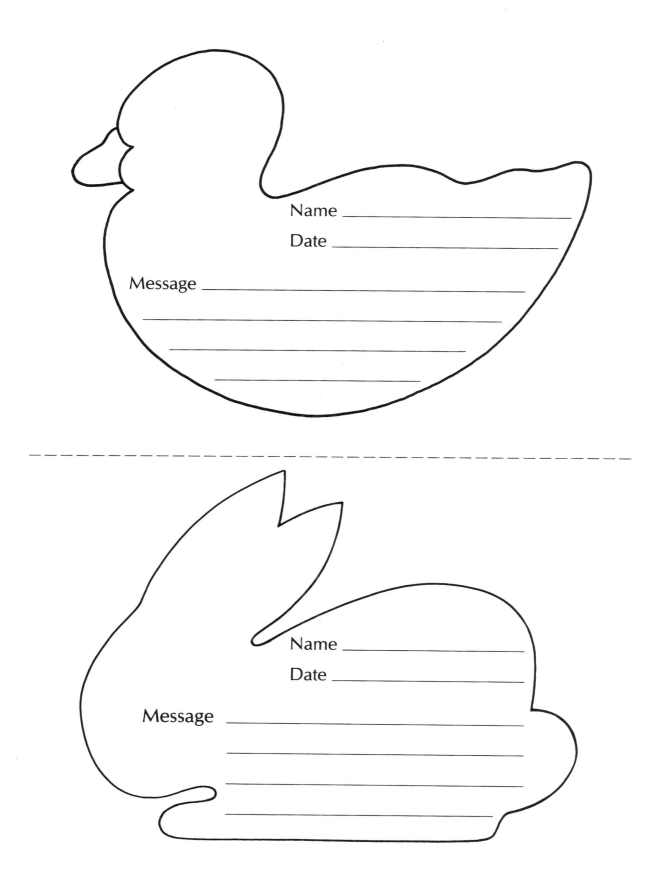

Name _____

Date _____

Message _____

_____

_____

_____

Name _____

Date _____

Message _____

_____

_____

_____

From *Skillstreaming in Early Childhood: Teaching Prosocial Skills* (3rd ed.), © 2012
by E. McGinnis, Champaign, IL: Research Press (www.researchpress.com, 800-519-2707).

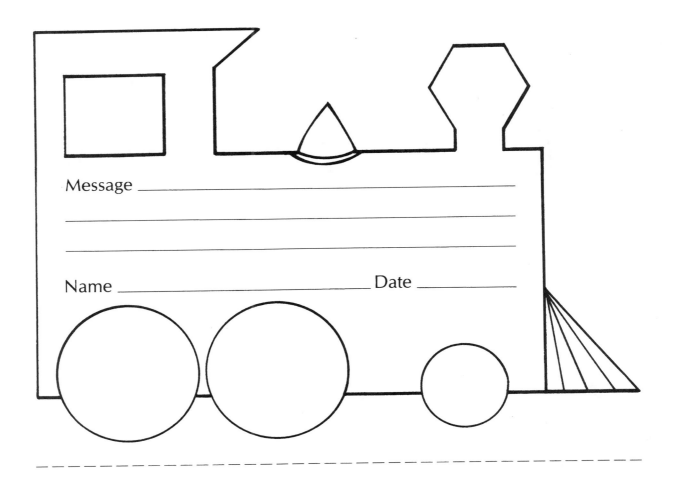

Message _____

_____

_____

Name _____ Date _____

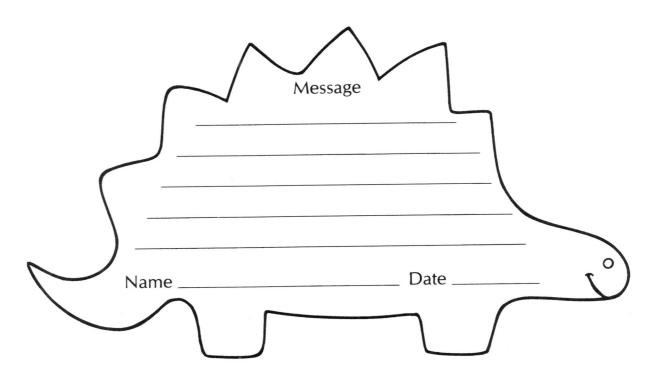

Message

_____

_____

_____

Name _____ Date _____

Skillstreaming

Award

Name _____

Date _____

School Skills Award

Name _____

Date _____

Skillstreaming

From *Skillstreaming in Early Childhood: Teaching Prosocial Skills* (3rd ed.), © 2012 by E. McGinnis, Champaign, IL: Research Press (www.researchpress.com, 800-519-2707).

Friendship Award

Name _____

Date _____

From *Skillstreaming in Early Childhood: Teaching Prosocial Skills* (3rd ed.), © 2012 by E. McGinnis, Champaign, IL: Research Press (www.researchpress.com, 800-519-2707).

Skillstreaming

Dealing with Feelings Award

Name _____

Date _____

Skillstreaming

From *Skillstreaming in Early Childhood: Teaching Prosocial Skills* (3rd ed.), © 2012
by E. McGinnis, Champaign, IL: Research Press (www.researchpress.com, 800-519-2707).

Keeping Your Cool Award

Name _____

Date _____

Dealing with Stress Award

Name _____

Date _____

From *Skillstreaming in Early Childhood: Teaching Prosocial Skills* (3rd ed.), © 2012 by E. McGinnis, Champaign, IL: Research Press (www.researchpress.com, 800-519-2707).

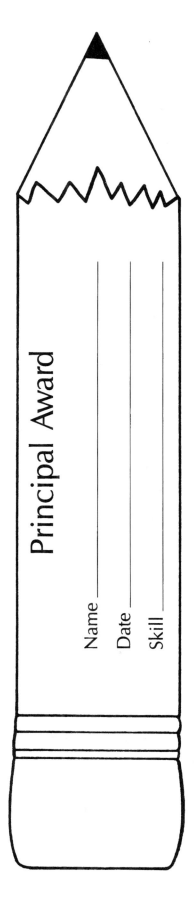

Principal Award

Name _____

Date _____

Skill _____

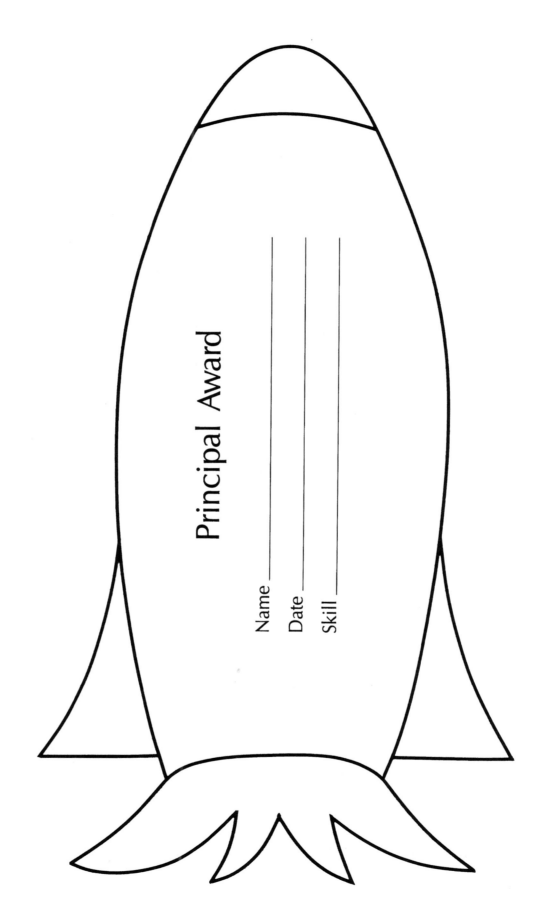

Principal Award

Name _____

Date _____

Skill _____

Skillstreaming

Parent Award

Name _____

Date _____

Parent Signature _____

Skill

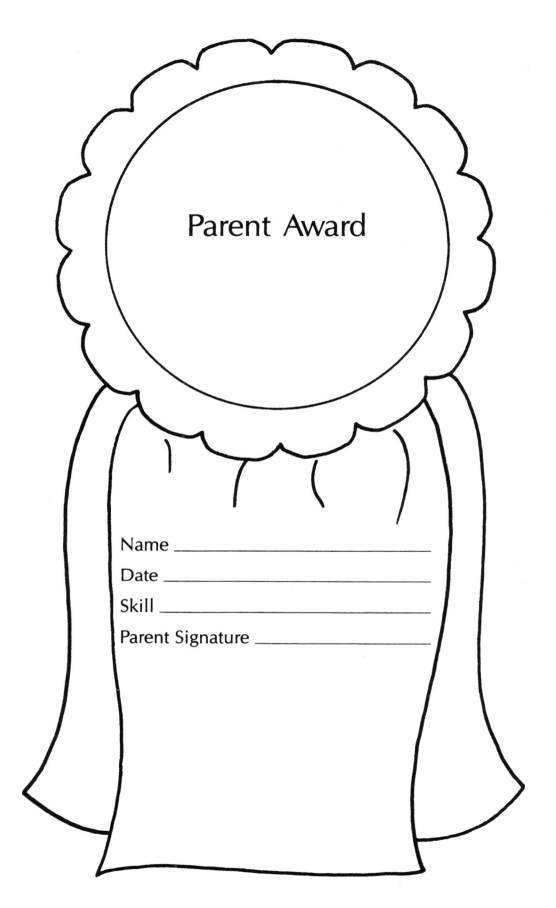

Parent Award

Name _____

Date _____

Skill _____

Parent Signature _____

Skillstreaming

From *Skillstreaming in Early Childhood: Teaching Prosocial Skills* (3rd ed.), © 2012 by E. McGinnis, Champaign, IL: Research Press (www.researchpress.com, 800-519-2707).

PARENT ORIENTATION NOTE

Date _____

Dear Parent or Guardian:

Your child and his or her classmates are learning to handle a variety of day-to-day concerns in positive ways. Sharing, taking turns, handling teasing and anger, and following directions are some of the concerns we are working on. We are all learning specific steps to social skills in order to handle these problems in acceptable ways.

The process we are using to learn these skills is called Skillstreaming. First, your child is watching someone else use the skill. Then he or she will try out the skill and receive feedback about how well he or she performed the skill from both peers and adults. Finally, your child will be asked to practice the skill in real-life situations.

Each week we will be sending home a note describing the skill and its steps. We hope that you review this note with your child and help your child practice the skill at home. Please feel free to call me or e-mail me if you have any questions.

Sincerely,

_____

Phone _____

E-mail _____

PARENT HOMEWORK NOTE I

Student _____ Date _____

Dear Parent or Guardian:

This week we are working on the following skill:

_____

This is a very important skill for your child to learn. The steps of the skill are:

_____

_____

_____

_____

_____

_____

Your child has completed a homework assignment on this skill. Please review this assignment with your child.

Please feel free to call or e-mail me if you have any questions.

Sincerely,

_____

Phone _____

E-mail _____

Skillstreaming

From *Skillstreaming in Early Childhood: Teaching Prosocial Skills* (3rd ed.), © 2012 by E. McGinnis, Champaign, IL: Research Press (www.researchpress.com, 800-519-2707).

PARENT HOMEWORK NOTE 2

Student _____ Date _____

Dear Parent or Guardian:

This week we are working on the following skill:

_____

This is a very important skill for your child to learn. The steps of the skill are:

_____

_____

_____

_____

_____

_____

Your child has learned this skill well but will need continued practice. Please watch for the skill at home! If you see a situation when the skill could be used, please encourage your child to use this skill. Enclosed is a Parent Award to complete and return to school when you see your child use this skill.

Please feel free to call or e-mail me if you have any questions.

Sincerely,

_____

Phone _____

E-mail _____

PARENT HOMEWORK NOTE 3

Student _____ Date _____

Dear Parent or Guardian:

This week we are working on the following skill:

_____

This is a very important skill for your child to learn. The steps of the skill are:

_____

_____

_____

_____

_____

_____

Your child has been asked to complete this skill at home. Please help your child to follow these skill steps.

Please sign and return this form to _____ with your comments (on the back) about quality of homework done and any questions/suggestions by _____.

Parent signature _____ Date _____

Skillstreaming

From *Skillstreaming in Early Childhood: Teaching Prosocial Skills* (3rd ed.), © 2012 by E. McGinnis, Champaign, IL: Research Press (www.researchpress.com, 800-519-2707).

SKILLSTREAMING REQUEST TO PARENTS

Student _____ Date _____

Dear Parent or Guardian:

Your child is working on the following skill(s):

_____

_____

_____

_____

The steps to these skills are attached to this note. Please help your child practice at home by doing the following:

- ▶ Remind your child to use the skill when you see a time the skill could be helpful.
- ▶ Respond positively to your child's skill use (allow the skill use to be successful).
- ▶ Reward your child's use of the skill. (You may use a Parent Award and have your child return this to school.)
- ▶ Ask your child to teach you (or a brother or sister) the skill.
- ▶ Other _____

Please write any comments on the back of this form about how your child is learning and practicing this skill at home.

Sincerely,

_____

From *Skillstreaming in Early Childhood: Teaching Prosocial Skills* (3rd ed.), © 2012 by E. McGinnis, Champaign, IL: Research Press (www.researchpress.com, 800-519-2707).

APPENDIX B

Program Integrity Checklists

LEADER'S CHECKLIST

INSTRUCTIONS: Leader(s) may complete this checklist at the conclusion of the Skillstreaming group by marking "yes" or "no" relative to each procedure implemented.

Group leader(s) _____

Date of group _____ Time of group _____

	Yes	No
Step 1: Define the skill		
1. The skill to be taught was defined, and the group understood its meaning.	☐	☐
2. Skill steps were presented and discussed (via poster or skill cards).	☐	☐
(For all sessions after the first)		
3. Group members' skill homework was discussed.	☐	☐
4. Appropriate reinforcement was provided for group members who completed homework.	☐	☐
Step 2: Model the skill		
5. Two examples of the skill were modeled.	☐	☐
6. Each skill step was identified as the modeling unfolded.	☐	☐
7. Modeling displays were relevant to group members' real-life circumstances.	☐	☐
8. Group members were directed to watch for the steps being modeled.	☐	☐
9. The model was friendly and helpful.	☐	☐
10. A coping model was presented if indicated.	☐	☐
11. The model used self-talk to illustrate the steps and thinking about skill performance.	☐	☐
12. The modeling display depicted positive outcomes.	☐	☐
13. The model was rewarded for skill performance (following the skill steps).	☐	☐
Step 3: Establish student skill need		
14. Each group member's need for skill use was defined (when, where, and with whom) and listed.	☐	☐
Step 4: Select the first role-player		
15. The main actor was selected for role-play (e.g., "Who would like to go first?")	☐	☐
Step 5: Set up the role-play		
16. Main actor selected a coactor who reminded him/her most of the real-life person with whom he/she has the skill need.	☐	☐
17. Main actor described the physical setting, events preceding the problem, mood/manner of the person, and any other relevant information.	☐	☐

Step 6: Conduct the role-play

18. Group members were assigned specific step(s) to observe. ☐ ☐
19. Main actor was instructed to follow the behavioral steps. ☐ ☐
20. Main actor was reminded to "think aloud." ☐ ☐
21. Coactor was reminded to stay in the role of the other person. ☐ ☐
22. Group leader assisted the main actor as needed (pointed to skill steps, coached). ☐ ☐

Step 7: Provide performance feedback

23. Coactor was asked to provide feedback (e.g., how he/she felt, how well the main actor enacted the steps). ☐ ☐
24. Group members were asked if the main actor followed each step. ☐ ☐
25. Leaders provided appropriate feedback (praise, approval, encouragement), identifying specific aspects of the main actor's performance. ☐ ☐
26. Reinforcement in an amount consistent with the quality of role-play was provided. ☐ ☐
27. Main actor was invited to give comments. ☐ ☐

Step 8: Select the next role-player

28. Volunteer participant asked to act as the main actor in the next role-play and coached in Steps 5 through 7. ☐ ☐
29. All group members were given a chance to role-play, or plans were made to role-play for those who did not have a chance. ☐ ☐

Step 9: Assign skill homework

30. Skill homework was assigned to each main actor. ☐ ☐
31. Assistance was provided as needed in identifying the day, place, with whom the skill will be used, and so forth. ☐ ☐

TOTAL YES _____   **TOTAL NO** _____

OBSERVER'S CHECKLIST

INSTRUCTIONS: A highly skilled observer may complete this observation checklist as the Skillstreaming group is taking place. The observer will note whether leader(s) completed each procedure with a low level of competence (score 1), medium proficiency (score 2), or a high level of skill (score 3). At the conclusion of the observation, the observer may provide leader(s) with recommendations for specific steps needing improvement.

Group leader(s) _____ Observers _____

Date of group _____ Time of group _____

	Proficiency Level		
	1	*2*	*3*
Step 1: Define the skill			
1. The skill to be taught was defined and the group understood its meaning.	☐	☐	☐
2. Skill steps were presented and discussed (via poster or skill cards).	☐	☐	☐
(For all sessions after the first)			
3. Group members' skill homework was discussed.	☐	☐	☐
4. Appropriate reinforcement was provided for group members who completed homework.	☐	☐	☐
Step 2: Model the skill			
5. Two examples of the skill were modeled.	☐	☐	☐
6. Each skill step was identified as the modeling unfolded.	☐	☐	☐
7. Modeling displays were relevant to group members' real-life circumstances.	☐	☐	☐
8. Group members were directed to watch for the steps being modeled.	☐	☐	☐
9. The model was friendly and helpful.	☐	☐	☐
10. A coping model was presented if indicated.	☐	☐	☐
11. The model used self-talk to illustrate the steps and thinking about skill performance.	☐	☐	☐
12. The modeling display depicted positive outcomes.	☐	☐	☐
13. The model was rewarded for skill performance (following the skill steps).	☐	☐	☐
Step 3: Establish student skill need			
14. Each group member's need for skill use was defined (when, where, and with whom) and listed.	☐	☐	☐
Step 4: Select the first role-player			
15. The main actor was selected for role-play (e.g., "Who would like to go first?")	☐	☐	☐

Step 5: Set up the role-play

16. Main actor selected a coactor who reminded him/her most of the real-life person with whom he/she has the skill need. ☐ ☐ ☐

17. Main actor described the physical setting, events preceding the problem, mood/manner of the person, and any other relevant information. ☐ ☐ ☐

Step 6: Conduct the role-play

18. Group members were assigned specific step(s) to observe. ☐ ☐ ☐
19. Main actor was instructed to follow the behavioral steps. ☐ ☐ ☐
20. Main actor was reminded to "think aloud." ☐ ☐ ☐
21. Coactor was reminded to stay in the role of the other person. ☐ ☐ ☐
22. Group leader assisted the main actor as needed (pointed to skill steps, coached). ☐ ☐ ☐

Step 7: Provide performance feedback

23. Coactor was asked to provide feedback (e.g., how he/she felt, how well the main actor enacted the steps). ☐ ☐ ☐
24. Group members were asked if the main actor followed each step. ☐ ☐ ☐
25. Leaders provided appropriate feedback (praise, approval, encouragement), identifying specific aspects of the main actor's performance. ☐ ☐ ☐
26. Reinforcement in an amount consistent with the quality of role-play was provided. ☐ ☐ ☐
27. Main actor was invited to give comments. ☐ ☐ ☐

Step 8: Select the next role-player

28. Volunteer participant asked to act as the main actor in the next role-play. Repeated Steps 5 through 7. ☐ ☐ ☐
29. All group members were given a chance to role-play, or plans were made to role-play for those who did not have a chance. ☐ ☐ ☐

Step 9: Assign skill homework

30. Skill homework was assigned to each main actor. ☐ ☐ ☐
31. Assistance was provided as needed in identifying the day, place, with whom the skill will be used, and so forth. ☐ ☐ ☐

TOTAL _____

      59 points or below   Group leader intervention needed.

      60–74 points   Continued monitoring of instruction necessary.

      75–83 points   Consultation with master leader available.

      84–93 points   Mastery of intervention demonstrated.

Comments:

Recommendations for improvement:

GENERALIZATION INTEGRITY CHECKLIST

Leader(s) _____

Group _____ Date(s) of review _____

INSTRUCTIONS: This self-rating checklist is designed to assist group leader(s) in enhancing generalization of student skill learning. While a numerical score is not computed, leader(s) may use this checklist to both plan instruction and evaluate the emphasis placed on generalization following instruction.

	Minimal	Average	Strong
Before session			
1. Instruction is provided to the same peers with whom the target students interact outside of the group.	☐	☐	☐
2. One instructor has ongoing, regular contact with the students.	☐	☐	☐
3. Skills likely to provide natural reinforcement are included.	☐	☐	☐
During session			
4. Students know the specific behavioral skill steps and can perform them well.	☐	☐	☐
5. Attempts made to create similarities between the instructional and real-life situations and settings.	☐	☐	☐
6. Numerous trials of correct skill performance provided.	☐	☐	☐
7. Variability of situations (range of settings, various people, variety of reasons for skill use, various cues) provided.	☐	☐	☐
8. When possible, instruction occured in the real-life environment where the skill is to be used.	☐	☐	☐
9. Some flexibility allowed in order to meet individual student needs and settings.	☐	☐	☐
After session			
10. Homework assignments provided after students competently performed the role-plays.	☐	☐	☐
11. Skill use prompted or coached when daily situations suggest skill use.	☐	☐	☐
12. Skill use reinforced with gradual thinning and delaying of reinforcement.	☐	☐	☐
13. Prompts and reminders gradually faded.	☐	☐	☐
14. Instruction in self-mediated generalization (e.g., self-recording, self-reinforcement) provided as appropriate to student need.	☐	☐	☐
15. Booster or coaching sessions are provided as needed.	☐	☐	☐
16. Plan for addressing competing behaviors developed and implemented as needed.	☐	☐	☐
17. Strategies for parent involvement implemented.	☐	☐	☐

Skillstreaming

From *Skillstreaming in Early Childhood: Teaching Prosocial Skills* (3rd ed.), © 2012 by E. McGinnis, Champaign, IL: Research Press (www.researchpress.com, 800-519-2707).

APPENDIX C

Behavior Management Techniques

Behaviors that both promote and inhibit skill learning can be influenced by behavior management techniques based on the principles of behavior modification. The effectiveness of behavior modification rests on a firm experimental foundation. Although not all of the techniques described in this appendix are equally valid for all age groups, a basic understanding of them is critical to managing the Skillstreaming group and to developing individual behavior intervention plans for those children and adolescents who need them. The techniques described are grouped under the behavioral principles of reinforcement and punishment.

Behavior modification techniques are derived from formal learning theory, systematically applied in an effort to change observable behavior and rigorously evaluated by experimental research. These procedures are based on the core premise that behavior is largely determined by its environmental consequences (Ferster & Skinner, 1957; Skinner, 1938, 1953). Operationally, this premise has been employed in techniques that contingently present or withdraw rewards or punishments (i.e., environmental consequences) to alter the behavior preceding these consequences. It is this contingent quality that has led to the use of the term *contingency management* to describe most of these activities.

REINFORCEMENT

Reinforcement can be of two types: positive or negative. Positive reinforcement is central to promoting enduring change in Skillstreaming and other learning efforts and is therefore discussed here at length. Negative reinforcement is far less common but does play a role in the classroom and Skillstreaming group.

Positive Reinforcement

A *positive reinforcer* is any event that increases the subsequent frequency of a behavior it follows. Presenting positive reinforcement to the student following and contingent upon the occurrence of appropriate behavior is an effective way to substitute appropriate for inappropriate behaviors. Teachers and other school-based staff have worked successfully with four types of positive reinforcers: material, social, activity, and token. (For a list of commonly used reinforcers, see Table 4 in chapter 6.)

Material reinforcers (sometimes called *tangible reinforcers*) are actual goods or objects presented to the individual contingent upon enactment of appropriate behaviors. Skill awards and skill tickets, discussed in chapter 5, are examples of specific types of material reinforcers. An important subcategory of material reinforcement, *primary reinforcement*, occurs when the contingent event presented satisfies a basic biological need. Food is one such primary reinforcer.

Social reinforcers—most often expressed in the form of attention, praise, or approval—are particularly powerful and are frequently used in the Skillstreaming group. Both teacher experience and extensive experimental research testify to the potency of teacher-dispensed social reinforcement in influencing personal, interpersonal, and academic student behaviors.

Activity reinforcers are events a child or adolescent freely chooses when an opportunity exists to engage in several different activities. Given freedom to choose, many youth will watch television or spend time on the computer rather than complete their homework. The parent wishing to use this type of activity reinforcer may specify that the youth may watch television or use the computer for a given time period contingent upon the prior completion of the homework. Stated otherwise, the opportunity to perform a higher probability behavior (given free choice) can be used as a reinforcer for a lower probability behavior.

Token reinforcers, usually employed when more easily implemented social reinforcers prove insufficient, are symbolic items (chips, stars, points, etc.) provided contingent upon the performance of appropriate or desirable behaviors. Tokens are then exchangeable for a wide range of material or activity reinforcers. A *token economy* is a system by which specific numbers of tokens are contingently gained and exchanged for the backup material or activity reinforcers.

In making decisions about which type of reinforcer to use with a given youth, the teacher should keep in mind that social reinforcement (e.g., attention, praise, approval) is easiest to implement on a continuing basis and is most likely to lead to enduring behavior change. Therefore, it is the type of reinforcement the teacher will wish to use most frequently. Unfortunately, in the initial stages of a behavior change effort—especially when aggressive, disruptive, and other inappropriate behaviors are probably being richly rewarded by teacher and peer attention, as well as by tangible reinforcers—the teacher will likely need to rely more on material and activity reinforcers.

A token reinforcement system may prove effective as the initial reinforcement strategy. Reinforcement preferences change over time, and teacher views of the appropriate reward value of desirable behaviors also change over time. Both variables are easily reflected in token-level adjustments. Some issues to be considered prior to implementing a token system (Kaplan & Carter, 2005) and are summarized as follows:

1. Identify what the student needs to do, the specific behaviors, to earn tokens.

2. Post a list of these contingent behaviors (e.g., somewhere in the classroom, on the student's desk) to remind him or her of the expectations.

3. Decide what the tokens will be. Tokens should be age appropriate and might include check marks, play money, stickers, tickets, and so forth. Provisions need to be made to prevent students from having tokens that they have not earned (e.g., accept only tokens validated with the teacher's signature).

4. Determine how many tokens the students will earn for given behaviors and how much students will be charged (in tokens) for the reinforcers.

5. Determine the backup reinforcers—for example, prizes, entitlements (privileges students normally receive without having to earn them), other privileges.

6. Decide who will give the tokens (typically the teacher, associate, peer tutor).

7. Determine when the tokens will be given. Typically, tokens should be given as soon after the behavior is demonstrated as possible and according to the reinforcement schedule that is being followed with a particular student.

8. Determine how the tokens will be given (e.g., Given directly to the student? Marked on a card? Placed in a bank?). This system should be kept simple.

9. Determine when the tokens will be redeemed. The primary consideration should be the student's needs (i.e., how long the student is able to wait before receiving the reinforcer). Activities or privileges that may be disruptive to the instructional setting will require additional consideration.

Tokens, as well as other tangible rewards, should be combined with social reinforcers. It is critical to remember that, with few exceptions, reliance on material, activity, or token reinforcement eventually should give way to reliance on more "real-life" social reinforcement.

The potency of many reinforcers is increased when the reward, in addition to being inherently desirable, also brings reinforcement from peers and others (e.g., ordering a DVD to watch as a group, earning extra gym or recess time for the class). A further benefit of certain activity reinforcers (e.g., playing a game with peers, helping in the principal's office) is the degree to which the activity, while serving as a reward, also helps the student practice one or more Skillstreaming skills.

Identifying Reinforcers

Identifying positive reinforcers for a given child or adolescent is often necessary prior to presenting such events contingently upon the occurrence of desirable behaviors. Given that almost any event may serve as a reinforcer for one individual but not another, how can the teacher decide which reinforcers may best be used? Simply, the youth may be asked straightforwardly which items he or she would like to earn. This direct approach may be insufficient because youth are unaware of the full range of reinforcers available to them or may discount in advance the possibility that a reinforcer will actually be given. When this is the case, other identification procedures must be employed. Carr (1981) and others have reported three procedures typically used for this purpose. First, the teacher can often make an accurate determination of whether a given event is functioning as a reinforcer by carefully *observing effects* on the youth. The event probably is reinforcing if the youth (a) asks that the event be repeated, (b) seems happy during the event's occurrence, (c) seems unhappy when the event ends, or (d) will work to earn the event. If one or more of these reactions are observed, chances are good that the event is a positive reinforcer and that it can be contingently provided to strengthen appropriate, nonaggressive, or interactive behaviors. Second, *observing choices* can be helpful. As noted earlier in connection with activity reinforcers, when a youth is free to choose from among several equally available activities, which one the youth chooses and how long he or she engages in it are clues to whether an event is reinforcing. Finally, *questionnaires* have been effectively used to identify positive reinforcers.

As noted earlier, which objects or activities will in fact be reinforcing for a given youth will vary from individual to individual and from time to time. In addition, the strength of selected reinforcers often decreases the more frequently they are used. Some teachers therefore find it useful to create a "reinforcement menu," or a list of rewards from which the student can choose. Such a menu may be in the form of an actual list, or it may be in the form of "coupons" for tangible and activity rewards. Each coupon may be a voucher for a particular amount of a given reinforcer (e.g., five minutes of computer time, five minutes playing with the gerbil). Using a reinforcement menu prevents students from becoming satiated with one reward when it is offered over a period of time and also allows them to make their own reinforcement choices.

Presenting Positive Reinforcers

As noted, a basic principle of contingency management is that the presentation of a reinforcing event contingent upon the occurrence of a given behavior will function to increase the likelihood of the reoccurrence of that behavior. A number of considerations influence the success of the reinforcement effort and should be reflected in the actual presentation of reinforcers.

Contingency

The connection between the desirable behavior and the subsequent reward should be made explicit. As is true for all contingency management efforts, this description should be behaviorally specific—that is, the connection between particular behavioral acts and reinforcement should be emphasized over behaviorally ambiguous concepts like "good behavior" or "being well behaved." Instead, comments like "Good job taking turns" and "Good listening" will help the student understand what has gained him or her the desired reinforcement.

Immediacy

The more immediately the reinforcer follows the desirable behavior, the more likely it is to be effective. Rapid reinforcement augments the message that the immediately preceding behavior is desirable, whereas delayed reinforcement increases the risk that an inappropriate behavior will occur between the positive behavior and the reinforcement. In other words, the following sequence occurs: A (desirable behavior), B (undesirable behavior), and C (reinforcement intended for A that in actuality reinforces B).

Consistency

The effects of positive reinforcement on behavior are usually gradual, not dramatic, working slowly to strengthen behavior over a period of time. Thus, it is important that positive reinforcement be presented consistently. Consistency means not only that the teacher must be consistent but also that the teacher must attempt to match his or her reinforcement efforts with similar efforts from as many other important persons in the student's life as possible. This means, ideally, that when the student enacts the behavior to be reinforced—in school in the presence of other teachers, at home in the presence of parents or siblings, or at play in the presence of peers—such reinforcement will be forthcoming.

Frequency

When first trying to establish a new appropriate behavior, the teacher reinforces all or almost all instances of that behavior. This high frequency of reinforcement is necessary to establish the behavior in the individual's behavioral repertoire. Once it seems clear that the behavior has actually been acquired, the teacher thins the reinforcement schedule, decreasing presentation so that only some of the student's desirable behaviors are followed by the reinforcement. This schedule, known as *partial reinforcement,* contributes to the continuation of the appropriate behavior because it parallels the sometimes reinforced/sometimes not reaction the appropriate behavior will elicit in other settings from other people. Partial reinforcement of the appropriate behaviors may be on a fixed-time schedule (e.g., at the end of each Skillstreaming session), on a fixed-number-of-response schedule (e.g., every fifth instance of the appropriate behavior), or on variable-time or number-of-response schedules. In any event, the basic strategy for reinforcement frequency remains a rich level for initial learning and partial reinforcement to sustain performance.

Amount

Learning (i.e., acquiring knowledge about how to perform new behaviors) and performance (i.e., overtly using these behaviors) are different aspects of behavior. The amount of reinforcement provided influences performance much more than it does learning. Children and adolescents will learn new appropriate behaviors just about as fast for a small reward as for a large reward, but they are more likely to perform the behaviors on a continuing basis when large rewards are involved. Yet rewards can be too large, causing a *satiation effect* in which youth lose interest in seeking the reinforcement because it is "too much of a good thing." Or rewards can be too small: too little time on the playground, too few tokens, too thin a social reinforcement schedule. The optimal amount can be determined empirically. If a youth has in the past worked energetically to obtain a particular reinforcer but gradually slacks off and seems to lose interest in obtaining it, a satiation effect has probably occurred, and the amount of reinforcement should be reduced. On the other hand, if a youth seems unwilling to work for a reinforcer believed desirable, it can be given once or twice for free—that is, not contingent on a specific desirable behavior. If the youth seems to enjoy the reinforcer or wants more, the amount used may have been too little. The amount can be increased and made contingent; observations will then show whether it is yielding the desired effect. If so, the amount of reinforcement offered is appropriate.

Variety

A type of reinforcement satiation parallel to a satiation effect due to excessive reinforcement occurs when the teacher uses the same approving phrase or other reward over and over again. Students may perceive such reinforcement as mechanical, and they may lose interest in or decrease responsiveness to it. By varying the content of the reinforcer, the teacher can maintain its potency. Thus, instead of repeating "Nice job" four or five times, using a mix of comments (e.g., "Well done," "Good work," "You really listened") is more likely to yield a sustained effect.

Pairing with Praise

As noted previously, social reinforcement is most germane to enduring behavior change, although there are circumstances under which material, activity, or token reinforcers are at least initially more appropriate. To move toward social reinforcement, the teacher pairs all presentations of material, activity, or token rewards with some expression of social reinforcement: an approving comment, a pat on the back, a wink, a smile, and

so forth. Walker (1979) has noted a major benefit of this tactic:

> By virtue of being consistently paired with reinforcement delivery, praise can take on the reinforcing properties of the actual reinforcer(s) used. This is especially important since teacher praise is not always initially effective.... By systematically increasing the incentive value of praise through pairing, the teacher is in a position to gradually reduce the frequency of (material, activity, or token) reinforcement and to substitute praise. After systematic pairing, the teacher's praise may be much more effective in maintaining the child's appropriate behavior. (p. 108)

Shaping

The first time a student practices an unfamiliar behavior, the performance may be rough or imperfect. This is true for classroom behaviors such as participating or paying attention, which a particular student may not have been exhibited often. Therefore, even a partial or flawed performance should be reinforced early on. As the student becomes more confident and skilled in performing the behavior, rewards are given for the improved skill behaviors and eliminated for the earlier and less adequate approximations. Gradually, the rewarded performance will come to approximate the target behavior. The student's performance is thus "shaped" by the teacher. Social behavior can be shaped according to the following guidelines, developed by Sloane (1976):

1. Find some behavior in which the student is currently engaging that is a better approximation of your goal than the student's usual behavior and reinforce this approximation each time it occurs.

2. When an approximation has become more frequent for several days, select a slightly better one for reinforcement and stop reinforcing the first.

3. Ensure that each approximation is only slightly different from the last one.

4. Let a new approximation receive many reinforcements before moving on to another approximation.

5. Reinforce any behavior that is better than that currently required.

Behavior Contracting

Behavior contracting, sometimes known as contingency contracting, does not rely on the management of contingencies, but it can be effectiveness in helping children and adolescents understand and change problem behaviors. A behavior contract is a written agreement between a leader and group member. It is a document each signs that specifies desirable behaviors and their contingent positive consequences, as well as undesirable behaviors and their contingent undesirable consequences. As Homme, Csanyi, Gonzales, & Rechs (1969) specify in their early description of this procedure, such contracts will more reliably lead to desirable behaviors when the contract payoff is immediate; approximations to the desirable behavior are rewarded; the contract rewards accomplishment rather than obedience; accomplishment precedes reward; and the contract is fair, clear, honest, positive, and systematically implemented.

Group Reinforcement

Children and adolescents are very responsive to the influence of their peers. This phenomenon can be used to encourage the performance of infrequent but desirable behaviors. In using group reinforcement, the teacher provides a reward (e.g., privilege, activity) to the entire group contingent on the cooperative behavior of individual group members. If the reward is meaningful and desirable to the entire group, group members are likely to put pressure on one another to behave appropriately. For example:

> For the last three sessions, Tammy has made statements about how "stupid and dumb" she thought the Skillstreaming group was. When Tammy made these remarks, other students joined in by adding their own de-

rogatory comments. The group leader decided to deal with this problem by telling the students that if, for the next three sessions, they encouraged one another's participation in the activities, they would earn an additional recess. The teacher prepared a small chart on which he wrote the dates of the next three sessions and a space for marking how frequently encouraging statements were offered. The extra recess was a desirable enough group reinforcer that when Tammy began her usual comments, the other students insisted that she stop disrupting the group.

Removing Positive Reinforcement

The teacher's behavior management goal with students who display aggressive or other problem behaviors is, in a general sense, twofold. Both sides of the behavioral coin—appropriate and inappropriate, prosocial and antisocial, desirable and undesirable—must be attended to. In a proper behavior change effort, procedures are simultaneously or sequentially employed to reduce and eliminate the inappropriate, antisocial, or undesirable components of the students' behavioral repertoires and to increase the quality and frequency of appropriate, prosocial, or desirable components. This latter task is served primarily by the direct teaching of prosocial behaviors via Skillstreaming participation and by the contingent presentation of positive reinforcement following skill use. Conversely, the contingent removal of positive reinforcement in response to aggressive, disruptive, or other negative behaviors is the major behavior management strategy for reducing or eliminating such behaviors. Therefore, in conjunction with the procedures discussed previously for presenting positive reinforcement, the teacher should also simultaneously or consecutively employ one or both of the following techniques for removing positive reinforcement.

Negative Reinforcement

Negative reinforcement is the removal of aversive stimuli contingent upon the occurrence of desirable behaviors. Negative reinforcement has seldom been used to modify behavior in a classroom context. The major exception to this rule is the contingent release of youth from time-out (an aversive environment), depending on such desirable behaviors as quietness and calmness. Such release serves as negative reinforcement for these behaviors. Unfortunately, negative reinforcement often proves important in a classroom context in a less constructive way. Consider a teacher-student interaction in which the student behaves disruptively (shouts, swears, fights), the teacher responds with anger and punishment, and the punishment brings about a temporary suppression of the youth's disruptiveness. The decrease in the student's disruptiveness may also be viewed by the teacher as a decrease in aversive stimulation, which functions to negatively reinforce the immediately preceding teacher behavior (in this case, punishment). The net effect of this sequence is to increase the likelihood that the teacher will use punishment in the future. Analogous sequences may occur and function to increase the likelihood of other ineffective or inappropriate teacher behaviors.

PUNISHMENT

Formally, punishment is the presentation of an aversive or negative stimulus contingent upon the performance of a given behavior, intended to decrease the future occurrences of that behavior. Two common forms are verbal punishment (e.g., reprimands) and physical punishment (e.g., paddling, spanking). Corporal punishment is no longer allowed in most schools, nor is it recommended in any setting, including the home.

In fact, it is a common finding that, when verbal and physical punishment does succeed in altering behavior, such effects are often temporary. A number of clinicians and researchers have assumed an antipunishment stance, seeing little place for punishment, especially in the classroom. This view corresponds to punishment research demonstrating such undesirable side effects as withdrawal from social contact, coun-

teraggression toward the punisher, violence, vandalism, modeling of punishing behavior, disruption of social relationships, failure of effects to generalize, selective avoidance (refraining from inappropriate behaviors only when under surveillance), and stigmatizing labeling effects (Azrin & Holz, 1966; Bandura, 1973; Mayer, 2001). Nelson, Lott, and Glenn (1993) state:

> Most teachers mean well when they administer punishment. They believe punishment is the best way to motivate students to behave properly. If the misbehavior stops for a while because of punishment, they may have been fooled into thinking they were right. However, when they become aware of the long-range effects of punishment on students, they naturally want to learn more respectful methods of motivating students to behave properly. (p. 78)

Because they are intended to reduce the frequency of behavior, extinction and time-out are, strictly speaking, also forms of punishment. These two techniques can be helpful in effecting behavior change in the Skillstreaming group if proper guidelines for their use are followed. Response cost and logical consequences can also have a place in helping children and adolescents decrease undesirable behavior.

Extinction

Extinction is the withdrawal or removal of positive reinforcement for aggressive or other undesirable behaviors that have been either deliberately or inadvertently reinforced in the past. This technique is the procedure of choice with milder forms of aggression (e.g., sarcasm, put-downs, or other low-level forms of verbal aggression).

Knowing When to Use Extinction

Determining when to use extinction is, of course, in part a function of each teacher's guiding group management philosophy and tolerance for deviant behavior. Each teacher will have to decide individually the range of undesirable behaviors that can be safely ignored. Taking a rather conservative stance, Walker (1979) suggests that extinction "should be applied only to those inappropriate behaviors that are minimally disruptive to classroom atmosphere" (p. 40). In any event, it is clear that the first step in applying extinction is knowing when to use it.

Providing Positive Reinforcement for Appropriate Behaviors

As noted earlier, attempts to reduce inappropriate behavior by reinforcement withdrawal should always be accompanied by efforts to increase appropriate behaviors by reinforcement provision. This combination of efforts will succeed especially well when the appropriate and inappropriate behaviors involved are opposite from, or at least incompatible with, each other (e.g., reward in-seat behavior, ignore out-of-seat behavior; reward talking at a conversational level, ignore talking loudly).

Identifying Positive Reinforcers Maintaining Inappropriate Behaviors

The reinforcers maintaining inappropriate behaviors are the ones to be withheld. The teacher should discern what the student is working for; what payoffs are involved; and what reinforcers are being sought or earned by aggression, disruptiveness, and similar behaviors. Very often, the answer will be attention. Looking, staring, yelling at, talking to, or turning toward are common teacher and peer reactions to a student's inappropriate behaviors. The withdrawal of such positive social reinforcement by ignoring the behaviors (by turning away and not yelling, talking, or looking at the perpetrator) is the teacher and peer behavior that will effect extinction.

Ignoring Low-Level Aggressive Behaviors

Carr (1981) has suggested guidelines for ignoring low-level aggressive behaviors (e.g., verbal comments). First, do not comment to the youth that you are ignoring. Long (or even short) explanations about why teachers, peers, or others are going to avoid attending to given behaviors pro-

vide precisely the type of social reinforcement that extinction is designed to withdraw. Ignoring behavior should simply occur with no forewarning, introduction, or explanation. Second, do not look away suddenly when the youth behaves inappropriately. Doing so may communicate the message that "I really noticed and was impelled to action by your behavior," the exact opposite of an extinction message. As Carr recommends, "It is best to ignore the behavior by reacting to it in a matter of fact way by continuing natural ongoing activities" (p. 38).

These guidelines should be followed only with behaviors that are not harmful to others. Observed incidents of verbal and physical aggression (or harassment) must be dealt with quickly and consistently in order to maintain an a safe school environment. Thus, extinction is not supported as a method for dealing with behaviors that could cause harm to the student or others.

Using Extinction Consistently

As is true for the provision of reinforcement, removal of reinforcement must be consistent. Within a given Skillstreaming group, this rule of consistency means that the teacher and students must act in concert and that the teacher must be consistent across time. Within a given school, consistency means that, to the degree possible, all teachers having significant contact with a given student must strive to ignore the same inappropriate behaviors. In addition, to avoid the student's making the discrimination "I can't act up here, but I can out there," parent conferences should be held to bring parents, siblings, and other significant real-world figures in the student's life into the extinction effort.

Using Extinction Long Enough

Disruptive behaviors often have a long history of positive reinforcement. Especially if much of that history is one of intermittent reinforcement, efforts to undo these behaviors must be sustained. Teacher persistence in this regard will usually succeed. There are, however, two types of events to keep in mind when judging the effectiveness of extinction efforts. The first is what is known as the *extinction burst.* When extinction is first introduced, it is not uncommon for the rate or intensity of the aggressive behavior to increase sharply before it begins its more gradual decline toward zero. It is important that the teacher not be discouraged during this short detour. In fact, the meaning of the increase is that extinction is beginning to work. Second, inappropriate behaviors that have been successfully extinguished will reappear occasionally for reasons that are difficult to determine. Like the extinction burst, this *spontaneous recovery* is transitory and will disappear if the teacher persists in the extinction effort.

Time-Out

In time-out, a child or adolescent who engages in aggressive or other inappropriate behavior is removed from all sources of reinforcement for a specified time period. As with extinction, the purpose of time-out is to reduce the undesirable behavior. It differs from extinction in that extinction involves removing reinforcement from the person, whereas time-out usually involves removing the person from the reinforcing situation.

In school-based practice, time-out has typically taken three forms. *Isolation* or *seclusion time-out* requires that the youth be removed from the classroom to a time-out room. Because isolation or seclusion time-out is now considered to be a type of restraint, individuals considering this type of intervention should consult their state and district policies and procedures.

Exclusion time-out is somewhat less restrictive but also involves removing the youth from sources of reinforcement; it is perhaps the most common form of time-out used in elementary school classrooms. Here the youth is required to go to an area of the classroom and perhaps to sit in a "quiet chair," which is sometimes behind a screen. The youth is not removed from the class-

room but is excluded from classroom activities for a specified time period. *Nonexclusion time-out* (also called *contingent observation*), the least restrictive time-out variant, requires the youth to sit and watch on the periphery of classroom activities, to observe the appropriate behaviors of other students. This variant combines time-out with modeling opportunities and thus is the preferred approach for Skillstreaming group use. The implementation of time-out in any of its forms optimally employs the procedures next described.

Knowing When to Use Time-Out

As noted, extinction is the recommended procedure for undesirable behaviors that can be safely ignored. Behaviors potentially injurious to others require a more active teacher response, possibly time-out. Exclusion or nonexclusion time-out is also the procedure to use for less severe forms of problematic behavior when the combination of extinction and positive reinforcement for more positive behaviors has been attempted and failed.

Whenever possible, the student should be verbally directed to use the time-out area. If he or she refuses to go, the rest of the class or group may be removed instead of the student causing the problem. This will leave the student with the same response—time-out from positive reinforcement. In certain situations where student safety is at risk, it may be necessary to move a student physically to time-out. This may be the case for children age 2 to 12 who display high rates of potentially dangerous or aggressive behaviors. Such physical intervention should be used only as a last resort to protect the safety of the student or others—and only after attempts have been made to deescalate the student's behavior. Many times, after deescalation the student will move to the time-out area independently.

Providing Positive Reinforcement for Appropriate Behaviors

As is the case for extinction, positive reinforcement for appropriate behaviors should accompany any extinction procedure, including time-out. When possible, the behaviors positively reinforced should be opposite to, or at least incompatible with, those for which the time-out procedure is used. Carr (1981) recommends an additional basis combining these two techniques:

> Although one important reason for using positive reinforcement is to strengthen non-aggressive behaviors to the point where they replace aggressive behaviors, there is a second reason for using reinforcement procedures. If extensive use of positive reinforcement is made, then time-out will become all the more aversive since it would involve the temporary termination of a rich diversity of positive reinforcers. In this sense, then, the use of positive reinforcement helps to enhance the effectiveness of the time-out procedure. (pp. 41–42)

Arranging an Effective Time-Out Setting

Time-out must be a boring environment, with all reinforcers removed. With exclusionary time-out, there should be no attractive or distracting objects or opportunities—no toys, books, posters, people, windows to look out, sounds to overhear, or other obvious or not-so-obvious potential reinforcers. When contingent observation is used, the youth will still hear the ongoing activity.

Sending a Student to Time-Out

The teacher can take a number of actions when initiating time-out to increase the likelihood of its effectiveness. As for positive reinforcement, immediacy is an issue. Time-out is best instituted immediately following the aggressive or other behavior to be modified. Having earlier explained to the student the nature of time-out, as well as when and why it will be used, the teacher should initiate the procedure in a more or less automatic manner following the undesirable behavior—that is, in a way that minimizes social reinforcement. This means sending the student to time-out without a lengthy explanation but with a brief description of the precipitating behavior. This process is best conducted in a calm and matter-of-fact manner. In addition, the effectiveness of time-out is further enhanced by its consistent application, when appropriate, by the same teacher on other occasions, as well as by other teachers.

Maintaining a Student in Time-Out

Two questions arise during a student's period in time-out: What is he or she doing? and How long should time-out last? Answering the first question by monitoring the student makes certain that the time-out experience is not in fact pleasant or positively reinforcing. For example, rather than being a removal from positive reinforcement, time-out may in reality help a youth avoid an aversive situation from which he or she would prefer to escape. Similarly, if monitoring reveals that the youth is singing or playing, time-out will be less effective. Unless the situation can be made essentially nonreinforcing, a different behavioral intervention may be required.

With regard to duration, most successful time-out implementations have been from 2 to 10 minutes long (2 to 3 minutes for preschoolers and kindergartners, 3 to 5 minutes for the elementary-age student, and 5 to 10 minutes for an adolescent, with clear preference for the shorter time spans in this range. If time-out periods are longer than necessary, the student may calm down and then act up again out of boredom or frustration. When experimenting to find the optimal duration for any given youth, it is best to begin with a shorter duration and to lengthen the time until an effective span is identified rather than to shorten an initially longer span. This latter approach would, again, risk the danger of introducing an event the student experiences as positive reinforcement when the teacher's intention is quite the opposite.

Excusing a Student from Time-Out

As noted earlier in connection with extinction, withdrawal of positive reinforcement frequently leads to an extinction burst in which more intense or more frequent problem behaviors appear before they begin to subside. This same pattern is evident with withdrawal from positive reinforcement—that is, time-out. The first few times a student is directed to use time-out, what might be termed a *time-out burst* of heightened aggression or other problem behaviors may occur. These outbursts will usually subside, especially if the teacher requires the time-out to be served and the outburst does not result in the suspension of the time-out.

The student's release from time-out should be conducted in a matter-of-fact manner, and the student should be quickly returned to regular Skillstreaming activities. Lengthy teacher explanations or moralizing are, once again, tactically erroneous provisions of positive reinforcement that communicate to the student that acting out in the classroom will bring a short period of removal from reinforcement and then a (probably longer) period of undivided teacher attention.

It is important once the student returns to ongoing activities that the teacher quickly reinforce the student for subsequent positive behaviors. The Skillstreaming group must be a positive place—a place where the student wants to be—or time-out will be perceived as a reward instead of a negative consequence.

Providing Prosocial Alternatives

The responsible group leader will plan instruction in specific skills that could serve as prosocial ways of dealing with the problem that led to the use of time-out. For example, the student could be guided through the steps of Waiting your Turn (Skill 16) or Sharing (Skill 17) to reduce the likelihood that the event will reoccur. In addition, the leader must attempt to deescalate future occurrences of such behavior through techniques like prompting.

Response Cost

Response cost involves the removal of previously acquired reinforcers contingent upon and in order to reduce future instances of inappropriate behavior. The previously acquired reinforcers

may have been earned, as when response-cost procedures are a component of a token economy, or they may have simply been provided, as is the case with a freestanding response-cost system. In either instance, reinforcers are removed (the cost) whenever the undesirable behaviors occur (the response). Response-cost procedures can be effective, especially when combined with the provision of positive reinforcement via a token-economy system, for increasing prosocial behaviors. However, response-cost systems should never be a first choice in dealing with problem behaviors. Although the cost can be framed as a fine for breaking the rules or engaging in other actions for adolescents, this procedure has frequently shown to elicit aggressive responses on its own. Response cost is not appropriate for use with preschool or children in the early elementary grades.

Logical Consequences

An encouraging environment teaches students to respect themselves and others and treats all students with dignity. Rarely are students exposed to reprimands or other forms of harsh punishment; however, clear and consistent limits on unacceptable behavior are set and enforced so all students have the opportunity to learn. Logical consequences to reduce the frequency of undesirable behavior are most often recommended. Logical consequences are related to the individual's action, and they make sense (i.e., there is a cause-effect relationship; McLeod, Fisher, & Hoover, 2003). Consequences hold the student accountable yet maintain the student's dignity. McLeod, Fisher, & Hoover (2003) state:

> Punishment does not teach alternative acceptable behaviors; in fact, it models just the opposite. Teachers use punishment out of anger, frustration, or lack of other strategies. Consequences, however, teach students the connection between how they choose to behave and the outcomes of that behavior. (p. 114)

These authors suggest using restitution (fixing or replacing damaged, lost, or stolen items), restoration (giving the student a respite by being away from the group for a brief period of time), restriction (limiting privileges for a length of time), and reflection (reflecting on a problem and developing a plan through problem solving).

Dreikurs and Cassel (1972) further define logical consequences. Such consequences are related to the misbehavior; are planned, explained, and agreed on by students in advance; are administered in a neutral way; and are given consistently. In addition, consequences are reasonable and demonstrate respect by giving students a choice (i.e., to engage in the inappropriate behavior and receive an unpleasant consequence or to engage in the appropriate behavior and receive positive reinforcement).

When planning logical consequences, teachers will need to keep in mind that these consequences must be reasonable, related to the misbehavior, and respectful to the student (Nelson et al., 1993). Examples of logical consequences include the following:

► For choosing to talk instead of completing a class assignment, the student must complete the work during an enjoyable activity.

► For choosing to fight when provoked at recess, the student must stay on a specific area of the playground where there is increased supervision.

► For choosing to take a notebook belonging to someone else, the student must make restitution.

Overcorrection

Overcorrection is a behavior modification approach developed by Foxx and Azrin (1973) for circumstances in which other behavioral strategies have failed and when few alternative appropriate behaviors are available to reinforce. Overcorrection is a two-part procedure, having restitution and positive practice as components. Restitution requires that the individual return the behavioral setting (e.g., the classroom) to its status prior to disruption or better. Thus, objects broken by an angry youth must be repaired, classmates struck in anger apologized to, papers scattered across the room picked up. The positive practice component of overcorrection requires that the youth then be made to repair objects broken by others, apologize to classmates who witnessed the classmate being struck, or clean up the rest of the classroom (including areas not disturbed by the youth). It is clear that the restitution and positive practice requirements serve both punitive and instructional functions.

References

Adams, M. B., Womack, S. A., Shatzer, R. H., & Caldarella, P. (2010). Parent involvement in school-wide social skills instruction: Perceptions of a home note program. *Education, 130*(3), 513–528.

Advancement Project/Civil Rights Project. (2000, February). *Education denied: The negative impact of zero tolerance policies.* Testimony before the U.S. Commission on Civil Rights, Washington, DC.

Ahmad, Y., & Smith, P. K. (1994). Bullying in schools and the issue of sex differences. In John Archer (Ed.), *Male violence.* London: Routledge.

Alberto, P. S., & Troutman, A. C. (2006). *Applied behavior analysis for teachers: Influencing student performance.* Upper Saddle River, NJ: Merrill/Prentice Hall.

Allen, K. E., & Marotz, L. R. (2000). By the ages: Behavior and development of children pre-birth through eight. Albany, NY: Delmar.

Andrews, S. P., Taylor, P. B., Martin, E. P., & Slate, J. R. (1998). *Evaluation of an alternative discipline program.* Chapel Hill: The University of North Carolina Press.

Applied Research Center. (1999). *Making the grade: A racial justice report card.* Washington DC: Author.

Asarnow, J. R., & Callan, J. W. (1985). Boys with peer adjustment problems: Social cognitive processes. *Journal of Consulting and Clinical Psychology, 53,* 80–87.

Ascher, C. (1994). *Gaining control of violence in the schools: A view from the field* (ERIC Digest No. 100). New York: ERIC Clearinghouse on Urban Education.

Azrin, N. H., & Holz, W. C. (1966). Punishment. In W. K. Honig (Ed.), *Operant behavior: Areas of research and application.* New York: Appleton-Century-Crofts.

Bandura, A. (1973). *Aggression: A social learning analysis.* Englewood Cliffs, NJ: Prentice Hall.

Bandura, A. (1977). *Social learning theory.* Englewood Cliffs, NJ: Prentice Hall.

Beane, A. (1999). *The bully-free classroom.* Minneapolis: Free Spirit.

Bender, W. N. (2009). *Beyond the RTI pyramid: Solutions for the first years of implementation.* Bloomington, IN: Solution Tree Press.

Blair, K. C., Fox, L., & Lentini, R. (2010). Use of positive behavior support to address the challenging behavior of young children within a community early childhood program. *Topics in Early Childhood Special Education, 30*(2), 68–79.

Blood, E., & Neel, R. S. (2007). From FBA to implementation: A look at what is actually being delivered. *Education and Treatment of Children, 30*(4), 67–80.

Bock, S. J., Tapscott, K. E., & Savner, J. L. (1998). Suspension and expulsion: Effective management for students? *Intervention in School and Clinic, 34*(1), 50–52.

Bourland, E. (1995). *RRFC Links 2*(3). (Available from Federal Resource Center for Special Education, Academy for Educational Development, 1875 Connecticut Ave. NW, Washington, DC 20009–1202)

Boyajian, A. E., DuPaul, G. J., Handler, M. W., Eckert, T. L., & McGoey, K. E. (2001). The use of classroom-based brief functional analyses with preschoolers at-risk for attention deficit hyperactivity disorder. *School Psychology Review, 30*(2), 278–293.

Brannon, D. (2008). Character education: A joint responsibility. *Kappa Delta Pi Record, 44* (Winter), 62–65.

Brendtro, L. K., Brokenleg, M., & Van Bockern, S. (2002). *Reclaiming youth at risk: Our hope for the future.* Bloomington, IN: National Educational Service.

Brownstein, R. (2010). Pushed out. *Teaching Tolerance,* March, 23–27.

Bruder, M. B. (2010). Early childhood intervention: A promise to children and families for their future. *Exceptional Children, 76*(3), 339–355.

Buhremester, D. (1982). *Children's Concerns Inventory manual.* Los Angeles: University of California, Department of Psychiatry.

Caldarella, P., & Merrell, K. W. (1977). Common dimensions of social skills of children and adolescents: A taxonomy of positive behaviors. *School Psychology Review, 26*(2), 264–279.

Camodeca, M., Goossens, F. A., Schuengel, C., & Terwogt, M. M. (2003). Links between social information processing in middle childhood and involvement in bullying. *Aggressive Behavior, 29,* 116–127.

Camp, B. W., & Bash, M. A. S. (1981). *Think Aloud: Increasing social and cognitive skills—A problem-solving program for children* (Primary Level). Champaign, IL: Research Press.

Camp, B. W., & Bash, M. A. S. (1985). *Think Aloud: Increasing social and cognitive skills—A problem-solving program for children* (Classroom Program, Grades 1–2). Champaign, IL: Research Press.

Caprara, G. V., Barbaranelli, C., Pastorelli, C., Bandura, A., & Zimbardo, P. (2000). Prosocial foundations of children's academic achievement. *Psychological Science, 11,* 301–306.

Carr, E. G. (1981). Contingency management. In A. P. Goldstein, E. G. Carr, W. Davidson, & P. Wehr (Eds.), *In response to aggression.* New York: Pergamon.

Carr, E. G., Dunlap, G., Horner, R. H., Koegel, R. L., Turnbull, A. P., Sailor, W., Anderson, J. L., Albin, R. W., Koegel, L. K., & Fox, L. (2002). Positive behavior support: Evolution of an applied science. *Journal of Positive Behavior Interventions, 4*(1), 4–16.

Carter, D. A., & Horner, R. H. (2007). Adding functional behavioral assessment to First Step to Success: A case study. *Journal of Positive Behavior Interventions. 9*(4), 229–238.

Cartledge, G. (2003, February 20). *Discipline, diversity and behavioral disorders: Issues and interventions.* Presentation made at the Midwest Symposium for Leadership in Behavioral Disorders, Kansas City, MO.

Cartledge, G., & Feng, H. (1996). The relationship of culture and social behavior. In G. Cartledge (Ed.), *Cultural diversity and social skills instruction: Understanding ethnic and gender differences.* Champaign, IL: Research Press.

Cartledge, G., & Johnson, S. (1997). Cultural sensitivity. In A. P. Goldstein & J. C. Conoley (Eds.), *School violence intervention: A practical handbook.* New York: Guilford.

Cartledge, G., & Kourea, L. (2008). Culturally responsive classrooms for culturally diverse students with and at risk for disabilities. *Exceptional Children, 74*(3), 351–371.

Cartledge, G., & Lo, Y. (2006). *Teaching urban learners: Culturally responsive strategies for developing academic and behavioral competence.* Champaign, IL: Research Press.

Cartledge, G., & Milburn, J. F. (1980). *Teaching social skills to children.* New York: Pergamon.

Cartledge, G., & Milburn, J. F. (1995). *Teaching social skills to children and youth: Innovative approaches* (3rd ed.). Needham Heights, MA: Allyn and Bacon.

Cartledge, G., & Milburn, J. F. (1996). A model for teaching social skills. In G. Cartledge (Ed.), *Cultural diversity and social skills instruction: Understanding ethnic and gender differences.* Champaign, IL: Research Press.

Caselman, T. D., & Self, P. A. (2008). Assessment instruments for measuring young children's social-emotional behavior development. *Children and Schools, 30*(2), 103–115.

Chan, K. S., & Rueda, R. (1979). Poverty and culture in education: Separate but equal. *Exceptional Children, 45,* 422–428.

Chapman, W. E. (1977). *Roots of character education.* Schenectady, NY: Character Research Press.

Chen, K. (2006). Social skills intervention for students with emotional/behavioral disorders: A literature review from the American perspective. *Educational Research and Reviews, 1*(3), 143–149.

Choi, D. H., & Kim, J. (2003). Practicing social skills training for young children with low peer acceptance: A cognitive-social learning model. *Early Childhood Education Journal, 31*(1), 41–46.

Cochrane, W. S., & Laux, J. M. (2007). Investigating school psychologists' perceptions of treatment integrity in school-based interventions for children with academic and behavior concerns. *Preventing School Failure, 51*(4), 29–34.

Cohen, J., Pickeral, T., & McCloskey, M. (April, 2009). Assessing school climate. *Education Digest, 74*(8) 45–48.

Coie, J. D., & Kupersmidt, J. B. (1983). A behavioral analysis of emerging social status in boys' groups. *Child Development, 54,* 1400–1416.

Cook, C. R., Crews, S. D., Wright, D. B., Mayer, G. R., Gale, B., Kramer, B., & Gresham, F.M. (2007). Establishing and evaluating the substantive adequacy of Positive Behavioral Support Plans. *Journal of Behavioral Education, 16,* 191–206.

Cook, C. R., Gresham, F. M., Kern, L., Barreras, R. B., & Crews, S. D. (2008). Social skills training for secondary students with emotional and/or behavioral disorders: A review and analysis of the meta-analytic literature. *Journal of Emotional and Behavioral Disorders, 16*(3), 131–144.

Costenbader, V., & Markson, S. (1998). School suspension: A study with secondary school students. *Journal of School Psychology, 36,* 59–82.

Crick, N. R., & Dodge, K. A. (1994). A review and reformulation of social information processing mechanisms in children's social adjustment. *Psychological Bulletin, 115,* 74–101.

Crick, N. R., & Dodge, K. A. (1996). Social information-processing mechanisms in reactive and proactive aggression. *Child Development, 67,* 993–1002.

Crone, D. A., Hawken, L. S., & Bergstrom, M. (2007). A demonstration of training, implementing, and using functional behavioral assessment in 10 elementary and middle school settings. *Journal of Positive Behavior Interventions, 9*(1), 15–29.

Crone, D. A., & Horner, R. H. (2003). *Building positive behavior support systems in schools: Functional behavioral assessment.* New York: Guilford Press.

Denham, S. A. (1998). *Emotional development in young children.* New York: Guilford.

Dereli, E. (2009). Examining the permanence of the effect of a social skills training program for the acquisition of social problem-solving skills. *Social Behavior and Personality, 37,* 1419-1428.

Dewey, J. (1938). *Experience and education.* New York: Collier.

Docksai, R. (2010). Teaching social skills. *Futurist, 44*(3), 12–13.

Dodge, K. A. (1983). Behavioral antecedents of peer social status. *Child Development, 54,* 1385–1399.

Dodge, K. A. (1985). Facets of social interaction and the assessment of social competence in children. In B. H. Schneider, K. H. Rubin, & J. E. Ledingham (Eds.), *Children's peer relations: Issues in assessment and intervention.* New York: Springer-Verlag.

Dodge, K. A., Coie, J. D., & Bralke, N. P. (1982). Behavior patterns of socially rejected and neglected preadolescents: The roles of social approach and aggression. *Journal of Abnormal Child Psychology, 10,* 389–410.

Dodge, K. A., Lockman, J. E., Harnish, J. D., Bates, J. E., & Pettit, G. S. (1997). Reactive and proactive aggression in school children and psychiatrically impaired chronically assaultive youth. *Journal of Abnormal Psychology, 106*(1), 37–51.

Dodge, K. A., Murphy, R. R., & Birchsbaum, K. C. (1984). The assessment of intention-cue detection skills in children: Implications for developmental psychology. *Child Development, 55,* 163–173.

Donovan, M. S., & Cross, C. T. (Eds.). (2002). *Minority students in special and gifted education.* Washington, DC: National Academy Press.

Dreikurs, R., & Cassel, P. (1972). *Discipline without tears.* New York: Hawthorne.

Dreikurs, R., Grunwald, B., & Pepper, F. (1971). *Maintaining sanity in the classroom.* New York: Harper & Row.

Dunlap, G., Strain, P. S., Fox, L., Carta, J. J., Conroy, M., Smith, B. J., Kern, L., Memmeter, M. L., Timm, M. A., McCart, A., Sailor, W., Markey, U., Markey, D. J., Lardieri, S., & Sowell, C. (2006). Prevention and intervention with young children's challenging behavior: Perspectives regarding current knowledge. *Behavioral Disorders, 32*(1), 29–45.

Dupper, D. R., & Bosch, L. A. (1996). *Reasons for school suspensions. Journal for a Just and Caring Education, 2*(2), 140–150.

Elksnin, L. K., & Elksnin, N. (2000). Teaching parents to teach their children to be prosocial. *Intervention in School and Clinic, 36*(1), 27–35.

Elliott, S. N., & Gresham, F. M. (1991). *Social skills intervention guide: Practical strategies for social skills training.* Circle Pines, MN: American Guidance Service.

Ellis, H. (1965). *The transfer of learning.* New York: Macmillan.

Entwisle, D. R., Alexander, K. L., & Olson, L. S. (2005). First grade and educational attainment by age 22: A new story. *American Journal of Sociology, 110*(5), 1458–1502.

Epps, S., Thompson, F. J., & Lane, M. P. (1985). *Procedures for incorporating generalization programming into interventions for behaviorally disordered students.* Unpublished manuscript, Iowa State University, Ames.

Farmer, T. W., Farmer, E. M. Z., Estell, D. B., & Hutchins, B. C. (2007). The developmental dynamics of aggression and the prevention of school violence. *Journal of Emotional and Behavioral Disorders 15*(4), 197–208.

Feindler, E. L. (1979). *Cognitive and behavioral approaches to anger control training in explosive adolescents.* Unpublished doctoral dissertation, West Virginia University, Morgantown.

Feindler, E. L. (1995). An ideal treatment package for children and adolescents with anger disorders. In H. Kassinove (Ed.), *Anger disorders: Definition, diagnosis, and treatment.* New York: Taylor & Francis.

Feindler, E. L., & Ecton, R. B. (1986). *Adolescent anger control: Cognitive-behavioral techniques.* New York: Pergamon.

Ferster, C. B., & Skinner, B. F. (1957). *Schedules of reinforcement.* New York: Appleton-Century-Crofts.

Fialka, J., & Mikus, K. C. (1999). *Do you hear what I hear?* Ann Arbor, MI: Proctor.

Fox, C. L., & Boulton, J. J. (2003). Evaluating the effectiveness of a social skills training (SST) programme for victims of bullying. *Educational Research, 45*(3), 231–247.

Foxx, R. M., & Azrin, N. H. (1973). A method of eliminating aggressive-disruptive behavior for retarded and brain-damaged patients. *Behaviour Research and Therapy, 10,* 15–27.

Friesen, B. J., & Stephens, B. (1998). Expanding family roles in the system of care: Research and practice. In M. H. Epstein, K. Kutash, & A. Duchnowski (Eds.), *Outcomes for children and youth with behavioral and emotional disorders and their families.* Austin, TX: PRO-ED.

Fullerton, E. K., Conroy, M. A., & Correa, V. I. (2009). Early childhood teacher's use of specific praise statements with young children at risk for behavioral disorders. *Behavioral Disorders, 34*(3), 118–135.

Gemelli, R. J. (1996). Understanding and helping children who do not talk in school. In N. J. Long & W. C. Morse (Eds.), *Conflict in the classroom: The education of at-risk and troubled students.* Austin, TX: PRO-ED.

Gibbs, J. C., Potter, G. B., & Goldstein, A. P. (1995). *The EQUIP program: Teaching youth to think and act responsibly through a peer-helping approach.* Champaign, IL: Research Press.

Gilliam, W. S. (2005). Prekindergarteners left behind: Expulsion rates in state prekindergarten systems. Retrieved May 22, 2011 from www.hartfordinfo.org/issues/wsd/education/NationalPreKExpulsionPaper

Glick, B., & Gibbs, J. C. (2010). *Aggression Replacement Training: A comprehensive intervention for aggressive youth* (3rd ed.). Champaign, IL: Research Press.

Goldstein, A. P. (1973). *Structured Learning Therapy: Toward a psychotherapy for the poor.* New York: Academic.

Goldstein, A. P. (1989). *The Prepare Curriculum: Teaching prosocial competencies.* Champaign, IL: Research Press.

Goldstein, A. P. (1999a). *Low-level aggression: First steps on the ladder to violence.* Champaign, IL: Research Press.

Goldstein, A. P. (1999b). *The Prepare Curriculum: Teaching prosocial competencies* (Rev. ed.). Champaign, IL: Research Press.

Goldstein, A. P., Gershaw, N. J., Klein, P., & Sprafkin, R. P. (1980). *Skillstreaming the adolescent: A structured learning approach to teaching prosocial skills.* Champaign, IL: Research Press.

Goldstein, A. P., Glick, B., Carthan, W., & Blancero, D. (1994). *The prosocial gang.* New York: Pergamon.

Goldstein, A. P., Glick, B., & Gibbs, J. C. (1998). *Aggression Replacement Training: A comprehensive intervention for aggressive youth* (Rev. ed.). Champaign, IL: Research Press.

Goldstein, A. P., Glick, B., Irwin, J. J., Pask-McCartney, C., & Rubama, I. (1989). *Reducing delinquency: Intervention in the community.* New York: Pergamon.

Goldstein, A. P., Glick, B., Reiner, S., Zimmerman, D., & Coultry, T. (1986). *Aggression Replacement Training: A comprehensive program for aggressive youth.* Champaign, IL: Research Press.

Goldstein, A. P., & Kanfer, F. H. (1979). *Maximizing treatment gains.* New York: Academic.

Goldstein, A. P., & McGinnis, E. (1988). *The Skillstreaming video: How to teach students prosocial skills.* Champaign, IL: Research Press.

Goldstein, A. P., & McGinnis, E. (1997). *Skillstreaming the adolescent: New strategies and perspectives for teaching prosocial skills* (Rev. ed.). Champaign, IL: Research Press.

Goldstein, A. P., & Michaels, G. Y. (1985). *Empathy: Development, training and consequences.* Hillsdale, NJ: Erlbaum.

Goldstein, S. E., Young, A., & Boyd, C. (2008). Relational aggression at school: Associations with school safety and social climate. *Journal of Youth Adolescence. 37,* 641–654.

Goleman, D. (1995). *Emotional intelligence.* New York: Bantam.

Graham, S., Harris, K. R., & Reid, R. (1992). Developing self-regulated learners. *Focus on Exceptional Children, 24,* 1–16.

Green, R. W. (2010). Calling all frequent flyers. *Educational Leadership, 68*(2), 28–34.

Greenbaum, S., Turner, B., & Stephens, R. D. (1989). *Set straight on bullies.* Malibu, CA: National School Safety Center.

Greenwood, C. R., Hops, H., Delquadri, J., & Guild, J. (1974). Group contingencies for group consequences in classroom management: A further analysis. *Journal of Applied Behavior Analysis, 7,* 413–425.

Gresham, F. M. (1998a). Social skills training: Should we raze, remodel, or rebuild? *Behavioral Disorders, 24*(1), 19–25.

Gresham, F. M. (1998b). Social skills training with children: Social learning and applied behavioral analytic approaches. In T. S. Watson & F. M. Gresham (Eds.), *Handbook of child behavior therapy.* New York: Plenum Press.

Gresham, F. M. (2002). Social skills assessment and instruction for students with emotional and behavioral disorders. In K. L. Lane, F. M. Gresham, &

T. E. O'Shaughnessy (Eds.), *Interventions for children with or at risk for emotional and behavioral disorders.* Boston: Allyn and Bacon.

Gresham, F. M. (2005). Methodological issues in evaluating cognitive-beahvioral treatments for students with behavioral disorders. *Behavioral Disorders, 30*(3), 213–215.

Gresham, F. M. (2009). Evolution of the treatment integrity concept: Current status and future directions. *School Psychology Review, 38*(4), 533–540.

Gresham, F. M., & Elliott, S. N. (1990). *Social Skills Rating System.* Circle Pines, MN: American Guidance Service.

Gresham, F. M., & Gansle, K. A. (1993). Treatment integrity of school-based behavioral intervention studies: 1980–1990. *School Psychology Review, 22*(2), 254–272.

Gresham, F. M., MacMillan, M. E., Beebe-Frankenberger, M. E., & Bocian, K. M. (2000). Treatment integrity in learning disabilities intervention research: Do we really know how treatments are implemented? *Learning Disabilities Research and Practice, 15*(4), 198–205.

Gresham, F. M., Sugai, G., & Horner, R. H. (2001). Interpreting outcomes of social skills training for students with high-incidence disabilities. *Exceptional Children, 67,* 331–344.

Gresham, F. M., Van, M. B., & Cook, C. R. (2006). Social skills training for teaching replacement behaviors: Remediating acquisition deficits in at-risk students. *Behavioral Disorders, 31*(4), 363–377.

Gresham, F. M., Watson, T. S., & Skinner, C. H. (2001). Functional behavioral assessment: Principles, procedures, and future directions. *School Psychology Review, 30*(2), 156–172.

Grizenko, J., Zappitelli, M., Langevin, J. P., Hrychko, S., El-Messidi, A., Kaminester, D., Pawliuk, N., & Stepanian, M. T. (2000). Effectiveness of a social skills training program using self/other perspective-taking: A nine month follow-up. *American Journal of Orthopsychiatry, 70*(4), 501–509.

Guerra, N. G., Boxer, P., & Kim, T. E. (2005). A cognitive-ecological approach to serving students with emotional and behavioral disorders: Application to aggressive behavior. *Behavioral Disorders, 30*(3), 277–288.

Guerra, N. G., & Slaby, R. G. (1989). Evaluative factors in social problem solving by aggressive boys. *Journal of Abnormal Child Psychology, 17,* 277–289.

Guzzetta, R. A. (1974). *Acquisition and transfer of empathy by the parents of early adolescents through Structured Learning training.* Unpublished doctoral dissertation, Syracuse University.

Harry, B., & Klingner, J. (2006). *Why are so many minority students in special education?* New York: Teachers College Press.

Hartup, W. W. (1983). Peer relations. In P. H. Mussen (Ed.), *Handbook of child psychology* (Vol. 4). New York: Wiley.

Hemmeter, M. L., Ostrosky, M., & Fox, L. (2006). Social and emotional foundations for early learning: A conceptual model for intervention. *School Psychology Review, 35*(4), 583–601.

Hickman, G. P., Bartholomew, M., Mathwig, J., & Heinrichs, R. S. (2008). Differential developmental pathways of high school dropouts and graduates. *Journal of Educational Research, 102*(1), 3–14.

Homme, L., Csanyi, A. P., Gonzales, M. A., & Rechs, J. R. (1969). *How to use contingency contracting in the classroom.* Champaign, IL: Research Press.

Hoover, J. H., & Oliver, R. (1996). *The bullying prevention handbook: A guide for principals, teachers, and counselors.* Bloomington, IN: National Education Service.

Horner, R. H., & Carr, E. G. (1997). Behavioral support for students with severe disabilities: Functional assessment and comprehensive intervention. *The Journal of Special Education, 31*(1), 84–104.

Hubbard, J. A., Dodge, K. A., Cillessen, A. H., Coie, J. D., & Schwartz, D. (2001). The dyadic nature of social information processing in boys' reactive and proactive aggression. *Journal of Personality and Social Psychology, 80*(2), 268–280.

Hune, J. B., & Nelson, C. M. (2002). Effects of teaching a problem-solving strategy on preschool children with problem behavior. *Behavioral Disorders, 27*(3), 185–207.

Individuals with Disabilities Education Act (IDEA) Amendments of 1997, Pub. L. 105–17.

Individuals with Disabilities Education Act (IDEA) Amendments of 2004, Pub. L. 180–446.

Ingram, K., Lewis-Palmer, T., & Sugai, G. (2005). Function-based intervention planning: Comparing the effectiveness of FBA function-based and non-function based intervention plans. *Journal of Positive Behavior Interventions, 7*(4), 224–236.

Jensen, E. (2000). *Brain-based learning.* San Diego: The Brain Store Publishing.

Jewett, J. (1992). *Aggression and cooperation: Helping young children develop constructive strategies.* (ERIC Document Reproduction Service No. ED351147)

Johns, B. H., Carr, V. G., & Hoots, C. W. (1995). *Reduction of school violence: Alternatives to suspension.* Horsham, PA: LRP.

Johnson, S. L. (2009). Improving the school environment to reduce school violence: A review of the literature. *Journal of School Health, 79*(10), 451–465.

Jolivette, K., McCormick, K. M., Jung, L. A., & Lingo, A. S. (2004). Embedding choices into the daily routines of young children with behavior problems: Eight reasons to build social competence. *Beyond Behavior, 13*(3), 21–26.

Jolivette, K., Scott, T. M., & Nelson, C. M. (2000). *The link between Functional Behavioral Assessments (FBAs) and Behavioral Intervention Plans (BIPs)* (ERIC Digest E592). Reston, VA: Council for Exceptional Children.

Jones, V. F., & Jones, L. S. (2008). *Comprehensive classroom management* (9th ed.). Boston: Allyn & Bacon.

Jones, K. M., Young, M. M., & Friman, P. C. (2000). Increasing peer praise of socially rejected delinquent youth: Effects on cooperation and acceptance. *School Psychology Review, 15*, 30–39.

Jung, L. A., Gomez, C., Baird, S. M., & Keramidas, C. L. G. (2008). Designing intervention plans: Bridging the gap between individualized education programs and implementation. *Teaching Exceptional Children, 41*(1), 26–33.

Kame'enui, E. J., & Simmons, D. C. (1990). *Designing instructional strategies: The prevention of academic learning problems.* Columbus, OH: Merrill.

Kaplan, J. S., & Carter, J. (2005). *Beyond behavior modification: A cognitive behavioral approach to behavior management in the school* (3rd ed.). Austin, TX: PRO-ED.

Karoly, P., & Steffen, J. J. (1980). Operant methods. In F. H. Kanfer & A. P. Goldstein (Eds.), *Helping people change.* New York: Pergamon.

Kauffman, J. M. (2005). *Characteristics of emotional and behavioral disorders of children and youth* (9th ed.). Upper Saddle River, NJ: Pearson.

Kauffman, J. M., Mostert, M. P., Trent, S. C., & Hallahan, D. P. (1998). *Managing classroom behavior: A reflective case-based approach* (2nd ed.). Boston: Allyn and Bacon.

Kazdin, A. E. (1975). *Behavior modification in applied settings.* Homewood, IL: Dorsey.

Keeley, S. M., Shemberg, K. M., & Carbonell, J. (1976). Operant clinical intervention: Behavior management or beyond? Where are the data? *Behavior Therapy, 7*, 292–305.

Kendall, P. C., & Braswell, L. (1985). *Cognitive behavioral therapy for children.* New York: Guilford.

Keogh, B. K., & Burnstein, J. D. (1988). Relationship of temperament to preschoolers' interaction with peers and teachers. *Exceptional Children, 54*, 456–461.

Kern, L., Hilt, A. M., & Gresham, F. (2004). An evaluation of the functional behavioral assessment process used with students with or at-risk for emotional and behavioral disorders. *Education and Treatment of Children, 27*(4), 440–452.

Knight, B. J., & West, D. J. (1975). Temporary and continuing delinquency. *British Journal of Criminology, 15*, 43–50.

Kohlberg, L. (1969). Stage and sequence: The cognitive-developmental approach to socialization. In D. A. Goslin (Ed.), *Handbook of socialization theory and research.* Chicago: Rand McNally.

Kohlberg, L. (Ed.). (1973). *Collected papers on moral development and moral education.* Cambridge, MA: Harvard University, Center for Moral Education.

Kounin, J. (1970). *Discipline and group management in classrooms.* New York: Holt, Rinehart and Winston.

Kulli, K. (2008). Developing effective behavior intervention plans: Suggestions for school personnel. *Intervention in School and Clinic, 43*(3), 140–149.

Ladd, G. W., Kochenderfer, B. J., & Coleman, C. C. (2000). Friendship and school adjustment: Friendship quality as a predictor of young children's early school adjustment. In W. Craig (Ed.), *Childhood social development: The essential readings.* Malden, MS: Blackwell.

Ladd, G. W., & Mize, J. (1983). A cognitive-social learning model of social skill training. *Psychological Review, 90,* 127–157.

Lane, K. L., Givner, C. C., & Pierson, M. R. (2004). Teacher expectations of student behavior: Social skills necessary for success in elementary school classrooms. *Journal of Special Education, 38,* 104–110.

Lane, K. L., Menzies, H. M., Barton-Arwood, S. M., Doukas, G. L., & Munton, S. M. (2005). Designing, implementing, and evaluating social skills interventions for elementary students: Step-by-step procedures based on actual school-based investigations. *Preventing School Failure, 49*(2), 18–26.

Lane, K. L., Wehby, J. H., & Cooley, C. (2006). Teacher expectations of students' classroom behavior across the grade span: Which social skills are necessary for success? *Exceptional Children, 72*(2), 153–167.

LaRue, Jr., R. H., Weiss, M. J., & Ferraioli, S. J. (2008). State of the art procedures for assessment and treatment of learners with behavioral problems. *International Journal of Behavioral Consultation and Therapy, 4*(2), 250–263.

Lassen, S. R., Steele, M. M., & Sailor, W. (2006). The relationship of school-wide positive behavior support to academic achievement in an urban middle school. *Psychology in the Schools, 43*(6), 701–712.

Loeber, R., & Dishion, T. (1983). Early predictors of male delinquency: A review. *Psychological Bulletin, 94,* 68–99.

Maag, J. W. (2006). Social skills training for students with emotional and behavioral disorders: A review of reviews. *Behavioral Disorders, 32*(1), 5–17.

Maag, J. W., & Swearer, S. M. (2005). Cognitive-behvioral interventions for depression: Review and implications for school personnel. *Behavioral Disorders, 30*(3), 259–276.

Maccoby, E. E. (1980). *Social development.* New York: Harcourt Brace Jovanovich.

MacNeil, A. J., Prater, D. L., & Busch, S. (2009). The effects of school culture and climate on student achievement. *International Journal of Leadership in Education, 12*(1), 73–84.

Mann, J. H. (1956). Experimental evaluations of role playing. *Psychological Bulletin, 53,* 227–234.

Manning, M., Heron, J., & Marshall, T. (1978). Styles of hostility and of social interactions at nursery, at school and at home: An extended study of children. In L. A. Hersov & M. Berger (Eds.), *Aggression and anti-social behavior in childhood and adolescence.* Oxford, UK: Pergamon.

Marx, G. (2006). *An overview of sixteen trends: Their profound impact on our future: Implications for students, education, communities, and whole of society.* Alexandria, VA: Educational Research Service.

Marzano, R. J., & Haystead, M.W. (2008). *Making standards useful in the classroom.* Alexandria, VA: Association for Supervision and Curriculum Development.

Marzano, R. J., Pickering, D., & McTighe, J. (1993). *Assessing student outcomes: Performance assessment using the dimensions of learning model.* Alexandria, VA: Association for Supervision and Curriculum Development.

Mayer, G. R. (2001). Antisocial behavior: Its causes and prevention within our schools. *Education and Treatment of Children, 245*(4), 414–429.

McConnell, S. R. (1987). Entrapment effects and the generalization and maintenance of social skills training for elementary school students with behavioral disorders. *Behavioral Disorders, 12,* 252–263.

McGinnis, E. (2012). *Skillstreaming the elementary school child: A guide for teaching prosocial skills* (3rd ed.). Champaign, IL: Research Press.

McGinnis, E., & Goldstein, A. P. (1984). *Skillstreaming the elementary school child: A guide for teaching prosocial skills.* Champaign, IL: Research Press.

McGinnis, E., & Goldstein, A. P. (1990). *Skillstreaming in early childhood: Teaching prosocial skills to the preschool and kindergarten child.* Champaign, IL: Research Press.

McGinnis, E., & Goldstein, A. P. (1997). *Skillstreaming the elementary school child: New strategies and perpectives for teaching prosocial skills* (Rev. ed.). Champaign, IL: Research Press.

McGinnis, E., & Goldstein, A. P. (2003). *Skillstreaming in early childhood: New strategies and perpectives for teaching prosocial skills* (Rev. ed.). Champaign, IL: Research Press.

McGlamery, M. E., & Ball, S. E. (2008). The case for social skills training in the primary school curriculum: A follow-up study of attention and theory of mind skills in first grade boys. *Curriculum and Teaching Dialogue, 10,* (1 & 2), 27–39.

McIntosh, K., Borgmeier, C., Anderson, C. M., Horner, R. H., Rodriguez, B. J., & Tobin, T. (2008). Technical adequacy of the functional assessment checklist: Teacher and staff (FACTS) FBA interview measure. *Journal of Positive Behavior Interventions, 10*(1), 33–45.

McIntosh, K., Flannery, K. B., Sugai, G., Braun, D. H., & Cochrane, K. L. (2008). Relationship between academic and problem behavior in the transition from middle school to high school. *Journal of Positive Behavior Interventions, 10*(4), 243–255.

McIntosh, K., & Mackay, L. D. (2008). Enhancing generalization of social skills: Making social skills curricula effective after the lesson. *Beyond Behavior, Fall,* 18–25.

McIntosh, R., Vaughn, S., & Zaragoza, N. (1991). A review of social interventions for students with learning disabilities. *Journal of Learning Disabilities, 24,* 451–458.

McLaren, E. M., & Nelson, C. M. (2009). Using functional behavior assessment to develop behavior interventions for students in Head Start. *Journal of Positive Behavior Interventions, 11*(1), 3–21.

McLeod, J., Fisher, J., & Hoover, G. (2003). *The key elements of classroom management: Managing time and space, student behavior, and instructional strategies.* Alexandria, VA: Association for Supervision and Curriculum Development.

Meichenbaum, D. H. (1977). *Cognitive-behavior modification: An integrative approach.* New York: Plenum.

Meier, C. R., DiPerna, J. C., & Oster, M. M. (2006). Importance of social skills in the elementary grades. *Education and Treatment of Children, 29,* 409–419.

Mendler, A. N., & Curwin, R. L. (1999). *Discipline with dignity for challenging youth.* Bloomington, IN: National Educational Service.

Mercer, C. D., & Pullen, P. C. (2005). *Students with learning disabilities.* Upper Saddle River, NJ: Pearson Education.

Miller, J. P. (1976). *Humanizing the classroom.* New York: Praeger.

Mize, J., & Ladd, G. W. (1984, April). Preschool children's goal and strategy knowledge: A comparison of picture-story and enactive assessment. In G. W. Ladd (Chair), *From preschool to high school: Are children's interpersonal goals and strategies predictive of their social competence?* Symposium conducted at the annual meeting of the American Educational Research Association, New Orleans.

Modro, M. (1995). *Safekeeping: Adult responsibility, children's right.* Providence: Behavioral Health Resource.

Moroz, K. B., & Jones, K. M. (2002). The effects of positive peer reporting on children's social involvement. *School Psychology Review, 31*(2) 235–245.

Morrison, R. L., & Bellack, A. S. (1981). The role of social perception in social skills. *Behavior Therapy, 12,* 69–70.

National Association for the Education of Young Children. (1993). NAEYC position statement on violence in the lives of children. *Young Children, 48*(6), 80–84.

Neilans, T. H., & Israel, A. C. (1981). Towards maintenance and generalization of behavior change: Teaching children self-regulation and self-instructional skills. *Cognitive Therapy and Research, 5,* 189–196.

Nelson, J., Lott, L., & Glenn, H. S. (1993). *Positive discipline in the classroom: How to effectively use class meetings and other positive discipline strategies.* Rocklin, CA: Prima.

Newman, D. A., Horne, A. M., & Bartolomucci, C. L. (2000). *Bully busters: A teacher's manual for helping bullies, victims, and bystanders.* Champaign, IL: Research Press.

Nickerson, A. B., & Martens, M. P. (2008). School violence: Associations with control, security/enforcement, educational/therapeutic approaches, and demographic factors. *School Psychology Review, 37*(2), 228–241.

Nowicki, S., Jr., & Duke, M. P. (1992). *Helping the child who doesn't fit in.* Atlanta, GA: Peachtree.

Olweus, D. (1991). Bully/victim problems among school children: Basic facts and effects of a school-based intervention program. In D. Pepler & K. H. Rubin (Eds.), *The development and treatment of childhood aggression.* Hillsdale, NJ: Erlbaum.

Olweus, D. (1993). *Bullying at school: What we know and what we can do.* Oxford, UK: Blackwell.

Osgood, C. E. (1953). *Method and theory in experimental psychology.* New York: Oxford University Press.

Partnership for 21st Century Skills. (2008). *21st Century skills, education, and competitiveness: A resource and policy guide.* Retrieved May 22, 2011, from www.p21.org/documents/21st_century_skills_education_and_competitiveness_guide.pdf

Patterson, G. R. (1982). *Coercive family process.* Eugene, OR: Castalia.

Patterson, G. R., Reid, J. B., Jones, R. R., & Conger, R. E. (1975). *A social learning approach to family intervention* (Vol. 1). Eugene, OR: Castalia.

Payne, R. (1998). *A framework for understanding poverty.* Baytown, TX: RFT Publishing.

Pelco, L. E., & Reed-Victor, E. (2007). Self-regulation and learning-related social skills: Intervention ideas for elementary school students. *Preventing School Failure, 51*(3), 36–41.

Perea, S. (2004). *The new America: The America of the moo-shoo burrito.* Denver, CO: HIS Ministries Publications.

Perry, P. G., Perry, L. C., & Rasmussen, P. (1986). Cognitive social learning mediators of aggression. *Child Development, 57,* 700–711.

Pettit, G. S., Bates, J. E., & Dodge, K. A. (2000). Supportive parenting, ecological context, and children's adjustment: A seven-year longitudinal study. In W. Craig (Ed.), *Childhood social development: The essential readings.* Malden, MS: Blackwell.

Piaget, J. (1962). *Play, dreams, and imitation in childhood.* New York: Norton.

Public Health Service. (2001). *Youth violence: A report of the Surgeon General.* Retrieved May 22, 2011 from www.surgeongeneral.gov/library/youthviolence/toc.html

Quinn, M. M., Osher, D., Warger, C. L., Hanley, T. V., Bader, B. D., & Hoffman, C. C. (2000). *Teaching and working with children who have emotional and behavioral challenges.* Longmont, CO: Sopris West.

Raine, A., Dodge, K., Loeber, R., Gatzke-Kopp, L. M., Lynam, D., Reynolds, C., Stouthamer-Loeber, M., & Liu, J. (2006). The Reactive-Proactive Aggression Questionnaire: Differential correlates of reactive and proactive aggression in adolescent boys. *Aggressive Behavior, 32,* 159–171.

Redl, F., & Wineman, D. (1957). *The aggressive child.* New York: Free Press.

Reid, M. J., Webster-Stratton, C., & Hammond, M. (2007). Enhancing a classroom social competence and problem-solving curriculum by offering parent training to families of moderate- to high-risk elementary school children. *Journal of Clinical Child and Adolescent Psychology, 36*(4), 605–620.

Rimm-Kaufman, S. E., Pianta, R. C., & Cox, M. J. (2000). Teachers' judgments of problems in the transition to kindergarten. *Early Childhood Research Quarterly, 15,* 147–166.

Robins, K. N., Lindsey, R. B., Lindsey, D. B., & Terrell, R. D. (2006). *Culturally proficient instruction: A guide for people who teach* (2nd ed.). Thousand Oaks, CA: Corwin Press.

Robins, L. N., West, P. A., & Herjanic, B. L. (1975). Arrests and delinquency in two generations: A study of black urban families and their children. *Journal of Child Psychology and Psychiatry, 16,* 125–140.

Rock, E. E., Fessler, M. A., & Church, R. P. (1997). The concomitance of learning disabilities and emotional/behavioral disorders: A conceptual model. *Journal of Learning Disabilities, 30,* 245–263.

Rose, L. C., & Gallup, A. M. (2004). *The 36th Annual Phi Delta Kappa/Gallup Poll of the public's attitude toward public schools.* Bloomington, IN: Phi Delta Kappa International.

Sanetti, L. M., & Kratochwill, T. R. (2008). Treatment integrity in behavioral consultation: Measurement, promotion, and outcomes. *International Journal of Behavioral Consultation and Therapy, 4*(1), 95–114.

Sanetti, L. M., & Kratochwill, T. R. (2009). Toward developing a science of treatment integrity: Introduction to a special series. *School Psychology Review, 38*(4), 445–459.

Sarason, I. G., Glaser, M., & Fargo, G. A. (1972). *Reinforcing productive classroom behavior.* New York: Behavioral Publications.

Schmoker, M. (1999). *Results: A key to continuous school improvement* (2nd ed.). Alexandria, VA: Association for Supervision and Curriculum Development.

Schneider, M., & Robin, A. (1974). *Turtle manual.* (ERIC Document Reproduction Service No. ED128680)

Schoenfeld, N. A., Rutherford, R. B., Jr., Gable, R. A., & Rock, M. L. (2008). *ENGAGE: A blueprint for incorporating social skills training into daily academic instruction.* Birmingham, AL: Heldref.

Scott, T. M., Anderson, C. M., & Spaulding, S. A. (2008). Strategies for developing and carrying out functional assessment and behavior intervention planning. *Preventing School Failure, 52*(3), 39–49.

Scott, T. M., & Nelson, C. M. (1998). Confusion and failure in facilitating generalized social responding in the school setting: Sometimes 2 + 2 = 5. *Behavioral Disorders, 23*(4), 264–275.

Simon, S. G., Howe, L. W., & Kirschenbaum, H. (1972). *Values clarification.* New York: Hart.

Skiba, R. J., Peterson, R. L., & Williams, T. (1997). Office referrals and suspension: Disciplinary intervention in middle schools. *Education and Treatment of Children, 20*(3), 295–315.

Skiba, R. J., & Sprague, J. (2008). Safety without suspension. *Educational Leadership, 66*(1), 38–43.

Skinner, B. F. (1938). *The behavior of organisms: An experimental analysis.* New York: Appleton-Century-Crofts.

Skinner, B. F. (1953). *Science and human behavior.* New York: Macmillan.

Skinner, C. H., Cashwell, T. H., & Skinner, A. L. (2000). Increasing tootling: Effects of a peer-monitored group contingency program on students' reports of peers' prosocial behaviors. *Psychology in the Schools, 37,* 263–270.

Slavin, R. E. (1980). *Using student team learning* (Rev. ed.). Baltimore: Johns Hopkins University, Center for Social Organization of Schools.

Slim, L., Whiteside, S. P., Dittner, C. A., & Mellon, M. (2006). Effectiveness of a social skills training program with school age children: Transition to clinical setting. *Journal of Child and Family Studies, 15,* 409–418.

Smith, P. K., & Levan, S. (1995). Perceptions and experiences of bullying in younger pupils. *British Journal of Educational Psychology, 65,* 489–500.

Smith, S. W., & Gilles, D. L. (2003). Using key instructional elements to systematically promote social skill generalization for students with challenging behavior. *Intervention in School and Clinic, 39*(1), 30–37.

Smith, S. W., Lochman, J. E., & Daunic, A. P. (2005). Managing aggression using cognitive-beahvioral interventions: State of practice and future directions. *Behavioral Disorders, 30*(3), 227–240.

Spivack, G. E., & Shure, M. B. (1974). *Social adjustment of young children.* San Francisco: Jossey-Bass.

Sprague, J., & Walker, H. (2000). Early identification and intervention for youth with antisocial and violent behavior. *Exceptional Children, 66*(3), 367–379.

Stokes, T. F., & Baer, D. M. (1977). An implicit technology of generalization. *Journal of Applied Behavior Analysis, 10,* 349–367.

Stormont, M., & Reinke, W. (2009). The importance of precorrective statements and behavior-specific praise and strategies to increase their use. *Beyond Behavior, 18*(3), 26–32.

Strain, P. S., & Timm, M. A. (2001). Remediation and prevention of aggression: An evaluation of the regional intervention program over a quarter century. *Behavioral Disorders, 26*(4), 297–313.

Sugai, G., Guardino, D., & Lathrop, M. (2007). Response to intervention: Examining classroom behavior support in second grade. *Exceptional Children, 73*(3), 288–310.

Sulzer-Azaroff, B., & Mayer, G. R. (1991). *Behavior analysis for lasting change.* San Francisco: Holt, Rinehart and Winston.

Technical Assistance Center on Social Emotional Intervention for Young Children (November, 2004). *Facts about young children with challenging behaviors.* Retrieved May 22, 2011 from www.challengingbehavior.org/do/resources/documents/facts_about_sheet.pdf

Thorndike, E. L., & Woodworth, R. S. (1901). The influence of improvement in one mental function upon the efficiency of other functions. *Psychological Review, 8,* 247–261.

Trussell, R. P., Lewis, T. J., & Stichter, J. P. (2008). The impact of targeted classroom interventions and function-based behavior interventions on problem behaviors of students with emotional/behavioral disorders. *Behavioral Disorders, 33*(3), 153–166.

Trzesniewski, K. H., Moffit, T. E., Caspi, A., Taylor, A., & Maughan, B. (2006). Revisiting the association between reading and antisocial behavior: New evidence of an environmental explanation from a twin study. *Child Development. 77,* 72–88.

Turner, N. D. (2003). Preparing preservice teachers for inclusion in secondary classrooms. *Education, 123*(3), 491–495.

Voltz, D. L., Sims, M. J., & Nelson, B. (2010). *Connecting teachers, students, and standards: Strategies for success in diverse and inclusive classrooms.* Alexandria, VA: Association for Supervision and Curriculum Development.

Walker, H. M. (1979). *The acting-out child: Coping with classroom disruption.* Boston: Allyn and Bacon.

Walker, H. M., Colvin, G., & Ramsey, E. (1995). *Antisocial behaviors in schools: Strategies and best practices.* Pacific Grove, CA: Brooks/Cole.

Walker, H. M., Ramsey, E., & Gresham, F. M. (2004). *Antisocial behavior in school: Evidence-based practices* (2nd ed.). Belmont, CA: Wadsworth/Thomson Learning.

Warden, D., & MacKinnon, S. (2003). Prosocial children, bullies, and victims: An investigation of their sociometric status, empathy, and social-problem-solving strategies. *British Journal of Developmental Psychology, 21,* 367–385.

Werner, E. E., & Smith, R. S. (1982). *Vulnerable but invincible.* New York: McGraw-Hill.

Whitted, K. S. (2011). Understanding how social and emotional skill deficits contribute to school failure. *Preventing School Failure, 55*(1), 10–16.

Wood, B. K., Umbreit, J., Liaupsin, C. J., & Gresham, F. M. (2007). A treatment integrity analysis of function-based intervention. *Education and Treatment of Children, 30*(4), 105–120.

Zahn-Waxler, C., & Radke-Yarrow, M. (1982). The development of altruism: Alternative research strategies. In N. Eisenberg (Ed.), *The development of prosocial behavior.* New York: Academic.

Zahn-Waxler, C., & Radke-Yarrow, M. (1990). The origins of empathic concern. *Motivation and Emotion, 14,* 107–130.

Zins, J. E., Bloodworth, M. R., Weissberg, R. P., & Walberg, H. J. (2004). The scientific base linking social and emotional learning to school success. In J. Zins, M. Bloodworth, R. Weissberg, & G. Walberg (Eds.), *Building academic success on social and emotional learning: What does the research say?* New York: Teachers College Press.

About the Author

Ellen McGinnis earned her Ph.D. from the University of Iowa in 1986. She holds degrees in elementary education, special education, and school administration. She has taught elementary and secondary students in the public schools in Minnesota, Iowa, and Arizona. In addition, she has served as a special education consultant in both public and hospital schools and as assistant professor of special education at the University of Wisconsin–Eau Claire. Dr. McGinnis also served with the Des Moines Public Schools as the principal of the education program at Orchard Place, a residential and day treatment facility for children and adolescents with emotional/behavioral disorders. She has been an executive director of student support services in both Iowa and Colorado and is currently a private consultant. The author of numerous articles on identifying and teaching youth with emotional/behavioral disorders, Dr. McGinnis collaborated with Dr. Arnold P. Goldstein on earlier Skillstreaming books and is author of the newly released third editions of *Skillstreaming the Elementary School Child* and *Skillstreaming the Adolescent*.

FOR PRESCHOOL AND KINDERGARTEN

SKILLSTREAMING IN EARLY CHILDHOOD

A Guide for Teaching Prosocial Skills

Dr. Ellen McGinnis

PROGRAM BOOK

A complete description of the *Skillstreaming* program, with instructions for teaching 40 prosocial skills.

Skill Areas

* Beginning Social Skills
* School-Related Skills
* Friendship-Making Skills
* Dealing with Stress
* Alternatives to Aggression
* Dealing with Feelings

8 ½ × 11, 352 pages (CD included)

SKILL CARDS

Convenient 3 × 5 cards, illustrated for nonreaders, listing the behavioral steps for each of the 40 early childhood skills. Eight cards provided for each skill—a total of 320 cards.

SKILL POSTERS

A set of 40 12 × 18 posters, illustrated for nonreaders and displaying the behavioral steps in each of the skills for preschool and kindergarten.

FOR ELEMENTARY SCHOOL STUDENTS

SKILLSTREAMING THE ELEMENTARY SCHOOL CHILD

A Guide for Teaching Prosocial Skills

Dr. Ellen McGinnis

PROGRAM BOOK

Instructions for teaching 60 prosocial skills, plus complete guidelines for running the *Skillstreaming* program.

Skill Areas

* Classroom Survival Skills
* Friendship-Making Skills
* Skills for Dealing with Feelings
* Skill Alternatives to Aggression
* Skills for Dealing with Stress

8 ½ × 11, 408 pages (CD included)

SKILLSTREAMING IN THE ELEMENTARY SCHOOL

Lesson Plans and Activities

Make *Skillstreaming* even more fun! This book provides supplementary activities for at least one week of additional instruction for each of the 60 elementary skills. Features 600 easy-to-use lesson plans and a CD including over 200 printable forms necessary to implement the lesson plans.

8½ × 11, 312 pages (CD included)

STUDENT MANUAL

Written for the elementary-age student, a concise guide describing the program, designed to promote active involvement in the *Skillstreaming* group. A useful reference and organizer.

8½ × 11, 80 pages

SKILL CARDS

In a convenient 3 × 5 format, cards list the behavioral steps for each of the 60 elementary *Skillstreaming* skills. Eight cards provided for each skill—480 cards total.

POSTERS

A set of 60 18 × 12 posters displaying the behavioral steps in each of the skills for elementary-age students.

DVD—For Student Viewing
PEOPLE SKILLS: DOING 'EM RIGHT!

A quick and easy way to show your students what *Skillstreaming* is all about. Illustrates the process of teacher modeling, student role-playing, and feedback to clarify the benefits of using skills and motivate students to participate.

Elementary DVD, 17 minutes (closed captioned)